How to get the MONEY to pay for COLLEGE

How to get the MONEY to pay for COLLEGE

GENE R. HAWES & DAVID M. BROWNSTONE

A Hudson Group Book

DAVID McKAY COMPANY, INC.
NEW YORK

Library of Congress Cataloging in Publication Data

Hawes, Gene R
   How to get the money to pay for college.

  "A Hudson Group book."
  Bibliography: p.
  Includes index.
  1. College costs.   I.   Brownstone, David M., joint author.   II.   Title.
LB2342.H39   378.3   77-18959
ISBN 0-679-50848-1
ISBN 0-679-50849-X pbk.

10 9 8 7 6 5 4 3 2 1

MANUFACTURED IN THE UNITED STATES OF AMERICA

Designed by Antler & Baldwin, Inc.

CONTENTS

How to get the MONEY to pay for COLLEGE

1

A TOTAL STRATEGY
FOR MEETING COLLEGE COSTS

ON a single day in March last year these things happened:

• A small liberal arts college in the northeast mailed notices to all students and parents telling of yet another fee increase for the coming school year. Total tuition, board, and miscellaneous fees were to go from the current $6,100 per year to a little under $6,700, an increase of just under 10 percent. The year before the increase had been from $5,500 to $6,100, a little over 10 percent.

• A graduate school in a big southwestern city increased its per-credit charges by 9 percent.

• A major state university increased its undergraduate room, board, and miscellaneous charges by an average of almost 10 percent. No additional financial assistance funds were made available.

• A big New York textbook publisher raised prices on several of its most widely circulated textbooks by an average of 12 percent.

• The American people were urged to exhibit that combination of courage and self-sacrifice that had made and would keep America great. Members of Congress settled down to spend their new, very large wage increases.

All was much as before. American students and their families nodded, agreed that they would try to keep America great, and continued to try to figure out how to get the money to pay for the skyrocketing costs of acquiring a college education.

The plain fact is that college costs are rising enormously fast, and neither incomes nor government assistance are rising nearly fast enough to offset the pace of rising costs.

Assume that you are a high school senior, headed for a liberal arts college in the northeast. At the current 9 to 10 percent per year fee increase rate of that college (and that rate is to be expected at similar schools throughout the country), you would pay $6,700 the first year, about $7,300 the second year, $8,000 the next year, and $8,700 in your senior year—a total of $30,700 for your four years of college (plus books, lab fees, and "incidentals"). And that's for a college "year" of about eight months—you have to live for the other four months and that costs money, too.

If you go on to, let us say, three years of an equally expensive law school, you face additional school costs of at least $30,000 more, as costs continue to rise.

Now let us assume that you are a parent, facing the prospect of paying the college costs of three children, two years apart, starting two years from now. You're determined to get them all college educations, no matter what it takes. You're careful, ready to get fully acquainted with all the financial aid possibilities, mean to start working and planning now to handle what you recognize as a major set of responsibilities coming right up.

Assume that you get some financial aid, and that your children attend a mix of private and public colleges, experience a mix of away-from-home and commuting-from-home college costs. That they average one year of graduate school. That they help out by working as much as possible.

The odds are that you still face an average expenditure of at least $3,000 per year per child at current cost levels for an average of five years each. Allowing for steeply rising college costs all during the period in which your children will be attending college, you probably face minimum costs amounting to a total of almost $77,000. Barring really massive new government help, which seems unlikely, that is the kind of minimum you may be facing. And under certain circumstances, it could be twice that.

The essence of the matter is that college costs have risen and will continue to rise far more steeply than incomes, and even more disproportionately relative to the rates of growth experienced by fixed assets and savings.

A couple of examples of the latter may help.

Let us say you invested one dollar in the stock market ten years ago, when the Dow industrial average was in the 800-to-900 range. That average is now in the 850-to-1,000 range. Assume you have a gain paralleling the market's showing, and show a gain of 10 to 15 percent. You also received some dividends over the years, amounting to an average of 4 percent per year, but of course you paid taxes on the dividends. On the face of it, you've gained some value, gotten some dividends.

Not quite. Assuming a rate of inflation of 7 percent per year for the ten-year period, your dollar is worth just a little over half what it was worth when you invested it. Assuming you reinvested every penny of posttax dividends, your investment has simply eroded by about 30 to 35 percent.

But perhaps you put the dollar into a savings account, averaged as much as 6 percent in taxable dividends over the ten-year period. After taxes your dollar probably eroded by 25 to 30 percent, depending on your tax bracket.

At best, you can expect your currently earned income to go up at roughly the same rate as the current rate of inflation. At worst, inflation will continue to outstrip income levels. And at best, you can only hope that your fixed assets and savings will rise in value as quickly as the rate of inflation.

However, there is no reason at all to believe that either current earned income or your assets will rise as quickly as college costs. College-cost increases have been soaring over income and asset increases for many years now, and will continue to do so for many years more.

The inescapable conclusion is that now, more than ever before, the cost of acquiring a college education is often the single largest, most concentrated expenditure in the entire lives of individuals and whole families. To meet college costs requires total individual and family planning, often for many years before and after the actual college years.

That's what this book is all about—totally planning how to get the money to pay for college.

IS IT WORTH IT?

In a sense, there is a previous question. Is all the planning and sacrifice worth it—for the student, for the family? Does it really make sense for a student to mortgage years of future earnings to pay off college loans? Does it make sense for parents, student wives and husbands to spend a large part of their most productive years planning and working to pay college bills? Is there a "law of diminishing returns" as more and more college graduates compete for jobs, a narrowing gap between the lifetime earnings expectations of college graduates and others?

We think it is worth it. It has been since there were colleges to graduate from. It still is.

One leading authority estimates that as of the mid-1970s male college graduates can expect lifetime earnings amounting to $230,000 more than male high school graduates, measured in current dollars.

In March, 1975, a period of deep economic recession, the unemployment rate for high school graduates was a little over 9 percent; for college graduates a little under 3 percent.

Those figures alone clearly make the case for getting a college degree. Beyond those figures, in a sense underneath those figures, we are continuing to see a long-term trend toward a general view of the college degree as "openers" for almost all the best-paying, most attractive kinds of work.

You cannot become a lawyer, doctor, dentist, accountant, clinical psychologist or enter any of the other major professions without a basic degree and usually graduate degrees beyond. There are very few people heading up large organizations of any kind who do not have degrees. You must have a degree to even be considered for most executive level corporate jobs, and increasingly a business degree besides.

Without the basic degree, it becomes very difficult to develop alternate career choices later in life. All too often, the woman now wanting to get back into the job market after years of raising a family is hampered by not having that basic degree on which to build a career specialty. All too often, women and men trained for one specialty who want to change careers later in life find it very difficult without that basic degree.

Yes, the sacrifice and planning are worth it. And if you are going to sacrifice and plan, let it be the most informed kind of planning possible. Sound planning minimizes personal sacrifice.

COST OPTIONS

To make practical plans to meet college costs, you must first know what those costs are and are likely to be. In this book, we will illuminate all the basic college-cost options and combinations now possible, all the way from eight years of undergraduate and graduate work in private colleges and universities and spent entirely away from home to a basic degree acquired at almost no cost part-time while living at home and holding a full-time job.

The cost options are extremely wide, though clearly not every option will fit every student or every chosen career. The low-cost "college on your own" alternative is especially good for mature students with self-discipline and self-generated drives toward their college educations. It may not be at all appropriate for the seventeen-year-old just out of high school, with little experience or self-discipline to fall back on when the sky is blue, the birds are singing, and the last thing anyone really wants to do is study.

Similarly, some of the most expensive options will be most appropriate for students headed for highly competitive graduate schools, though there is considerable room for effective planning within those options—and a need to plan even more carefully if you're planning for seven or eight years of college costs, rather than for the basic four-year costs. Chapter 2 discusses the wide range of college-cost options available.

PERSONAL INVENTORY

The starting point for sound money-for-college planning is the personal financial resources inventory. You need to know what financial resources you have right now and how much money you can draw upon from them for college costs. And in planning for future needs, you must be able to make a good estimate of how much your current resources will be worth when you need them.

This is not quite the same process as doing a personal financial statement for a bank loan, in which you list and add up what you have and what you owe to get a statement of personal net worth.

For example, you're a parent sending children to college. You own a house on which you still have a mortgage of $15,000. Without going into the ins and outs of assessments and bank evaluations, assume that the fair market value of the house is now $50,000; that is, you can probably sell it for that much. For net worth purposes you might reasonably call it an asset worth $35,000.

But you're not likely to plan to sell your house to put your children through college. People have done that often enough, but it's not something to plan on. Therefore for college cost planning purposes you're not going to use the $35,000 figure. Instead, you'll inquire around a little at local banks and see what kind of remortgage amount is to be reasonably expected. In many parts of the country, you'll find 75 percent of fair market value a mortgage top on an older house, for example. Then you would take 75 percent of $50,000, which is $37,500, subtract the $15,000 mortgage, and get a remaining rough "cash available" figure of $22,500. In some parts of the country, you'd also have to subtract as much as $1,500 for new closing costs and attorneys' fees, thus netting $21,000 in cash.

Then, continuing to work out the example, you would see what the new monthly payments were, as compared with the payments under the old mortgage. You would be carrying a much larger mortgage and probably at a much higher interest rate, meaning that you might be paying a relatively great deal more monthly. You would need to total up the differences in payments over the years your children would be in college and then estimate your tax savings from the increased interest to get a reasonable rough estimate of the extra costs of the new mortgage during the period. If the additional costs came to $4,000 during the period, you'd subtract that from the $21,000 "cash available" figure to get a real college money source amounting to $17,000.

After all that, you'd think two or three times about remortgaging your house for college costs, quite correctly figuring that remortgaging should be a last resort since it is one of the most expensive ways to go. On the other hand, the remortgage money you can liberate from your house and property is often a very important factor in your total financial picture, and a number you should know.

In figuring the worth of your current resources for college money purposes you cannot reasonably include such personal property as clothes, furniture, and automobiles, as you won't be converting these kinds of property into money for college. They are part of your net worth, but not directly part of your college money source inventory.

The main current money-for-college resources are analyzed in Chapter 3.

HANDLING RESOURCES AND CURRENT INCOME IN MEETING COLLEGE COSTS

Very few of us can expect to pay for college entirely out of current income. Most of us expect to use existing assets and current income, to borrow against future income, and to secure some financial aid.

You can moderate the impact of college costs by careful attention to the way you spend your income—starting a good deal earlier than the day college money starts being spent.

For example, a student with summer job earnings should put away as much as possible for college-cost purposes. But bear in mind that existing student savings can directly reduce the amount of financial aid available. Therefore if, for example, you plan to buy a car before going to college, by all means do it before you fill out the Student's Financial Statement portion of your applications for financial aid. Holding the money as cash means diminishing financial aid possibilities, while holding the same amount of resources converted into a car means taking the money out of college cost resources entirely. That car may be part of your net worth, as is your clothing, but it doesn't count at all for financial aid purposes.

Similarly, while it is crucially important for the whole famly to save to meet coming college costs, it is equally important to know how to increase those savings during the preparatory years and as much as possible right on through the college years. One of the main things to bear in mind is that the rate of college-cost increases far outstrips whatever rates of interest you can safely get on your savings.

Current income will need to be allocated carefully before and during the entire college period. All too often, vacations, clubs, entertainment— all the discretionary income items—must be curtailed. Unless money is just not a question for you, cutting back and care during the college years can mean far smaller debts after those years. It's not much fun to pay high interest rates on long-term loans for many years, and it is often possible to minimize that kind of drain with prudent spending policies when you need them.

Current family income can often be augmented during the college years. More and more, women with children in college who have been at home for many years are going back into the working world. Very often they go solely because they want to build careers and independent lives now that their children are grown. More often they go back to work both to build independent careers and to help pay for college.

There's a trap here many women fall into. They find themselves back in the working world without the skills, current training, formal credentials, and experience they need to maximize both income and job satisfaction; they find that they must "take whatever they can get" to help pay for the enormous and immediate costs of college. The result is often low pay coupled with terrible dissatisfaction, not a very good combination for either marriages or college costs.

The answer again lies in early planning. Going back to school and to work while children are in high school makes sense; it helps guarantee that when those college bills come in there will be two effective career-building breadwinners sharing the load in that family.

There is no contradiction, either, in spending money to educate and train a woman who wants to go back to work while at the same time trying to put aside as much as possible for college-bound teenagers. There is no better investment, nothing that can even begin to touch the high rate of return on the investment. The difference between what an entry-level file clerk can earn and what an entry-level mature woman in any profession can earn is very large. Where else can you get at least $5,000 a year, every year, on an investment in training and credentials that can't be much larger than $10,000 all together?

MORTGAGING YOUR FUTURE

That college costs usually involve borrowing is a painful fact of current American life. In this book, we will carefully examine the borrowing alternatives available for students and their families.

One main question is, who does the borrowing? For example, the "cost of money" difference between a federally guaranteed student loan and a so-called student or college loan taken by a student's family at ordinary commercial bank interest rates is often very large. On the other hand, students and their families are often reluctant to mortgage a student's future earnings, especially when they may be relatively small during the early years. To know the borrowing alternatives and costs in this area is to be able to make an informed decision.

 Loan sources are discussed in Chapters 8 and 12.

TAX QUESTIONS

Astute tax planning is an important element of money-for-college planning. A caution here: All tax considerations should be taken up with your accountant or other tax adviser. No book can be specific enough to give precise advice fitting your particular personal situation. Usually the money you spend on long-term tax planning advice comes back to you manyfold over the years.

We will be discussing many tax aspects of money-for-college planning throughout this book as an integral part of many of the planning strategies suggested.

For example, those parents who are self-employed, especially those running family businesses employing others, need to give early thought to the possibility of hiring on their children during those long, long college intersessions and vacations. Talk to your accountant about what it takes to do so, what rates of pay are possible, whether or not you can handle items like a child's car insurance through the business. Remember, every dollar of college expenses you can share with Uncle Sam and the state and local taxing authorities is probably something like half a dollar saved for you.

HEDGING YOUR BETS

Illness, disability, and death are part of the human condition. We try to protect ourselves and those we love by insuring against those contingencies.

As always in discussing insurance, your aim is to get the protection you need, not more and not less, at the lowest possible cost. Insurance is never properly to be viewed as an investment. It is always to be viewed as contingency protection.

In the money-for-college area, careful assessment of all your insurance coverages is a vital necessity. You certainly don't want those to whom you are committed and who are depending on you to get partway through college to not be able to go on because you had not properly insured yourself. On the other hand, you don't want, for example, to spend thousands of dollars over a period of many years on life insurance that is far too expensive and the wrong kind for the job you want done. Chapter 3 discusses several aspects of insurance coverage.

STUDENT JOBS AND BUSINESSES

Student moneymaking ability is an important facet of money-for-college planning.

A full-time student should not, if at all possible, count on making all or most of college costs currently; a part-time student often does just that.

Family-supported students can supplement that support substantially by working part-time while school is in session and if at all possible full time during the balance of the year.

It is often very difficult for students to get work that can generate meaningful amounts of money for college, especially in recession years when students have in many instances been all but squeezed out of the work force. But there are significant moneymaking possibilities, both on and off campus.

 Student and family sources of additional income are discussed in Chapter 11.

FINANCIAL AID SOURCES

College-bound students and their families should not expect to find order and consistency in the ways in which financial aid for college is provided in the United States. There is no one underlying principle or overarching system that, when once understood, makes everything clear. The American approach to financial aid for college is piecemeal and diverse rather than systematic. You should expect to find the whole spectrum of financial aid initially confusing.

For instance, most financial aid awarded to college students today is adjusted in amount according to their family's financial need. But athletic scholarships for students who are specifically recruited to play varsity sports cover full costs for room, board, and tuition regardless of need at most of the country's colleges that have strong football and basketball teams (notably excepting the Ivy League colleges—Brown, Columbia, Cornell, Dartmouth, Harvard, Pennsylvania, Princeton, and Yale, which have no athletic scholarships as such and adjust all aid awards by need).

✗ Financial need also has no bearing on the payment of an average of $1,320 a year in Social Security educational benefits to each of some half-million college students who currently qualify for them. ✗

Moreover, students who join units of the ROTC (Reserve Officer Training Corps of the army, navy or air force) at scores of colleges receive substantial financial aid (payment of room, board, tuition plus a monthly stipend) regardless of financial need. Also providing a rigorous college education on an expense-paid basis plus pay without regard to need are not only the four U.S. armed service academies (West Point, Annapolis, Air Force, and Coast Guard), but the maritime academies of several states (New York and California among them).

As another example, there should be one best way for estimating the financial need of families for college aid. But there are at least five large-scale systems for determining financial need, each of which calls for you to fill out its own confidential financial statement form if you apply for aid from a source using that system. The five are:

1. College Scholarship Service (CSS) system of the College Entrance Examination Board or CEEB (which has the FAF form).

2. Student Need Analysis Service (SNAS) of the American College Testing Program (ACT) system (which uses the FFS form)

3. National Merit Scholarship Corporation (NMSC) system

4. Basic Educational Opportunity Grant (BEOG) system of the federal government

5. Tuition Assistance Program (TAP) system of New York State

All these systems are quite similar—they're based largely on your income-tax return data—but that still doesn't spare you the trouble of possibly having to get and fill out more than one of their forms. (Things are getting simpler, though, thanks to recent developments. For instance, starting in 1978, you can take the form of either system 1 or 2 to apply for a grant in system 4.)

On top of all this, the thousands of scholarship programs sponsored independently by colleges and by private agencies such as companies, foundations, churches, labor unions, veterans groups, and fraternal organizations each have their own eligibility rules, schedules, application forms, requirements, and selection criteria.

And if all this were not complicated enough, you can also choose among many options provided in a whole alternative approach—that of indirectly giving financial aid by offering college education for low-tuition or no-tuition charges. This is the approach of state universities and colleges, community colleges, external-degree colleges, and still other institutions in a whole large sector of American higher education.

Nevertheless, you can cope successfully with financial aid and benefit by possibly hundreds or thousands of dollars with some patience and the help of this book. We explain all the major things you need to know about financial aid here, so that you will be able to take advantage of it in much the same way you already take advantage of the similarly unsystematic American approach to merchandising all the things you buy.

A total strategy for meeting college costs requires thorough student and family understanding of costs, resources, income possibilities, financial aid available, and loan sources. The next chapter discusses that all-important first question: How much will it cost?

2

WHAT YOU FACE:
YOUR RANGE OF COLLEGE-COST
OPTIONS

INCREDIBLE as it may sound, the person generally viewed as the nation's highest education official recently resigned because the job did not pay enough for him to afford education for his children!

You can imagine the type of education he felt he couldn't afford as the U.S. Commissioner of Education at an annual salary of $37,800. Yes, it was college education—just what you yourself are facing.

"I will soon have three sons entering college," Terrel H. Bell explained when announcing his resignation as U.S. Commissioner on April 19, 1976. He noted that the first son would start college that fall, and that his new job paid 40 percent more than the federal one—some $11,000 more a year. The new job was commissioner of higher education and chairman of the board of regents in his home state, Utah.

But also incredible about Commissioner Bell's case is that he seemed reluctant to act on the wide range of cost options for college open to any American family. More than 95 percent of all families with children in college right now have annual incomes of less than $37,800, with some ranging down to $4,000 or less.

Knowing the full range of these basic cost options can be vital to you as a family or individual right at the start of planning how to meet your college costs. For you cannot possibly tell how much money you'll need until you know which broad cost options you might choose. Knowledge of them can even spell the difference between getting and not getting a college education.

The options range all the way from actually being paid to go to college on through your paying some $7,650 per year ($30,600 in all) for a four-year college education. And between these extremes you can combine many varieties of cost-cutting possibilities. (MIT—Massachusetts Institute of Technology—actually has the highest 1977–78 student expense budget for full-time dorm students of any well-known four-year college in the country —$7,950. But Harvard's corresponding $7,650 is used in illustrative examples in this book because MIT seems to represent a rather special case, with study programs concentrated heavily in science and engineering fields.)

WHAT MAY BE YOUR BIG STUMBLING BLOCK: THE PRESTIGE QUESTION

Before we look at concrete details of your basic cost options, let's first talk about likely beliefs of yours which might keep you from using some options that could save you the most money. After all, it's no good to you to know about the cost options if you feel some would be out of the question.

Parents and students in this country generally have deeply rooted prejudices and stereotypes about what kinds of colleges are best to attend. Those vaguely defined but socially recognized as high-prestige colleges are generally held in highest esteem by middle-class families. Though the fact is not often consciously realized, these are the colleges to which American families with the greatest social and financial status send their children.

There's an amazingly simple way to tell which colleges these are among the private institutions. They are with few exceptions the most expensive colleges in the country or in their regions—the colleges or universities that have the highest undergraduate tuition charges. These are colleges like Dartmouth and Princeton, Duke and Tulane, Caltech and Stanford.

Many American families of middle-class or higher status prefer to have their children go to such colleges as these. Their gut feeling is that their daughter or son at such a college will mingle with "the right people" for getting ahead.

That gut feeling is also protective, for parents also feel that at such colleges their children will not have to mingle with the crude, the vulgar, the common hoi polloi of no account who use bad language and may have corrupting habits and life-styles.

Feelings like this can easily be hidden in the case of such colleges, though, for these colleges are also ones that (for reasons too involved to go into here) have generally also developed the strongest academic prowess. So, what's wrong with wanting to go to a Harvard or Yale, a Stanford or Duke? Don't they give the best education?

What's Wrong with Fixation Only on High-Prestige Colleges

Two things are seriously wrong for a great many people who harbor ambitions along these lines, however. One is that feature already noted—their tendency to charge top-of-the-market prices. The possible hazard from peak costs appears in what admissions officers at Ivy League colleges call their "admit-deny" students. These are applicants for admission with financial aid who are granted admission but are denied financial aid. Denial of aid is based on lack of sufficient college aid funds; these students have at least some substantial need for aid that has been carefully ascertained by the college. And the admissions directors observe that quite a few of the admit-deny students accept and attend anyway, finding the money God knows how. As such admit-deny cases suggest, a blind admiration of yours for one of these colleges could lead you to positively sacrificial spending for college.

More cruelly wrong about lusting after an expensive prestige college to the point of obsession is that it blocks out much more humane and effective alternatives for many a student. This can be acutely agonizing to a son or daughter who doesn't quite have the supercapability scholastically (about top 5 percent nationwide) and special personal pizzazz accepted by these elite colleges (or the combination of poverty–minority status and promise of gifts for supercapability and pizzazz with which the colleges commendably season their entering classes). Given sufficient pressure from parents, such a young person who is in fact extremely capable—ranking, say, in the top 10 percent nationwide instead of the top 5 percent—may easily be rejected by these colleges and wind up feeling like an utter failure at seventeen.

Most middle-class parents and students are more reasonable, though, and find lesser though acceptable levels of prestige at colleges that have campuses resembling country estates (or country clubs) and "good reputations"—mainly small, private liberal arts colleges and strong state universities that in each case steadily generate favorable publicity. It is also felt important for prestige to have the son or daughter "go away to college" or at least live on campus rather than at home when they attend such acceptable institutions.

As Prestige Drops, Where Do You Say No?

Alternatives for attending college beyond these feature prestige of decreasingly acceptable levels for middle-class families until levels "out of the question" in the eyes of many families are reached. Here are a few possibilities across the range of those levels in roughly decreasing order of acceptability on grounds of social prestige or status. (And, significantly, in roughly decreasing order of cost.) Do you reach an "out-of-the-question" point for yourself as you go down the list?

1. Student lives at home and commutes by car to a four-year college that's private with a country-estate campus.

2. Student lives at home and commutes by car to a four-year state college with a rural but tacky campus and many students from lower-income families.

3. Student lives at home and commutes by mass transit to a four-year public college that's in a dense urban area (perhaps a slum) and has no green, grassy campus and many low-income students.

4. Student lives at home and commutes by mass transit to a two-year public college, a "community college" that's in several floors of an office building in a run-down business section of the city and is overcrowded with poverty and minority group students.

Gradations of college social prestige (or lack of it) as illustrated by these alternatives, from top to bottom, cannot be evaluated with any degree of accuracy or objectivity. But they are still quite real, though individually varying, for every American who's involved with college in any way. Wherever you may stand in the scale of aspiration for college prestige, we're not asking you to ignore your attitudes about such prestige. But we are urging you to be enlightened and even shrewd about those attitudes in the interest of saving yourself perhaps thousands of dollars. And we briefly give you ideas in the next section on how to be shrewd.

Ways to Get Both Prestige and Lower Costs in Going to College

To reap the benefits of both acceptable prestige and minimized costs from college, you should keep two general rules in mind. These are:

1. Substantial to quite high prestige for practical purposes (jobs, graduate schools) accrues to any student who develops an exceptionally outstanding record of performance both in studies and activities (college, social service, interest/hobby or career activities), regardless of the kind of college attended (as long as the college is "regionally accredited," as most colleges are). This holds true because high performance in itself still commands considerable social prestige in America, regardless of one's past social setting and connections.

2. If least college costs are important for you but you still want attendance at a college of at least some prestige, you should combine getting much or most of a college education at a low-cost college with finishing for a degree at a higher-cost, prestige college.

Many American families today apply rule 2 by having the student complete the first two college years through commuting to a local community college and then transferring to a four-year college of acceptable prestige for the last two years. However, many other combinations are possible. For example, the student might commute to a city or state four-year college for the bachelor's degree and then earn a one-year master's degree from a prestige college or university. Or the student might complete the first three years in commuting to a city or state four-year college and then transfer to a prestige college for only the senior year and bachelor's degree (though a few prestige colleges require two years of full-time attendance instead of just one for the bachelor's degree).

A strategy like this of low-cost early years and higher-cost later years at a prestige institution might be especially advisable for you if you or a child plan graduate professional study beyond the bachelor's—as in law, medicine, dentistry, librarianship, business administration (for the two-year M.B.A., master of business administration degree), or engineering.

Some students start college at a prestige institution and then transfer to a lower-cost option after a year or two. This can be used to establish lifelong social ties with the prestige college, if you like, for these colleges commonly consider as alumni "nongraduates" who may have attended full time for only one academic year.

Should you plan to transfer (or go on to graduate study) up in the academic-social scale, be careful to do two things. First, check the standards and requirements for transfer (or graduate) admission at the later, higher-prestige college and make sure they can be met. Second, act on rule 1 to rack up the highest possible performance at the earlier, low-cost college because doing so is valuable both in itself and in applying for transfer or graduate admission.

Now, here are specific details illustrating your basic college cost options, roughly in order from least to most expensive. These are the broad options you might combine in a strategy of your own for maximum prestige at minimum cost. Or you might act on them simply for minimum cost, period. Most but not all involve choices of higher or lower prestige as you will see.

BEING PAID TO GO TO COLLEGE AT THE FIVE U.S. SERVICE ACADEMIES

The cost option representing one extreme for college attendance—actually being paid to go to college—is offered at all five of the U.S. service academies (given below in about their order of familiarity to the public):

U.S. Military Academy (West Point)
U.S. Naval Academy (Annapolis)
U.S. Air Force Academy
U.S. Coast Guard Academy
U.S. Merchant Marine Academy

Acting on this option requires at least tolerance by the student of spending some years either in military service or at sea, as well as considerable capability in academy study programs heavily concentrated in engineering and administration subjects. From four to six years' active service after graduation with the bachelor's degree from any of these academies is required. After that, though, graduates can (and many do) pursue non-military (or landlubber) careers. Also, the option is open only to the few thousand students a year admitted by the academies.

Women as well as men are now eligible. Admission requirements are being nominated by an official (most often your U.S. Congressperson, but the Coast Guard Academy requires no nomination), having fairly but not extremely high academic qualifications for success in the competitive selections, and meeting strict physical and health stipulations (and also being in the seventeen-through-twenty-one age bracket, never married, and a U.S. citizen with a clean criminal and moral record).

But what does it pay? In addition to free tuition and fees, room and board, books and supplies and medical care, more than $300 a month at all but the Merchant Marine Academy. Merchant Marine students get the same things free and an annual allowance of some $575 a year for three years and, for the one year of four that they spend at sea, they are paid about $300 a month.

> If this special but valuable cost option (worth upwards of $40,000) appeals to you, write for current details to the director of admissions at (choose ones you prefer) U.S. Air Force Academy, Colorado Springs, Colo. 80840; U.S. Coast Guard Academy, New London, Conn. 06320; U.S. Merchant Marine Academy, Kings Point, N.Y. 11024; U.S. Military Academy, West Point, N.Y. 10996; and U.S. Naval Academy, Annapolis, Md. 21402.

BIG MONEY-SAVER (UP TO $4,000 OR MORE) AT ALL OTHER COST OPTIONS: EARNING COLLEGE-DEGREE CREDITS BY EXAMINATIONS

Fairly bright and academically motivated students at good college-preparatory high schools almost always have the chance today to complete as much as a full year's work toward their college degrees while still in high school. Any student who does this obviously saves the cost of a year's full-time college study—ranging in cost up to $7,000 or more a year. Not so obviously, the student in addition very probably saves the loss of earnings through a year that would otherwise have to be spent in college. That amount realized in otherwise lost earnings might reasonably be valued at a minimum of $4,000.

In consequence, a student who completes a year's college work in high school can increase the family's financial resources (or his or her own resources) by this $4,000 or more plus whatever a year of college costs in that individual case—$3,000 to $4,000 on the average, say, for a total of some $7,000 or more. Hard and serious studying in high school can in this way be quite well-paid work for a teenage youngster, especially since the study effort for college-credit work in high school often does not need to occupy substantially more of the student's time than just working to get good grades in regular high school courses.

How You Can Get Credits toward Your College Degree While Still in High School

College-level courses in high school have become widely available through the Advanced Placement Program (APP) of the College Entrance Examination Board (CEEB). Descriptions of twenty college-level courses in some fifteen subjects (including courses in art, mathematics, English, the sciences, history, foreign languages) high schools can offer are published by the CEEB. High schools widely give as many of these courses as their teachers and students show interest in having. The courses are open to students after they complete regular high school courses in the different subjects (usually by the time the students are high school juniors or seniors).

AP examinations on the basis of which 1,500 or more colleges grant credit are also offered by the CEEB for each APP course, with the exams being administered nationwide each May. Exams are scored on a scale ranging from a low of 1 to a high of 5. While each college sets its own policy on what credits by AP examination it will grant, AP exam marks of 3 or more are high enough to be worth course credits toward degrees at many hundreds of colleges.

You would get credits toward your college degree by having reports of your AP exam scores (and possibly other information) sent to the college that had admitted you and that you had agreed to attend (when you are a graduating high school senior). The college would grant you credit according to its policies.

Even if a student's high school does not offer one or another (or any) AP courses, any very ambitious student can get literature on them from X the CEEB and can study with the individual help of interested teachers (or on the student's own) and take AP exams for possible credit.

Any AP course work or good exam scores a student can get will be of benefit even if cost savings are not sought. AP achievements on a student's high school transcript (record of academic work in high school) enhance the student's chances of admission to sought-after colleges. For example, Harvard University especially values the AP entrant and for a number of years has admitted some 10 percent of each entering class with sophomore standing on the basis largely of AP results (course marks and exam scores), thus granting each of these students credit for a full year of Harvard study that currently costs dorm students more than $7,000.

A year's college credit, you might note, would normally amount to four or five yearlong AP courses and/or exams. Students who complete two or three AP courses/exams for a half-year's credit could, of course, benefit by saving a half-year's college costs and lost earnings.

Some 200 colleges and universities will admit you with sophomore (second-year) standing if you get AP exam scores acceptable to the college on three or more AP exams. The colleges include Princeton, Yale, and the universities of Hawaii, Kentucky, Missouri, Utah, and Wisconsin.

> For current details about your AP opportunities, inquire at your high school guidance office or write: Advanced Placement Program, College Entrance Examination Board, 888 Seventh Ave., New York, N.Y. 10019.

You Can Also Widely Earn Degree Credits by Examination While You Are in College

Many thousands of bright and ambitious students a year also cut down on both their college tuition costs and classroom boredom through earning degree credits by examinations while they are in college. They do this through two other programs of examinations that many hundreds of colleges recognize for granting credits toward their degrees—the "College-Level Examination Program" ("CLEP") of the CEEB and the "Proficiency Examination Program" ("PEP") of the American College Testing Program (ACT).

You might be especially interested to know that one group of these examinations—the "CLEP General Examinations"—can be used to earn almost a full year of credits at many colleges (up to about twenty-six semester-hour credits, compared to the normal average of thirty semester-hour credits for a full-year's full-time study in college courses).

The CLEP Generals are not impossibly difficult exams. Thousands of college students (as well as many adults beyond the usual college age) have earned credit-qualifying scores on them. They consist of five exams, each with a ninety-minute time limit, so that they may all be taken in a single day's testing. The five are English composition, humanities (literature and fine arts subjects), mathematics, natural sciences, and social sciences-history (social sciences include economics, sociology, and anthropology). Lively cultural interests that have long been cultivated, wide reading, and a good, well-rounded education in and beyond high school should prepare your child or you to do well on the CLEP Generals.

Other CLEP and PEP examinations each cover the content (and are worth the credit) of one-year or one-semester college courses. You would thus have to earn credit-qualifying scores on four or five of the exams (ones worth the credits of one-year courses) in order to get credits equal to about a year's college attendance.

If you want to gauge readiness or see specifically how to prepare for CLEP or PEP exams, you can get descriptive and study-guide material on them without charge by writing:

College-Level Examination Program, College Entrance Examinati
Board, 888 Seventh Ave., New York, N.Y. 10019; or

Proficiency Examination Program, American College Testing
gram, Box 168, Iowa City, Iowa 52240 (or, if you are in New York
State, write to the agency that originated the program: New York
State Education Department, College Proficiency Examination Program, 99 Washington Ave., Albany, N.Y. 12230).

Each college sets its own individual policies on what credits (if any)
it gives for which of the CLEP or PEP exams. You should therefore be sure
to check with any individual college in question at the start of your CLEP
or PEP exam inquiries. Rest assured, though, that many hundreds of
colleges do recognize these exams for credit—more than 1,200 colleges,
for instance, in the case of CLEP exams.

It might be helpful for you to understand two things concerning the
content covered on any of these exams. One is that demonstrating knowledge of the content on one of the exams can spare a student the boredom
of having to cover essentially the same content in course attendance. The
other is that colleges do not grant exam credit for any exam that covers
essentially the same content as a course through which a student has
already earned degree credit.

Two Similar Savers of up to a Year's "Lost Earnings": College "Early Admissions" Plans and College Summer Sessions

Two other types of offerings by colleges enable industrious and bright high
school students to graduate a semester or year early from college—and thus
save a half-year or year of earnings otherwise lost through college attendance. These offerings are "early admissions" plans and college summer
session courses open to high school students.

Colleges with early admissions plans admit especially capable students
a semester or a year before their high school graduation. Some colleges with
summer sessions permit qualified high school students to take degree-credit
courses in summers both before and after the student's senior year in high
school.

Look for word of these types of offerings in college directories, catalogs,
or announcements if they interest you. Some scores of colleges across the
country have them. And don't confuse "early admission" with "early
decision" plans. Early decision plans of colleges are ones in which the
college notifies early decision applicants of acceptance or rejection early
(usually by about December 1 of the high school senior year), but do not
provide for admission before high school graduation.

LEAST COST IN AN UNCONVENTIONAL MODE: SOUND NEW ROUTES TO AN "EXTERNAL DEGREE"

Getting a college education and degree at just about rock-bottom cost is open to you or your child through any one of three new institutions dedicated entirely to awarding "external degrees." The three are:

Regents External Degree Program of the University of the State of New York

Thomas A. Edison College of the State of New Jersey

Board for State Academic Awards of the State of Connecticut

Each of these three institutions awards regular college degrees— bachelor's degrees just like those you would get on graduating from regular four-year colleges and associate's degrees just like those gotten on graduating from two-year colleges. The educational authorities of each of their sponsoring states fully back these external degrees, and the degrees have become about as widely recognized—for employment or for admission to higher-degree studies—as similar degrees awarded by regular state universities and colleges.

Many unusual advantages are open to you if you choose to get your college education via an external degree. Among these advantages are:

1. *Rock-bottom costs*, running as low as only some $600 or $700 for an entire bachelor's degree program (or half that for an associate's degree program).

Each external-degree institution recognizes programs of examinations for degree credit, including those described in the previous section. Students can earn external degrees entirely by examinations if they wish. Those who opt for this pay only annual external-degree program fees of some $25 to $50, examination fees ranging mainly from $15 to $35 per examination, and costs of books they use to learn college subjects by independent self-study (and thus prepare for the exams). Total costs when proceeding in this way (entirely by examination) currently come to as little as $600 or $700 for a bachelor's degree.

Earning a college degree by exams usually takes special maturity, initiative, and determination. But it can save from $12,000 to $25,000 or more in direct college costs—a thought that may help spur determination.

2. *Studying wherever you happen to be*, for the external degree institutions have no attendance requirements whatever; students in all states of the United States and even many foreign countries have already earned external degrees. Examinations through which you would earn credits toward your degree are given several times a year at colleges throughout the country and are also available in many foreign countries.

3. *Studying while you are working or raising a family full time*, because the institutions have no schedule requirements as well as no attendance

requirements. You can advance at any pace practical for your individual needs. Some unusual individuals have completed all work for bachelor's degrees in as little as a year or two while also holding a job. Others take as much longer as they choose than the conventional four years for a bachelor's.

This feature can prove a very large money-saver on college costs. One of the highest costs of college is hidden—the cost in lost earnings while attending college. And earnings need not be lost if you go for an external degree.

4. *Applying credit from college attendance and credit by exam toward your degree in any combination you want.* The three external-degree institutions also accept credits you have earned in attending college courses. External degrees can and have been awarded entirely on the basis of transfer of college course credits, usually credits from a number of different colleges. You can thus combine credits from attendance and from external-degree study in any way you want (being careful to plan your studies to meet external degree "distribution" requirements for amounts of credit in kinds of subjects).

This feature can prove a godsend to persons who must leave college and go to work before finishing because they don't have enough money. Indeed, the new external-degree institutions—introduced only in this decade—have enabled a number of persons who had been in exactly this fix to become college graduates.

5. *Degree credits for college-level learning you have gained in cultural experience or work.* If you have learned some skills or special bodies of knowledge that are taught in college-credit courses, you can get degree credits for them from the external-degree institutions. For instance, fluency in speaking and writing a foreign language that you may have learned from parents or grandparents while you grew up might be used to earn credit by examination. Or skill in industrial photography, business management, or any of a great many other specialties could be appraised for degree credits through carefully designed procedures for special assessment.

Full information on your very unusual opportunities through external degrees (including information on study guides helpful in preparing for the exams) may be obtained on request from the institutions:

Regents External Degree Program of the University of the State of New York, 99 Washington Ave., Albany, N.Y. 12230

Thomas A. Edison College, Forrestal Center, Forrestal Rd., Princeton, N.J. 08540

Board for State Academic Awards, 340 Capitol Ave., Hartford, Conn. 06115

ALSO FINANCIALLY FEASIBLE WHILE WORKING FULL TIME: NIGHT COLLEGE OR "WEEKEND COLLEGE" AND NEW NONRESIDENCE STUDY PROGRAMS

Should you (or your son or daughter) have to work full time while going to college, night classes offered by many colleges in large cities represent a time-honored way for getting a college education. It does take high interest and a high energy level for a student to go this route, though many thousands have. Those who do generally find that getting a degree takes about twice as long as in full-time study—that is, about eight years for a bachelor's degree.

Night-college costs are also not inconsiderable. For an entire degree program, they are essentially the same as those for full-time commuting students (ones who live at home and commute to college classes). At 1977–78 levels of college charges, these total costs for a bachelor's would average $9,944 at a public four-year college and $17,324 at a private four-year college (according to *Student Expenses at Postsecondary Institutions 1977–78*, Elizabeth W. Suchar et al., New York: CEEB, 1977—subsequently referred to as *Student Expenses 1977–78*. Cost figures given in it and in this chapter are essentially costs for one nine-month academic year).

But night-college study does have the advantage of spreading these costs over more years than usual and (for students working full time) of offsetting these costs by current earnings (which hopefully may increase as fast as inflation in college costs over the years of college study). Night-college students usually can't qualify for financial aid.

In recent years colleges have introduced new programs designed to be more convenient for working adults than part-time evening study. These programs generally require less or very little attendance at the college, and have been launched by many colleges throughout the country (and particularly by colleges in or near big cities).

"Weekend college" is a frequent name for one type of new program for working adults. In weekend college programs, students attend classes only on weekends and can finish a bachelor's degree in four years. Regular tuition rates are charged.

In still other new programs, students study largely on their own and are required to attend sessions with college faculty members only every few months or only a few weeks a year. These programs have many different names, but they are all identified in announcements and ads as programs especially for adults leading busy lives. For convenience we call them nonresidence study programs here because they do not require students to meet the usual residence (attendance) requirements. Tuition is charged in all of them.

Because required attendance is infrequent in nonresidence programs, you might select one at a college a long distance away and still be able to get your college education and degree through it.

You may find nonresidence programs by inquiring at colleges or watching for news announcements or ads about them in your area. Some of the larger or older nonresidence programs that offer college degrees and from which you can obtain information are:

Empire State College, 2 Union Ave., Saratoga Springs, N.Y. 12866. This nonresidence college of the State University of New York operates at some twenty centers throughout the state and has students from other states and even a few foreign countries. Students may enroll on a half-time (or even quarter-time) study basis.

External Degree Programs, California State University and Colleges Consortium, 5670 Wilshire Blvd., Los Angeles, Calif. 90036. Various institutions among the nineteen state universities and colleges in this statewide system offer nonresidence programs on the college junior- and senior-year levels.

TV College, City Colleges of Chicago Central Office, 180 N. Michigan Ave., Chicago, Ill. 60601. Two-year associate in arts degrees may be earned entirely through courses broadcast on the educational TV station WTTW in this nonresidence program. The Chicago station has a range of about seventy-five miles.

Open University, University College, University of Maryland, College Park, Md. 20742. Attendance at only one weekend seminar per semester in introductory courses is required; bachelor's degree study can be completed in about six years of study, with study time averaging some twelve to fifteen hours a week.

College of Liberal Studies, University of Oklahoma, Norman, Okla. 73069.

Adult Degree Program, Goddard College, Plainfield, Vt. 05667. Campus sessions in this program are also available in Pacific Grove, Calif.

Independent Study Programs of Syracuse University, Room 21, 610 Fayette St., Syracuse, N.Y. 13202.

Metropolitan State University of Minnesota, St. Paul, Minn. 55101. Offers nonresidence programs on the college junior- and senior-year levels.

Coordinated Off-Campus Degree Program, Upper Iowa University, Fayette, Iowa 52142.

University Without Walls, Union for Experimenting Colleges and Universities, Antioch College, Yellow Springs, Ohio 45387. Some thirty colleges and universities across the country offer nonresidence programs under University Without Walls auspices. Most students in the UWW programs, however, pursue degree study on a full-time basis.

LEAST-COST CONVENTIONAL WAY: COMMUTING TO COMMUNITY COLLEGE

For many families and students pressed to save money on college, the most common least-cost alternative is to live at home and commute to a public two-year college—often called a community college. At community colleges, students can usually take two-year "transfer" programs and then transfer to four-year colleges for their last two years and bachelor's degrees. Or they can take two-year programs (also leading to associate's degrees) that prepare them to go to work right after community college graduation, often in rather lucrative fields with brisk employment demand such as registered nurse, veterinarian's assistant, X-ray technologist, or technician in one of many engineering specialties.

Tuition and other fees required for commuting students represent the core cost of this option. Such "tuition and fees" costs now average nationally some $400 per academic year, compared to corresponding figures of about $2,500 at private four-year colleges or about $620 at public four-year colleges.

You would have to scrape up some hundreds of dollars a year more than tuition and fees for community college tuition and fees (averaging $400). Averages for other kinds of expenses you would incur (according to *Student Expenses 1977–78*) include some $400 for commuting costs and about $200 for books and supplies. Further expenses also include another $460 for personal costs of such things as clothes replacement, laundry, toilet articles, and recreation, plus an allocation of about $860 for room and board to cover partial costs of living at home as well as meals and snacks bought on campus.

Families would probably have to pay for the $460 in personal expenses and $860 in room and board anyway were the son or daughter living at home without going to college. Leaving these cost items out gives a year's out-of-pocket expense of community college attendance of about $1,000 (again, as a national average). Adding these two cost items in gives a corresponding year's cost of $2,300.

That last $2,300 figure is not much lower than the total cost of some $2,500 (also a national average) for commuting to a public four-year college (state college or university).

Actual charges for tuition and fees vary by some hundreds of dollars in different parts of the country. California continues to keep its community college costs low (and opportunities abundant), charging only fees (and no tuition) that run less than $50 a year. Tuition and fees at public two-year colleges in Texas run from $150 to $300; in Illinois, from $300 to $500; in Pennsylvania, around $500 to $600; and in New York State, some $700 to $800 or more (but with this cost being offset by the state's Tuition Assistance Program [TAP] aid that is available to all state residents attending colleges in the state).

POPULAR ECONOMICAL WAY: IN-STATE STATE COLLEGE OR UNIVERSITY

As just noted, commuting to a four-year state college or university generally costs only a few hundred dollars more a year than commuting to a community college—some $220 a year more on the core cost of tuition and fees using national averages of some $400 for community colleges vs. about $620 for public four-year colleges.

Commuting to a four-year state college or university has consequently proven popular as an economical avenue to college education—for those lucky enough to live within commuting range of these four-year institutions. For students whose aim is a bachelor's degree and college prestige with reasonable economy, this option would probably be more desirable than commuting to a community college for the first two years.

Attending a four-year state college or university as a dorm student instead of a commuter also proves a low-cost option for many families and students who think it very important to live on campus. At these public four-year colleges, total cost budgets per year run some $2,500 for commuter students vs. about $2,900 for dorm students (in national averages according to *Student Expenses 1977–78*).

You should also realize that some of these state universities are among the highest-prestige colleges in their regions (these are often but not always regions in which private colleges of very high prestige have not been developed). Among such high-prestige state universities are the University of Virginia at Charlottesville, the University of North Carolina at Chapel Hill, "Ole Miss" (the University of Mississippi in Oxford, where novelist William Faulkner lived), the universities of Minnesota, Wisconsin at Madison, Iowa, Texas at Austin, Washington, and (before the 1960s) the University of California at Berkeley.

Costs of tuition and fees vary by states among these public four-year colleges, or even within states. Tuition and fees at California state colleges and universities run some $200, but at campuses of the University of California system they run more than $600. State university tuition-and-fees charges run around $400 or $500 in Arkansas, around $450 to $550 in Arizona, Kentucky, and North Carolina, around $650 in Massachusetts, and some $800 or more in New York State (these are academic-year figures for in-state residents; out-of-state students are charged from $500 to $2,000 more).

What about going to a state university as an out-of-state student? This usually costs about the same as going as a dorm student to middle-range private four-year colleges in your region. For instance, total cost budgets for out-of-state dorm students at the University of Arizona or the University of Maryland are some $4,500—compared to some $4,800 as the comparable cost budget at private four-year colleges (national average). State university costs for out-of-state dorm students might run somewhat lower, though, in specific cases—for instance, some $4,000 for the University of Massachusetts at Amherst or $2,900 at the University of Arkansas at Fayetteville.

EARNING UP TO HALF YOUR COLLEGE COSTS IN A CO-OP WORK-STUDY PROGRAM

Some colleges offer co-operative work-study programs in which students alternate periods of on-campus study with periods of paid employment—usually in a field related to the student's area of study and career interest. Students can often earn up to about half of their college costs in such co-op work-study jobs. They also benefit by getting two or more years of on-the-job experience in their career areas by the time of college graduation, which in turn usually brings opportunities for more responsible and higher-paid jobs.

Among important features of these programs for prospective students are that co-op jobs are most often located by the college and need not be found by the student. Many, though by no means all, co-op programs are in engineering and business fields. In some of the programs, five years rather than the customary four years of full-time study are needed to complete work for the bachelor's.

As an example of how earnings and costs work in such programs, co-op students at Northeastern University in Boston can earn as much as $11,000 in its five-year bachelor's program. And five-year costs for co-op dorm students there run about $23,000.

Among other colleges well known for their co-op programs are Antioch College in Ohio, Auburn University in Alabama, Drexel Institute in Philadelphia, Illinois Institute of Technology in Chicago, and the University of Cincinnati (which originated co-op work-study programs).

A current list of more than 900 co-op programs ("Undergraduate Programs of Cooperative Education in the United States and Canada" booklet) may be obtained free on request from: National Commission for Cooperative Education, 360 Huntington Ave., Boston, Mass. 02115.

THE FEW PRIVATE COLLEGES WHERE ALL STUDENTS WORK TO CUT THEIR COSTS—AND A FEW OTHER SPECIAL LOW-COST COLLEGES

At a small handful of private colleges, all students work to run the college's physical plant (and sometimes related enterprises like farms) and also thus cut their college costs to only several hundred dollars a year or less. These colleges generally operate this way mainly to benefit students from low-income families in their locales, though they admit some low-income students from distant homes. They claim benefits to education and character in having all students work for the college community, in some cases even putting up college buildings.

These are all regionally accredited colleges that provide sound education in the liberal arts and sciences and/or career areas. Should they interest you, you may write them for details, as follows:

> *Alice Lloyd College*, Pippa Passes, Ky. 41844. (This is the only one that is a two-year college; the others all award bachelor's degrees.)
>
> *Berea College*, Berea, Ky. 40403
>
> *School of the Ozarks*, Point Lookout, Mo. 65726.
>
> *Warren Wilson College*, Swannanoa, N.C. 28778. (Work scholarships here involving fifteen hours a week of work by all students realize financial aid of more than $600 a year for the student.)

Among a few other special colleges that offer most unusual, low-cost options are two private colleges that for many years made no student charges but now have very low charges:

> *Cooper Union*, Cooper Square, New York, N.Y. 10003. (This is a college mainly for engineering, architecture, and art studies with $200 a year tuition and fees and no dorms.)
>
> *Webb Institute of Naval Architecture*, Crescent Beach Rd., Glen Cove, Long Island, N.Y. 11542. (Webb has free tuition, charges $1,850 for room and board, and awards bachelor's degrees only in naval architecture and marine engineering.)

State maritime academies also offer special low-cost opportunities, combining the attractions of low state-college fees with a $600-a-year grant (from the U.S. Maritime Administration) for any student who is a U.S. citizen. Students graduate with both a bachelor's degree (in nautical science or marine engineering) and a third mate's or third assistant engineer's license in the merchant marine (with good prospects for jobs paying more than $10,000 a year and no living expenses while living at sea). Among these academies are:

> *California Maritime Academy*, Box 192, Vallejo, Calif. 94590.
>
> *Maine Maritime Academy*, Castine, Me. 04421.
>
> *State University Maritime College*, Fort Schuyler, Bronx, N.Y. 10465.

LESS-EXPENSIVE PRIVATE COLLEGES

If you're looking for a private, four-year college of the less-expensive variety, you'll be lucky to settle on one that has costs around the national averages for such colleges—annually, around $2,500 for tuition and fees, and some $4,800 in total cost budget for dorm students (or $4,300 for commuting students). For instance, here are costs at representative colleges of this type in various parts of the country:

	'77–'78 tuition & fees	'77–'78 total budget, dorm student
Baylor University, Texas	$1,800	$4,800
Southwestern at Memphis, Tenn.	2,950	5,250
Marietta College, Ohio	3,124	4,900
Creighton University, Neb.	2,600	4,800
Westminster College, Pa.	2,670	4,500
Presbyterian College, S.C.	2,450	4,215
Wake Forest University, N.C.	2,600	4,450

But costs of this order are generally higher than those of state colleges and state universities in your state (national averages per year: About $620 in tuition and fees, $2,900 total cost budget for dorm students).

You probably can find a few regionally accredited, private four-year colleges with costs lower than those of your own state's college and universities. These are likely to be in the South and West, where colleges generally have lower costs than those in the Middle Atlantic and New England states. But such very inexpensive private colleges are most likely quite small and little-known outside their immediate areas. One, for example, is Blue Mountain College in Blue Mountain, Miss. It has some 300 students, and its '76–'77 costs were $1,130 for tuition and fees, and $2,610 as the total annual cost budget for a dorm student.

MOST-EXPENSIVE PRIVATE COLLEGES

You would face a total annual cost budget of some $7,500 or more at one of the country's most-expensive private colleges, with tuition and fees alone often running well over $4,000 a year. Colleges like this represent your most extreme college cost option on the high end.

As examples, here are most of the current "price leaders" on total student expense budgets among four-year colleges today (in order of total budget for dorm students, 1977–78):

	'77–'78 tuition & fees	'77–'78 total budget, dorm student
Massachusetts Institute of Technology (MIT)	$4,500	$7,950
Harvard University (Harvard & Radcliffe)	4,100	7,650
Brown University	4,810	7,630

University of Pennsylvania	4,450	7,575
Columbia University		
(Columbia College)	4,350	7,500
Princeton University	4,650	7,495
Bennington College	5,500	7,465
Dartmouth College	4,530	7,425
Hampshire College	5,000	7,400
California Institute of the Arts	3,450	7,380
Stanford University	4,695	7,365
Cornell University	4,450	7,200
Bryn Mawr College	4,725	7,165
Skidmore College	4,270	7,050
California Institute of Technology		
(Caltech)	3,939	7,044
Williams College	4,220	7,020

A few words may be in order to ease your shock at the thought of perhaps actually paying four years of costs like these. For one thing, colleges with such costs are also generally colleges that award the largest amount of their own funds in financial aid.

Behind their high-charges/high-aid approach stands a certain view. Key canons in that credo include not giving "hidden scholarships" to very affluent families by setting tuition and other charges far lower than the college's actual cost of education. They also want to avoid becoming ghettos of the rich. They accordingly admit highly qualified students across a fairly representative range of economic status in the United States and offer aid in proportion to financial need to as many accepted applicants as their funds permit.

The result is that their peak rates are not fixed price tags for many students acceptable to them who also have financial need. They charge such students, in effect, on a sliding scale. This is illustrated concretely in Chapter 8 "Getting Aid from Colleges."

But if you don't have financial need—or otherwise don't get offered financial aid—college costs in this $7,000-a-year-and-up bracket could represent an actual cost option to you at the high extreme. Probably well over one-fourth of all families sending students to such colleges really do pay the costs shown. Such families include one who, the colleges figure, can afford the costs. Also among them are families of admit-deny aid applicants (mentioned before) who the colleges figure cannot afford the costs but who go anyway, some through sacrificial spending.

KEY POINT FOR YOUR PLANNING: PROBABLY SPREAD YOUR BETS ACROSS SEVERAL COST OPTIONS

It would probably be wise for you to spread your alternatives across several of these basic cost options for college. You would do this in planning for actual college and financial aid applications, as outlined later in Chapters 6 through 8. Your strategy in planning might be to try for high-cost (and probably high-prestige) options that you could afford if you get enough aid, while also setting up successively lower-cost options—some that would be financially feasible for you without aid and others that would be actual money-savers for you.

For quick reference in planning, here's a summary list of the basic options we've covered (roughly in order from lowest to highest cost, as covered):

Your Basic Cost Options for College	*Financial Impact on You*
U.S. service academies	Pays all costs plus $300 a month to the student
Credit by examination (in high school or college)	A supplement—can save up to a year's college costs— some $1,500 to $7,500
"Early admission" plans or early college summer sessions	Can also save up to a year's college costs
External degree	Costs only about $600 to $700 for an entire bachelor's degree program if done all by exams
Night college, or new "weekend college" or nonresidence study programs	Can also save four years of lost earnings
Commuting to community college	Costs about $1,000 to $2,300 a year
In-state state university or college	
Commuting	Costs about $2,500 a year
Dorm student	Costs about $2,900 a year
Co-op work-study program	Earnings cover about half of total college costs
Very few colleges where all students work (and a few other special colleges)	Can mean little or no cost for college (with aid from other sources, in some cases)
Less-expensive private colleges	
Commuting	About $4,300 a year
Dorm student	Some $4,800 a year
Most-expensive private colleges (dorm student)	$7,000 to $7,650 a year

    Several examples of how you might spread the options you choose among these alternatives are given in Chapter 6.

But while we're introducing you to the whole question of college costs in this chapter, we should briefly explain one point about costs that's crucial for what is defined as your "financial need"—and hence for the amounts of money you might get in a great many financial aid programs today.

The crucial point is that the cost figures of individual colleges that are used in official determinations of your financial need are those given in each college's "student expense budget." This student expense budget is worked out and used by the college's financial aid office. In many cases, it isn't published in the college's own catalogs and other literature (though there's a current trend for increasing numbers of colleges to include it in information pieces on their financial aid).

Student expense budgets include (as you might expect) the traditionally published college charges for tuition and fees (fees charged all students), room and board. But they also include average figures for the following inherent costs that are not necessarily charged students by the college:

Transportation (to and from the student's home)
Personal expenses (replacement clothes, laundry, and the like)
Books and supplies

Student expense budgets can directly affect your pocketbook in this way. The large majority of financial aid programs today adjust the amount of aid you get according to your officially defined financial need. To determine your need, agencies first calculate what they expect you should provide out of your income and assets toward college costs. They use elaborate procedures of "need analysis" to do this. The dollar total they expect from you will be the same for any college in any one need analysis system; there are various ones.

Your need at any one college is then figured by taking the student expense budget at the college and subtracting from it the total expected dollar amount for you. For instance, a total student expense budget of $5,000 less $3,000 expected from you equals a financial need in your case of $2,000 at that college. And naturally, for a college at which your student expense budget would total $3,000, you would have no financial need (were your total expected still the same $3,000).

About the only general source of these crucial "student expense budget" costs at almost all colleges is the annual *Student Expenses at Postsecondary Institutions* booklet that was often quoted from and cited earlier in this chapter. As the booklet shows, any one college actually has different student expense budgets for different types of students. The four types of students for whom this booklet gives total budget figures are those living on campus in dorms, those living at the college in off-campus private housing, commuter students living at home, and self-supporting students not dependent on their parents.

Student expense budgets seem to give some financial advantage to commuting students who live at home. They commonly include an allowance for the room and board of the student living at home that's more than half of what room and board at college costs for dorm students. But families would often be paying those at-home room-and-board costs even if the offspring weren't going to college. The result is apparently to inflate somewhat need-based awards made to commuting students, compared to need-based awards made to dorm students.

3
SEEING YOUR ASSETS
AS MONEY-FOR-COLLEGE SOURCES

IN considering your assets as potential money-for-college sources, there are several things to keep in mind.

First, you are trying to evaluate each asset as a college money source, not as part of your net worth. Some assets can be worth a great deal, but at the same time can be useless as college money sources, as in the instance of a partially owned family business you couldn't sell if you wanted to and can't even borrow money on.

You have some basic questions to ask about each asset.

1. What is it worth now? Even though your ultimate question about each asset has to do with its use as a college money source, the underlying worth of that asset now is basic knowledge you must have. Bear in mind that in some instances, such as businesses and real estate, your estimate of what an asset is worth will be approximate.

2. What is the asset likely to be worth when you need it? Just as you must take the negative impact of inflation into account in assessing college costs, so must you take into account the positive impacts of interest and growths in value between now and when you may need to use the asset to help pay for college costs (and the possible negative impact of losses in value between now and when you may need to use it).

For example, a savings account will grow by its compounded rate of interest if you leave it alone. Of course, you'll pay taxes on that interest, which must be taken into account when figuring how much the savings account has really grown.

Or an investment in common stock may grow in value a great deal more than a savings account—or lose a great deal of its value between now and when you may want to use it for covering college costs.

3. Can the asset be sold? For how much now? For how much when you may want to use it? What additional costs if any are involved in selling it? In taxes and professional fees?

4. How much cash, if any, now and later can you borrow on the asset? What additional costs may be involved in doing so?

Several kinds of assets can be used as collateral for loans. Which assets can be so used and how much can be borrowed varies with time, economic conditions, the financial picture of the borrower, federal and state laws and regulations.

For example, you may have a life insurance policy with "cash surrender value" that you may want to borrow on. That can be done anytime, quickly, easily, and with no additional costs.

On the other hand, you may be considering remortgaging your home to help pay for college costs. As we discussed in Chapter 1, this is often one of the most expensive ways to pay for college. You will probably find a combination of much higher interest rates and new legal and other closing fees make this a most unattractive way to go—even though your home may be the single largest store of value you possess.

5. How much can the asset be grown between now and when you may want to use it? The associated question here is: Do you want to hold onto this asset and use it as a source of college money, or would it be wiser to cash it in (if you can) and put it to work in what you hope will be a more productive way?

These are always difficult questions, depending as they do on so many factors out of your control. The country is full of rueful former stock market investors who thought they would be paying for their children's college educations out of the profits generated by their stock market investments of the mid-sixties, and who instead are in many cases still paying the debts generated by investments that turned sour.

Nonetheless, it is an important set of questions and must be approached. One rule of thumb worth considering: If an asset is so fragile that you find it extremely hard to assess what it may be worth a few years hence, then value it low, very low as a potential college money source. Then if you've underestimated, wonderful. On the other hand, you won't find yourself with a great big hole in your money for college planning, either. Putting it differently, speculations are usually a poor idea. But if you must speculate, do it with speculation money, not the money you need for food, clothing, housing, retirement, and college costs.

6. What tax aspects, if any, must be considered in relation to this asset?

Some kinds of investments are tax free; some partly tax free. Some defer taxes until future dates. Some are real tax shelters. Others seem to offer tax shelter, but may be successfully challenged by the Internal Revenue Service, causing you large penalties in future years coupled with risky investments now.

The tax aspects are often "make or break" in terms of your decision on where to put investment money. They are neither simple nor fixed for all time; the tax law, court, and administrative interpretations of that law change continually. Our general approach in sizing up assets as potential college money sources is to look very warily at the "tax opportunities" offered by speculative investments and to pay maximum attention to the underlying potential of the assets themselves.

7. What is the impact of the existence of this asset upon your ability to get financial aid to help handle college costs?

A large set of interlocking and overlapping systems have grown up in the last quarter century, aimed at trying to develop a reasonably fair way to assess family and individual financial needs, so that those funds available for financial aid can be fairly distributed. The total of all financial aid funds available is never enough to cover more than a fraction of the total need for financial aid, and the situation is worsening, as college costs escalate and financial aid funds diminish relative to total college costs.

We will discuss the entire process of financial need analyses in Chapter 5 since it is central to the question of securing financial aid. In discussing how to see assets as potential sources of college money, we will deal only with how specific assets impact on your ability to get financial aid.

TIMING AND RISKS

Beyond the basic questions about each kind of asset, there is the general question of timing, of when to start thinking of assets as college money sources. The only possible advice in that area is to start thinking and planning to meet college costs as soon as you have a pretty good idea you or someone you love will need to go to college.

Early and complete planning will make it possible to create the kinds of money-producing assets you need to meet college costs.

The standard advice, which runs something like "Just put a couple of thousand a year away in a nice, safe savings account," is, to put it gently, somewhat unrealistic. But early and complete planning can and should make it possible to create the best kinds of assets for your purposes out of current income and present assets.

As a general rule, what seems likely to guarantee the most asset growth is also usually the riskiest investment. And there is no free lunch, no riskless investment that will "make you a million."

When remembering that, always also remember that there are investment professionals and investment organizations out looking, and looking hard, for investment opportunities—just as you are. They understand clearly that there is an enormous difference between both the profits and the risks as between the 5-percent return and the 10-percent return. It's not that 10 percent is twice 5 percent, as the casual, unprofessional eye sees. It's the difference in the way the growth compounds.

Seeing Your Assets as Money-for-College Sources **35**

Look at it this way. Forgetting about the tax aspects for purposes of the example, $1,000 growing at the rate of 5 percent annually for thirty years, with interest left to grow, becomes $4,322. The same $1,000 growing at 10 percent annually becomes $17,449. That's over four times as much!

Bear in mind, therefore, that you must not let the sometimes staggering-looking size of the money-for-college obligations you face cause you to speculate, to plunge, to take high risks. Keep in mind the short-lived "real estate syndication" boom of a decade ago, in which thousands of older people, faced with too little capital to generate the kind of interest they needed for retirement, put their retirement money into "guaranteed 10 percent yearly returns," only to find out later that the "interest" was often paid out of their own invested capital.

Spread your assets, and as long as college costs are a critically important factor in your planning, keep your assets at least fairly able to be converted into cash as needed or easily borrowed against even in adverse economic circumstances.

In the mid-sixties, it was perfectly obvious to all but a relatively few old-fashioned holdouts that the place to be financially was "in the market." Where but in a portfolio of common stocks was there the kind of growth opportunity you needed to create a fortune? And the long-term trend was up, even if stocks might suffer a short-term "adjustment" down now and then. Oh, keep a little in a savings account, have adequate life insurance, but the main action was "in the market." To be safe, "diversify your port-folio" to spread the risk properly.

What nonsense it was. By taking some advice properly tendered to the very rich and distorting that advice out of context, millions of small investors were drawn into a game they knew nothing about and should not have been in. A diversified portfolio of common stocks is sensible for some-one who has major business interests, income-producing real estate, bonds, perhaps tax-free municipals—but not as the main element of investment strategy for middle-class people trying to provide for such crucial matters as college costs and retirement.

Spread the risks. Some common stocks, long-term "blue chips," especially those that can easily be used as collateral for loans. Some savings, some real estate perhaps, your own business growth if appropriate, skills development for all the breadwinners in the family. Five or ten years from now, don't you be the one who has a sad story to tell about how "the market," "options," "straddles," "municipals," or whatever the next investment game in town is felled you with a low blow. Investment naiveté is pathetic. Investment stupidity on the part of the informed is merely stupidity.

SAVINGS ACCOUNTS

Savings accounts, especially those with an automatic, timed, forced savings feature, are a very old-fashioned, very tried and true way of preparing for the financial burdens of a college education.

Even with a forced savings feature, such as allocating a part of each paycheck to savings, savings accounts require self-discipline. To be done successfully, savings must become a long-term habit, and savings dedicated to a college education must remain just that. Once you begin to invade college savings for other purposes, no matter how important those purposes seem at the time or how "temporary" that taking from college savings is intended to be, you are in grave danger of losing the benefit of those savings altogether.

The interest paid on savings accounts varies with kind of bank and length of time you are willing to commit the deposit. It also varies over the years as competition continues to develop between lending institutions and government regulations change. Generally, commercial banks pay the smallest rates of interest, going a little under 5 percent except in some time deposit instances, in which they currently may go as high as 7 to 8 percent. Savings banks and savings and loan associations tend to yield somewhat higher rates of interest—in the neighborhood of one-quarter to three-quarters of 1 percent more than the commercial banks.

Distinguish here between two kinds of savings accounts:

1. There is the savings account you should basically hold as a store of emergency cash. This is a relatively small sum of "rainy day" money amounting to perhaps enough to sustain you and your family for 3 to 4 months at a very basic level. You hold it on the assumption that if you suddenly need it, it's there and on demand. Usually the sum is small enough so that the decision as to where to hold it is mostly a matter of convenience, and people often hold such an account in the commercial bank in which they do the rest of their banking business.

Of course, under extraordinary circumstances, such as bank failure, that emergency fund may be there in the sense that it's federally insured, but may not be there on demand—you may have to wait for it. You would generally guard against that kind of unusual tie-up of emergency funds by holding those funds in as strong and well-regarded a bank as you can find.

2. Then there is the special purpose savings account—the college education fund, in this instance. That account should be held precisely where it safely draws the most interest—a strong, well-regarded, federally insured savings bank or savings and loan association. Bear in mind that over a period of ten years, which is not an unusual time period when discussing college education savings funds, an interest difference of as little as 1 percent on savings of $5,000—the difference between 6 and 7 percent, for instance—amounts to $882 more in your college fund.

The differences between storing money in a savings account bearing 5 percent interest and a long-term account bearing as much as 8 percent are even greater. The same $5,000 held for ten years at 5 percent yields $8,144, or interest of $3,144. In an 8-percent account, it yields $10,795, or interest of $5,795, close to double the interest of the 5-percent account.

Be sure that any savings account you have is federally insured and that you hold no more than $40,000 in all accounts of any kind in your name in that bank to guarantee that insurance. Should you hold joint accounts or should other members of your family hold accounts in that bank under their own names, those accounts are also protected up to $40,000 each.

Don't think that a state-insured bank is just as well protected as a federally insured bank. It hasn't happened yet, but it's quite possible that some time in the near future, a state-insured bank failure will be followed by discovery that the insurance fund of that state is not as fully solvent as it was thought to be.

Don't under any circumstances put your savings in any institution that is uninsured for depositor losses. People still do—it's a very basic, potentially very costly mistake.

By timing your savings account withdrawals properly over the entire period of college cost obligation, you will be able to get maximum interest from your accounts and minimize any potential interest losses due to premature withdrawals.

You'll pay taxes on the interest your savings yield at ordinary income tax rates. That will diminish your yield very substantially.

On the other hand, tax payments out of the rest of your income can act in a sense as an additional "forced savings" feature. You won't necessarily feel the taxes you pay on savings dividends very much, especially if you have offsetting deductions in some years. What you will see, year after year, is the growth of your college education fund, with the accelerator of compound interest built in. You'll see it keeping up with inflation, sometimes even seeming to outpace inflation in some years, and you'll know that whatever money you have and can add to those savings accounts is money you can be sure will be there when you need it for college costs.

Be aware that there are two sides to the attempt to minimize taxes by using gifts to build up college funds in children's names. Yes, you will avoid considerable taxes on dividends that way, as children may pay no taxes at all or very minimal taxes on the dividends from their savings accounts.

On the other hand, a dependent student's assets are treated far more harshly in determining "financial need" for student financial aid purposes than are parents' assets. Parents' assets are given an "asset protection allowance" and then taken into account for financial aid purposes at a much lower rate than are student assets. Student assets are treated as if almost wholly available for college education purposes, which means that a student with substantial savings accounts built up as a college fund may not be eligible for financial aid at all, solely because taxes were avoided on saved family funds.

The insurance policy, which is really a forced savings annuity for college funds purposes, is also vulnerable in student financial aid terms. The savings annuity matures just before the student enters college, the student suddenly has substantial assets, and financial aid that should have been forthcoming can disappear.

You can borrow on your savings accounts if you wish, without disturbing the balances in those accounts or the long-term buildup of interest. That can be useful for short-term personal purposes, but should not be used as a means of invading the principal in your college fund accounts. You should not borrow on your savings accounts to pay for college costs, as you will always pay more in interest on your borrowings than the interest you get from your savings. Banks are in the business of holding and paying interest to you on your money so that they may lend your money to others for more than the interest they pay you. It doesn't make much sense for you to pay more interest on a loan than you get on your savings unless it's a very short-term loan indeed.

INSURANCE

Insurance is for hedging your bets. We all need it—to protect our loved ones against our death or disability, to protect our homes and businesses, to pay medical and dental bills.

And our best-laid college financing plans can be destroyed without insurance protection. It certainly makes sense for family breadwinners to protect their college-bound dependents with life insurance and themselves with major medical and sometimes disability insurance so that family assets will not be wiped out by illness or disability.

When protecting college-bound dependents with life insurance, though, be aware of the financial aid hazard discussed in the last section. If you should die, and substantial life insurance is subsequently paid to your college-bound children, their assets may suddenly be so large that they simply can't qualify for any meaningful financial aid. It is far better, if possible, for husband and wife to insure each other, with the survivor using insurance to pay for college educations behind the shield of the asset protection allowance and less stringent asset rules applied to families.

Of course, there are all kinds of circumstances that may cause families to want to make life insurance benefits directly payable to surviving children. If personal considerations make that necessary, then let it be done with the clear knowledge that the financial aid possibilities may be substantially diminished by insurance proceeds.

Millions of Americans hold "whole life" insurance policies—that is, policies that combine actuarially determined premium payments for insurance in the event of death with premium payments that create forced savings in the insurance policy. The forced savings so created are called "cash surrender values."

Whole life insurance policies usually pay dividends on the forced savings or cash surrender values at the very low rate of about 3 percent per year. Therefore, they are at the very bottom of the investment scale in terms of interest yield.

Their sole advantage, if it can be called that, is that they are a form of forced savings and that the "cash surrender values" can be borrowed against, usually up to 90 to 95 percent of the cash surrender value and at a usual simple interest rate of 6 percent.

For the forced savings aspect, we think it far better to put your money in a long-term savings account plan and then buy "term" insurance at much lower than whole life rates, placing the savings in a savings account or in some other form of investment vehicle.

Of course, if you have had a whole life policy for many years, you are probably in a certain sense wedded to it, as this kind of insurance is often sold on a level premium basis, meaning that any term insurance now bought may well be just as expensive as the whole life insurance you already have, with its premiums based on your age at the time you bought it. In that case, the cash surrender values in the whole life policy may be a useful source of college funds at the proper time. Or you may prefer to borrow on the cash surrender values and use the cash derived in better-producing investments. Caution: If you use your cash surrender values for current expenses or for speculation, you may be destroying a relatively safe, though slow-growing, store of value to your own disadvantage.

GOVERNMENT SECURITIES

Until recently, federal, state, and municipal securities of all kinds have been considered sound, conservative, sometimes very tax-advantaged opportunities. Some government securities, notably those of the U.S. government, are as sound as they ever were, but some state and municipal securities should now be treated very warily, especially as college money sources.

Savings Bonds

A very popular device has been the use of U.S. government Series E and Series H savings bonds as a means of building a tax-free college fund.

It has been done basically by buying Series E bonds in the child's name, then either filing a federal income tax return at the end of the first year of the child's ownership indicating the child's intent to report the interest annually, or by buying the bonds in the child's name and having the child report interest as income only when the bonds are cashed many years later. Either way, a relatively modest long-term investment in the savings bonds would result in a substantial tax-free interest bonus to the child.

The tax advantage has been attractive and still is. However, relatively substantial student assets may once again operate to substantially disqualify an otherwise qualified student from receiving financial aid.

Your decision here has to be an early one. The tax advantages fully apply only if you start a modest and continuous savings program—perhaps $25 to $75 per month—ten to fifteen years before your child will need the college funds. Either you form a very early opinion that your income and assets will be such that when your child goes to college he or she wouldn't qualify for financial aid anyway, or you seriously consider the possible adverse financial aid impact of the assets you'll be building up in your child's name.

If you have been building up such a tax-free fund for future college costs, you may want to take another look and study alternatives that may give the college fund just as much net return without the financial aid risks.

You are currently able to cash in U.S. savings bonds after holding them for at least two months. However, you will forfeit all interest if you cash them in within six months of purchase. You will also forfeit considerable interest on E bonds if you cash them in before maturity, as they pay interest on a graduated scale to encourage holding to maturity. And they cannot be used as collateral for other loans. If you choose this savings technique, be sure to get your timing right so that you cash in only mature bonds.

Other U.S. Government Securities

There are a number of other kinds of U.S. government securities. They include short-term treasury bills, medium-term treasury notes, and long-term treasury bonds. They all share the characteristics of being backed by the full faith and credit of the U.S. government, of being entirely and easily salable at any time, and of being usable as collateral for loans.

You are unlikely to include short-term treasury bills in your college fund planning, but may have been attracted to their relative security and the rather high interest yields some treasury notes and bonds carried in the early 1970s. Whether to hold, sell, or buy more of these securities is a matter for you to reevaluate as with any securities or other stores of value you may hold.

There are a couple of dozen other kinds of federal securities available, issued by federal agencies as their own securities. They are mostly not directly guaranteed by the federal government, but indirectly well enough guaranteed to be quite safe. Like the treasury securities, they are salable, though not quite as easily, and can be used as collateral for loans.

STATE AND MUNICIPAL SECURITIES

State and municipal securities have for decades been favorite investment vehicles for the very rich, because interest on them has been exempt from federal taxes. Even at the rather low interest rates they have paid, those in very high tax brackets have often come out way ahead by investing in them.

With the historic long-term decline of the stock market starting in the late 1960s, many stockbrokers attempted with some success to create a new market for tax-free state and municipal securities among those hundreds of thousands of middle-class investors who deserted the stock exchanges.

You may have bought some of these securities and may still be buying some in the hope that their combination of fixed interest and tax advantages will allow you to keep up and perhaps get a little ahead of inflation. You may have decided to buy them through one of the new mutual funds specializing in these securities.

We urge you to seriously consider whether or not these are the kinds of securities you want to include in your money-for-college funds. Some of them are undoubtedly good investments; some are not. The key observation to make is that without being entirely conversant with the financial and political affairs of the states and municipalities you are investing in, you have no way of making an informed investment decision.

Recent experience with New York City securities certainly bears this out. If you had invested in the future of New York City, which is what you do when you buy a city's promise to pay you back your investment plus interest, and depended on the funds invested to finance college costs, you would have been sorely disappointed. You would have found yourself unable to look forward to timely collection of interest or principal, and at the same time unable to sell your bonds except at a huge loss.

Those risks continue to be very real throughout the country. Many cities and some states are simply very poor investment risks, and the federal government shows no eagerness to bail them out.

Nor are the mutual funds specializing in these securities necessarily a good substitute for your own judgment, any more than the mutual funds specializing in corporate common stocks were in the late 1960s and early 1970s. When the market went down, so did the mutual funds.

CORPORATE BONDS

When you buy a corporate bond, you lend money to that corporation and expect to get your money back plus a fixed rate of interest. No corporation is as good a risk as the U.S. government, and corporations therefore have to offer somewhat higher rates of interest than the federal government.

Knowing that there are somewhat greater hazards involved, many people building money-for-college funds have quite properly decided to invest in the triple A–rated bonds of the very largest and strongest American corporations—such as American Telephone and Telegraph, Citibank, and General Motors. If you have done so, good. The debt obligations of those kinds of corporations are currently good risks, entirely salable, offer very little potential loss due to fluctuation in value, and can be borrowed against.

Of course, you must watch them as you would any other investment of any kind. Even a Citibank can become overextended and suffer huge unanticipated losses due to international developments. Even a General Motors can, over a period of years, find its competitive position gravely damaged by a combination of unanticipated conditions, such as protracted gasoline shortages and moves to alternate means of transportation.

A corporate bond, like any other debt, is only as good a risk as the corporation itself. Bond defaults happen. Companies get into serious trouble, and even short of defaults you can run into serious drops in the values of bonds you hold. Even more seriously, you can find yourself holding corporate bonds you're unable to sell or borrow against just when you need the money to pay for college. Limit your corporate bond purchases for college money costs to only the safest of companies, and forgo the higher interest rates paid by the less secure companies.

COMMON STOCK

When you buy a corporate stock, you're literally buying a share in the corporation. As millions of Americans have learned to their sorrow in the last decade, that's risky no matter how large and stable the corporation is. The same large corporation that is a relatively safe bond purchase risk may be a poor stock purchase risk when you're buying that stock as part of a money-for-college fund. The problem is that even the best of stocks can go down sharply when the whole market goes down—even though the underlying value of the stock and its dividend payments remain unchanged. And it can happen just when you're ready to cash in that stock to pay for college, leaving you with a great big loss and an equally big hole in your college funding.

If you have stocks and are holding onto them to help pay for college costs, be sure to value them low for planning purposes.

And be very sure—this is critically important—to hold the stocks of large, stable companies that are actively traded on the New York Stock Exchange. Those stocks that are usually called "blue chips" are the stocks you can reasonably count on borrowing against if you need college money and selling would result in serious losses. If you have any doubt at all about how "borrowable" any stocks you own are, make a list of them and take them to your banker. Your banker won't be able to promise you that when you might need to borrow against your stocks they will be borrowable, but he or she can tell you just how good they would be as collateral right now. That's something you need to know.

COMMODITIES

Commodity futures, options, straddles—whatever the latest wrinkles in speculation at the time you read this book—are most emphatically not proper ways to try to build a money-for-college fund. Why? Because you can lose your shirt.

If you are speculating, doing it with your eyes wide open, and doing it with money that is not needed for basics like college costs, then that is nothing we have a right to question.

If, on the other hand, you're speculating in commodities or anything else with money-for-college funds, we suggest you take a long, sober look at what you're doing. You may come up rich, but you're more likely to come up broke.

Silver and gold are no different from other commodities for college fund purposes. Western Europe is full of gold speculators who bought gold only a few years ago for almost $200 per ounce, only to see it quickly lose close to half its value soon after.

COLLECTIBLES

People collect all kinds of things, and some of the things they collect for fun can become startlingly valuable. Many a coin collection, stamp collection, some pieces of old furniture handed down for generations, old paintings, even comic book collections have helped finance college educations.

If you have such collections or pieces you think may be of considerable value, by all means get them appraised by professionals. Find out their worth and figure them into your college fund possibilities.

Be sure to figure them low, however. Not all collectibles grow in value over the years. Those that grow in value do so unevenly.

If you have valuable collectibles and are fairly sure you'll need them to help finance college, plan to sell them well before you actually need the money, perhaps as much as a year or two before. In that way, you'll be able to watch the market, sell at the most favorable prices, perhaps take the gain on them most advantageously for tax purposes. Don't postpone the selling decision and then sell when you're right up against tuition payments. You'll almost always lose money doing it that way, sometimes a great deal.

Some people who are not basically collectors have been investing in collectibles in recent years on the theory that some collectibles have grown in value faster than the pace of inflation and faster than their previous investment in the stock market. They have gone into all kinds of collectibles, including original art, prints, books, coins, stamps, jewelry, antiques, silver plates, old bottles, and a multitude of other items. Some of them have made money; some have lost it. Much of the gain is on paper, as they tend to hold onto their acquisitions, sharing the widespread illusion that what goes up must continue to go up, as if by some natural law. They tend not to realize that they are the stuff panics are made of, and that when hundreds of thousands of people start selling silver plates, for example, there will be no way in the world that anyone will be able to keep the prices of those plates at anything above the underlying value of the silver in the plates. Paper gains will vanish, and losses will be real.

Collectibles are often hard to sell, especially when everybody else is selling. They are hard to borrow against, as their underlying value is often hard for a banker or other lender to determine. They pay no interest or dividends and are in that sense purely a means of tying up investment capital in the hope of substantial growth in values.

Therefore, while your collections and family possessions may have substantial value and be excellent sources of money for college, we think it unwise to invest in collectibles as part of money-for-college plans.

YOUR HOME

Many a college education has been partially financed with the proceeds of a refinanced first mortgage, a second mortgage, or even part of a somewhat redirected home improvement loan.

The fact is that the main asset possessed by an enormous number of American families is their home, and that facing the huge costs of sending family members to college, they are forced to try to somehow use the stores of value represented by their homes to raise money for college.

One way to do it is to sell outright. That's fairly rare, but sometimes done, as with a move from a large family house to a smaller house, co-op, condominium, or rented apartment.

There are tax consequences connected with the outright sale unless the seller is sixty-five or older or unless the new home is purchased for substantially the same amount for which the old home was sold—which is obviously self-defeating, as one of the main objects of sale in this situation is to free money for college.

But there are often far more compelling reasons not to sell your home. Often, the home you are carrying on a low 6-percent mortgage or with no mortgage at all is far less expensive than anything you might secure with anywhere nearly comparable living arrangements. Equally often, young family members in college go to school little more than seven months a year and need a place to live for the other five months, meaning that your space needs are really substantially unchanged. And often there are two or more children entering college over a period of years, with the family home needed as much as ever while you are beginning to try to cope with college costs.

The most usual way of using the family home to raise college money is the refinanced first mortgage. As we discussed in Chapter 1, this is an extraordinarily expensive way to raise money, carrying with it the multiple impacts of a much higher mortgage obligation over a longer term, higher monthly payments just when you're trying to cut costs, and the far higher rates of interest you will almost always pay on the new mortgage. Bankers love exchanging 8-percent mortgages for 6-percent mortgages; home owners like it a lot less.

But, on the other hand, refinancing is often the only way a family can raise a net $10,000 to $30,000 all at once, and that can mean the difference between college or not for one or more family members.

Before you do it, though, be sure you've exhausted all other reasonable financing alternatives. Beyond that, be sure that you want to pay the price involved. Sometimes, when faced with and fully understanding this sort of decision, families are willing to reexamine the prestige college choices in favor of much lower-cost alternatives that may be quite as good educational choices as the prestige schools.

Another way to use the store of value represented by your home is the second mortgage. This involves using the equity in your home as security for a mortgage you carry concurrently with your first mortgage for a period usually running three to ten years.

This is almost always a poor idea. It involves you in rather high interest rates, often in very substantial hidden charges, and in paying off two mortgages at the same time just when you are facing college costs. If you decide that you must use your home to raise college money, you will find that the refinanced first mortgage is almost always the better way to go.

BUSINESSES, FARMS, OTHER INCOME-PRODUCING PROPERTY

Family farms, other businesses, and income-producing property of all kinds are often very important sources of college funds, both as assets and producers of current income for all family members, including those in college.

You are unlikely to sell your farm or business to help pay college costs. You very well may, however, borrow from cash held in your business, taking care to consult your accountant, to set up the loan so as to minimize tax liability.

It is also possible to use your business, or property held by you or your business, as collateral for other kinds of loans that can be applied to college costs.

Or you may take more out of the business as salary in some years of high need than in other years, if the business will stand it.

Family farms and businesses offer a unique opportunity to employ the student members of a family, and in that way help pay for college costs with pre-tax rather than after-tax dollars. It is often entirely possible to use those months of the year that away-from-home students are not at school and all year for students commuting from home to provide income for students that can be used to pay college costs. And, if carefully set up, with the student as a bona fide employee, it may be possible for both the family and the student to get the benefit of the student's exemption for tax purposes.

This technique of using pre-tax business dollars to pay for college costs rather than after-tax personal dollars can in some instances cut college costs by as much as one-third. It is particularly useful in those situations in which financial aid is unlikely because of family income, and assets and salaries paid to students will not cut into financial aid possibilities. And it is in those very situations that the tax savings will be highest, with parents paying at very high tax rates and students paying at very low rates.

Very often there are seeming contradictions between going into your own business and doing sane, long-range college fund planning. Starting a business often involves considerable personal financial risk, and new businesses often fail, pulling all savings and other personal assets with them as they fail. Yet, at the same time, it is clear that for many families the personal financial growth resulting from building a successful business seems to far outweigh the substantial risks involved.

We would only suggest that if you are not in your own business now and decide to go into business while at the same time building money-for-college funds, it will be very important to you not to lose sight of the money-for-college fund in the drive to build a successful business. You will be wise to adopt some form of forced savings plan, no matter how small, constantly and carefully review your exposure to risk, and carefully hedge your bets with personal insurance.

4

HOW TO PROVE
YOUR NEED FOR FINANCIAL AID

THE area of student financial aid often seems little more than a bureaucratic thicket, a maze of ill-understood forms to fill out, "confidential" financial statements that can't possibly be held confidential and still perform their stated functions, "aid" that turns out to be just another way of mortgaging your future, and administrators who try hard but can't really overcome the plain fact that there's always too little money to help all those who really need help.

Often, students and their families simply give up—sometimes after starting and then throwing up their hands at the forms, sometimes without even trying to get aid that should rightfully be theirs. And often students and their families get far less aid than they should because they don't understand some of the basic things they must know when trying to get needed aid.

THE MEANING OF "FINANCIAL AID"

Unfortunately, the term "financial aid" has acquired a wider and wider meaning over the years. It now includes most aid from the colleges themselves, much federal and state money, much of the scholarship aid available from private sources.

For example, "financial aid" includes Basic Educational Opportunity Grants from the federal government, which consists of over $1 billion a year in no-strings grants. It also includes federally guaranteed student loans, which makes it possible for many students to borrow on a long-term basis from commercial lenders, with the federal government paying part of the interest charges. In each instance, the financial aid forms must be gone through.

Even campus jobs often depend on proving financial need, as many are funded wholly or partly by government sources. The student and his or her family must go through the whole process of financial aid application, complete with "need analysis" and "confidential" questionnaires, so that the student may be granted the privilege of working on campus at a job that probably pays something very close to the minimum wage.

In one way or another, the process of "proving need" through financial aid application will most probably have to be embarked upon. Therefore, it is wise for dependent students and their families, and for self-supporting students and their families, to settle down several months before financial aid applications have to be done and collect the basic data that will be needed one way or another for all the different applications.

PREPARING A PERSONAL FINANCIAL STATEMENT

Essentially, you'll be wisest to prepare what amounts to a personal financial statement once, add to it as facts change, and use your federal and state tax returns as basic associated documents. That summary statement should include a list of everything you own aside from personal property such as cars and clothes and of what everything is worth, stating value and what's owed on it. It should include everything you owe as well. If you have a business, farm, or other income-producing property, include summary figures on what they are worth.

Where you have to estimate what something is worth, such as the fair market value of your home or business building, figure reasonably low. A high estimate may adversely affect student ability to get needed financial aid, and a low estimate takes into account the possibility that your estimate of value may be unrealistic. Many a business owner has been very surprised at how much less a business was worth when up for sale than it was thought to be worth.

It's probably a good idea to prepare that statement with the help of your accountant, especially if business and property are involved. What you pay your accountant for that help may prove to be an excellent investment. And, during the college years, you and your accountant may find a number of entirely legal ways to reduce your gross income by pushing income into subsequent years and by holding down some kinds of business income. During the college years, some aspects of tax planning can prove doubly advantageous when taking financial aid possibilities into account.

Financial aid applications are best treated like tax returns—you'll have to do one, and if you're going to do it you might as well do it as knowledgeably as possible, so that you can get the most possible needed aid.

For financial aid purposes, a very important distinction is made between dependent students and self-supporting students. Aid to dependent students is based upon an analysis of the total financial assets and income of student and parents or guardians. Aid to the self-supporting student is based upon an analysis of the financial assets and income only of the student and spouse. Therefore, self-supporting students often have far better chances of securing meaningful financial aid than dependent students.

To be classified as a self-supporting student for financial aid purposes —during the year for which the financial aid is asked, and for the year during which you're applying, and for the preceding calendar year—that is last year, this year, and next year, you must satisfy these qualifications:

1. You can't have lived with your parent or guardian for more than two consecutive weeks at any time. Note that you may have lived with your parent or guardian more than two weeks in total, but the yardstick used is two *consecutive* weeks.

2. You didn't receive and won't receive more than $600 in cash or equivalents—like a car or clothes—from your parent or guardian. Note that this does not preclude you from working in a family business or on a family farm—but if you do, make sure that any money or equivalents received are clearly identified as payment for work performed.

3. You haven't been and won't be claimed as an exemption on anyone else's federal income tax return—except your wife or husband. Note again that payments to you as an employee of a family farm or business are not exemption deductions even though they are deductible expenses to the business or farm.

Note that in determining financial aid qualification, dependent student assets and current income are treated very differently from the assets and current income of the students' families. In both asset and current income areas, this can mean that substantial penalties in lost financial aid may result from early and probably erroneous college fund planning that stressed building up substantial assets in the student's name.

Samples of the main forms used (and required) coast to coast for determining financial need follow. These are Financial Aid Form (FAF) of the College Scholarship Service (of the College Entrance Examination Board), and the Family Financial Statement (FFS) of the American College Testing program. The Basic Educational Opportunity Grants program (a federal program) accepts either of these forms as a Basic Grant application.

Your financial need would be determined through one of these forms, very briefly, like this. The amounts for your income, assets, and debts that you give on the form would be put through a standard computation. Such calculations would yield sums viewed as reasonable allowances you could afford toward college costs. The final result is a certain dollar amount. It represents what the "need analysis" process indicates you should be able to spend toward the college costs of an individual student (one of your children or yourself) through the next academic year. In this book we call it the "total expected" (though it has other official names).

Your financial need would not be this "total expected." As explained earlier, it would be the difference between the "total expected" and the "student expense budget" applicable to the student concerned at a specific college. Your need accordingly can vary from college to college, depending on the costs at each college. You would have no need at a college at which your "total expected" was larger than the total of the "student expense budget." You may have need at some colleges and not others.

An approximation of your "total expected" and financial need may be obtained in the early high school years of a student through the Early Financial Aid Planning Service of the College Scholarship Service. Such approximations, which include indications of your eligibility for a Basic Grant, are offered for a $3.50 fee. Information and applications for the Early Planning Service should be available in high school guidance offices.

Here are:

1) A reprinted portion of the very helpful booklet, *Meeting College Costs*, issued by the College Scholarship Service of the College Board. It includes a filled-in Financial Application Form.

2) The College Scholarship Service forms and instructions for the 1978–79 school year, with our comments added. The circled numbers on the face of the form refer to our annotations, which are at the end of the chapter.

3) The American College Testing Program forms and instructions for the 1978–79 school year, with our comments added.

How Much Does College Cost?

There are different kinds of postsecondary education institutions to choose from — community colleges, vocational and technical schools, public or private universities near home or far away. Costs can differ greatly from one institution to another, so you should make an estimate of expenses for each college you are considering.

You can see from the examples below the types of expenses you will need to consider. There are direct educational costs such as tuition, fees, and books and supplies; and living costs, including room, board, transportation, and personal expenses such as clothes, laundry, and recreation. You must also consider whether you plan to live at home and commute to the campus for classes or reside on or near the campus.

Don't let an estimate of high expenses discourage you. Higher cost institutions generally have the financial aid available to help students meet the expenses of their institutions.

To find out about individual college costs, write to each institution you are considering for a copy of its latest catalog and any other booklets on expenses and financial assistance.

Two publications that can help you estimate total costs are *The College Handbook* and *Student Expenses at Postsecondary Institutions,* both published by the College Entrance Examination Board. Your counselor or librarian should have a copy. You should use the information in these publications only as a guide; individual college catalogs should be consulted when you are ready to make definite plans.

Examples of typical students (expenses given are for a 9-month period)	Andrea Commuting student (living at home) at an in-state 2-year public institution	Beth Resident student at an in-state 4-year public institution	Carlos Resident student at an independent (private) institution	Estimating your own expenses Name of institution	Name of institution	Name of institution
1. Tuition and fees	$ 375	$ 625	$2,500	$	$	$
2. Books and supplies	175	200	200			
3. Student's room	Not applicable	700	700			
4. Student's board/meals	850*	700	700			
5. Personal (clothing, laundry, recreation, medical)	450	500	450			
6. Transportation**	400	200	225			
7. Other (such as costs of child care, extra expenses because of handicap)	0	0	0			
A. Total budget (Add 1 through 7)	$2,250	$2,925	$4,775	$	$	$

*You will want to consider these expenses to your family if you live at home.

**If you are planning to live on campus, you should estimate the cost of the round trips you will make to your home. Colleges usually estimate that a student makes two or three round trips during the year. Students living at home should figure the costs of daily transportation to the college.

How to Determine Your Need

Postsecondary institutions, states, and other organizations award financial aid on the basis of demonstrated need. They believe that parents and students have a responsibility to pay as much as they can toward educational costs.

A method of determining how much families may be able to pay has been developed by the College Scholarship Service (css). The css, a part of the College Entrance Examination Board, is composed of postsecondary institutions, high schools, and scholarship programs throughout the country. Representatives of these institutions, economists, and other experts in financial aid develop the need analysis guidelines that are used nationally by colleges and scholarship programs to figure a family's ability to pay for college costs. Changes are made each year to reflect such factors as increases in living costs, so that a family who may not have qualified for aid one year may be eligible the next.

Table for 11 Family size allowance

Family size (including applicant)	Standard maintenance allowance
2	$ 4,970
3	6,200
4	7,650
5	9,030
6	10,560
7	11,760
8	12,960
9	14,160
10	15,360
11	16,560
12	17,760

Table for J Parents' expected contribution

Adjusted available income (or item I)	Taxation rate
$ 1-$4,440	22%
4,441- 5,560	$ 976 plus 25% of AAI over $4,440
5,561- 6,670	1,256 plus 29% of AAI over 5,560
6,671- 7,780	1,577 plus 34% of AAI over 6,670
7,781- 8,890	1,954 plus 40% of AAI over 7,780
8,891 or more	2,398 plus 47% of AAI over 8,890

Table for K Parents' contribution (when more than 1 family member is in college)

Number of family members attending college in the same year	Percentage of standard contribution to be contributed for each student
1	100%
2	60
3	45
4 or more	35

Table for 14 Adjustments for business or farm

Net worth	Adjustment rate
$ 1-$ 20,000	40% of net worth
20,001- 60,000	$8,000 plus 50% of excess over $20,000
60,001- 100,000	$28,000 plus 60% of excess over $60,000
100,001 or more	$52,000 plus 100% of excess over $100,000

Table for 18 Asset protection allowance

Age	Two-parent family	One-parent family
44 or less	$10,220	$12,670
45-49	11,780	14,560
50-54	13,890	17,000
55-59	16,670	20,110
60-64	20,670	24,450
65 or more	24,000	28,000

This procedure is intended to give you a general idea of what you and your family might be expected to contribute to your college costs. The analysis that the css makes will be based on more detailed and specific information. Financial aid administrators, who make the awards for their institutions, consider the css analysis and any other pertinent facts you have given them before determining how much aid you will be awarded.

Through the Financial Aid Form (FAF) families have the opportunity to state their financial situation. The CSS then uses the same procedures for measuring each student's need for financial aid. The resulting expected contribution varies according to such factors as income, assets, number of children, and family expenses.

The procedure given in this booklet can help you see if you are eligible for financial aid. To find out how much money you will require from aid sources, follow these four steps:

1. Estimate your educational expenses using the space on page 3.

2. Figure the amount your parents might be expected to contribute toward these costs on these two pages.

3. Figure your own contribution (page 6).

4. Subtract the contributions that you calculated for yourself and your parents from the total costs (page 6). The resulting figure is your financial need.

Estimating Parents' Contribution

	Andrea 4-member family, both parents work, age of primary wage earner is 50	Beth 1-parent family, nontaxable income only, some assets, 2 children in family, age of parent is 44	Carlos 5-member family, income from a business, 2 children in college, age of wage earner is 58	Your parents' estimate
1977 INCOME				
1. Father's yearly wages, salaries, tips, and other compensation	$10,700	$ 0	$22,000	$
2. Mother's yearly wages, salaries, tips, and other compensation	4,800	0	0	
3. All other income of mother and father (dividends, interest, social security, pensions, welfare, etc.)	20	8,200	2,000	
B. Total income (Add 1, 2, 3)	15,520	8,200	24,000	
EXPENSES				
4. Adjustments to income such as sick pay, moving expenses, employee business expenses (the amount allowed on U.S. income tax return)	90	0	0	
5. U.S. income tax parents expect to pay on their 1977 income (not amount withheld from paycheck)	1,490	0	2,992	
6. Social Security (FICA) tax (5.85% times each salary to a maximum of $965 each)	906	0	965	
7. State and other taxes (Enter 8% of B)	1,241	656	1,920	
8. Medical and dental expenses not covered by insurance allowed as a deduction for U.S. income tax purposes (or amount in excess of 3% of B)	584	0	400	
9. Casualty and theft losses such as flood or fire damage, allowed as a deduction for U.S. income tax purposes	0	0	0	
10. Employment allowance. If both parents work, take lower salary, enter half of the salary up to a maximum allowance of $2,000; in single-parent household take half of income for salaries up to $4,000 (maximum allowance $2,000)	2,000	0	0	
11. Standard maintenance allowance (See Table for 11)	7,650	6,200	9,030	
C. Total allowances against income (Add 4, 5, 6, 7, 8, 9, 10, 11)	13,961	6,856	15,307	
D. Available income (Subtract C from B)	1,559	1,344	8,693	
ASSETS				
12. Home equity (total estimated value of your home on the current market less any unpaid balance on your mortgage)	15,840	0	15,000	
13. Other real estate equity (value minus unpaid balance on your mortgage)	0	0	0	
14. Business or farm (Figure total value less indebtedness and then take percentage shown in table. If your family is only part owner of the farm or business, list only your share of the net value	0	0	21,000	
15. Cash, savings and checking accounts	900	6,000	2,000	
16. Other investments (current value)	0	0	0	
E. Total assets (Add 12, 13, 14, 15, 16)	16,740	6,000	38,000	
DEDUCTIONS				
17. Major debts, such as outstanding medical expenses for 1976 or previous years (Do not list mortgages or loans for car, appliances, etc.)	105	300	0	
18. Asset protection allowance (See Table for 18)	13,890	12,670	16,670	
F. Total allowances against assets (Add 17 and 18)	13,995	12,970	16,670	
G. Remaining assets (Subtract F from E)	2,745	−6,970	21,330	
H. Income supplement from assets (Multiply G by 12% if G is positive; by 6% if G is negative and D is less than $4,440. Enter zero if G is negative and D is $4,440 or more)	329	−418	2,559	
I. Adjusted available income (Add D and H)	1,888	926	11,252	
J. Parents' expected contribution (Multiply I by taxation rate amount given in Table for J)	415	203	3,508	
K. Parents' expected contribution if more than one family member is in college (Use Table for K only if there is more than one family member in college at least half time)			2,104	

Estimating Your Contribution

		Andrea	Beth	Carlos	Your estimate
		Some savings	No assets but summer savings	Savings plus two local scholarships	
19.	Savings and other assets such as stocks and bonds multiplied by 35%	$ 175	$ 0	$ 300	$
20.	Educational benefits for student such as social security and veterans' educational benefits	0	0	0	
21.	Savings from summer earnings (for the summer before freshman year, allow $500. Add $100 or $200 for each subsequent year)*	500	500	500	
22.	Other gifts you have already received	0	0	600	
L.	Student resources (Add 19, 20, 21, 22)	675	500	1,400	
M.	Total family contribution (Add J and L. Use figure for K instead of J if there is more than one child in college)	$1,090	$703	$3,504	$

*If you are unable to find a summer job or to save the amount suggested, you should report this to the college.

How Much Aid Do You Need?

After you have listed budgets for the colleges you are considering and figured parents' expected contribution and student resources, you can determine if you will need some form of financial aid to attend the colleges you have in mind. To figure your need, subtract the amounts you and your parents can contribute from the total costs.

If you show need, you should apply for financial aid. Even if you don't show need here, but you feel that your resources are inadequate, you should apply.

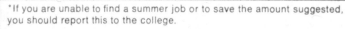

		Andrea	Beth	Carlos	Your estimate of need		
		Some need	Considerable need	Some need	Name of institution	Name of institution	Name of institution
A.	Total expenses (from page 3)	$2,250	$2,925	$4,775	$	$	$
M.	Total family contribution	1,090	703	3,504			
N.	Need (Subtract M from A)	$1,160	$2,222	$1,271	$	$	$

What an Aid Package Looks Like

Most colleges, state agencies, and other noncollege sponsors that use the CSS need analysis services endorse the principle that the amount of aid awarded to a student should depend on his or her financial need. They believe that aid awarded according to this principle will be most effective in helping the greatest number of students.

Whether you will need a lot of aid or just a little, institutions will do their best to help you find the combination of resources you need to attend. The box below shows how our three examples were able to meet college costs.

	Total family contribution	Basic Educational Opportunity Grant	State scholarship	Institutional grant	Supplemental Educational Opportunity Grant	College Work-Study	National Direct Student Loan	Guaranteed Student Loan	Total resources for college
Andrea	$1,090		450				700		$2,240
Beth	$ 703	450			400	750	600		$2,903
Carlos	$3,504			250				1,000	$4,754
Record your awards									

Sample Filled-In FAF

Most colleges and state or other scholarship programs will ask you to complete the Financial Aid Form (FAF). The FAF collects financial information these institutions and programs use to determine your need for financial aid. Students applying for financial aid in 1978-79 should submit the 1978-79 FAF after January 1, 1978. The sample FAF reproduced here lets you see what type of information you will need to provide. Note that you will need a social security number.

The FAF is designed so that information can be filled in easily and accurately by referring to the parents' (or

student's, if appropriate) U.S. income tax returns. To prevent delays in processing be sure to fill out the FAF completely.

Also, note that some colleges may request a copy of your parents' latest income tax return to verify the data on which an award is based.

The information reported on the form is kept confidential. Only those institutions and scholarship programs indicated by you will receive a copy of the FAF along with a need analysis report.

Financial Aid Form (FAF)
Academic Year 1978-79

STUDENT'S INFORMATION

Student's name: ZIEGLER, ANDREA J.
Social Security Number: 012 34 567 8
Permanent mailing address: 2311 NORTH OAK, FINDLAY, OH 45840

Date of birth: 01 18 59

PARENTS' CONFIDENTIAL STATEMENT

Father, Stepfather, or Male Guardian
Name: JAMES B. ZIEGLER, AGE 50
Home address: 2311 NORTH OAK, FINDLAY, OH 45840
Occupation: BOOKKEEPER
Employer: ACME DISTRIBUTING CO.
Social Security Number: 877-61-5532, OH, NUMBER 3

Mother, Stepmother, or Female Guardian
Name: RUTH H. ZIEGLER, AGE 49
Home address: 2311 NORTH OAK, FINDLAY, OH 45840
Occupation: TYPIST
Employer: KELLO COMPANY
Social Security Number: 766-55-4321, OH, NUMBER 4

Parents' Annual Income and Expenses

Parents' Assets and Indebtedness

Student's Income and Expenses

Student's Educational Benefits

Student's Assets and Indebtedness

Student's Additional Information

Occupation: SALESCLERK — PART TIME
Employer: BROWN'S DEPT. STORE

Divorced Separated Parents

Institutions and Programs to Receive This FAF

	NAME	CITY	STATE	CSS CODE NO.
	BRADLEY UNIVERSITY	PEORIA, IL		1070
	OHIO STATE UNIVERSITY	COLUMBUS, OH		1592
	COLLEGE OF WILLIAM AND MARY	WILLIAMSBURG, VA		5115
	OKLAHOMA CITY UNIVERSITY	OKLAHOMA CITY, OK		6543

Basic Educational Opportunity Grant Program

Certification and Authorization

Signature: Andrea J. Ziegler
James B. Ziegler
Ruth B. Ziegler
Telephone: (419) 555-1378
Date Completed: 02 05 78

financial Aid form

ACADEMIC YEAR 1978-79

COLLEGE SCHOLARSHIP SERVICE OF THE COLLEGE BOARD

WHAT IS THE FINANCIAL AID FORM?

The *Financial Aid Form* (FAF) is a document used to collect information for determining a student's need for financial aid. You submit the FAF to the College Scholarship Service (CSS), an activity of the College Board, where it is analyzed. The information you report on the FAF is confidential and is sent only to the recipients you indicate.

The CSS does not award financial aid; rather it evaluates your financial ability to contribute to the costs of education beyond high school.

The FAF may be used to apply for:

- the Basic Educational Opportunity Grant Program
- state scholarship and grant programs
- financial aid administered by colleges and other institutions of education beyond high school

The decision to award financial aid rests with the individual institutions and programs, which directly inform students whether or not they are eligible for financial aid. Some of these may also request completion of separate financial aid applications.

WHO COMPLETES THE FAF?

The FAF is completed by parents, in behalf of their children, and by students who are applying for financial aid for the academic year 1978-79.

If you answer "Yes" to ANY part of Items 13, 14, or 15 for ANY of the years indicated, your parents MUST complete the parents' section (Items 17-48) of the FAF. Refer to the definition of "parents" in the Instructions for Completing the FAF.

Even if you answer "No" to Items 13, 14, and 15 for all years, the institution you are applying to may require parents' information. You should follow any specific instructions you receive from the institution or program.

When parents' information is required and your parents are separated or divorced, Items 17-48 should be completed by the parent who has (or had) custody of you. Information may also be required of parent's present spouse, if any. See the Instructions for Completing the FAF.

WHEN SHOULD THE FAF BE COMPLETED?

The FAF should be completed *after January 1, 1978.* Mail this form as soon as possible, preferably at least one month or more before the earliest financial aid deadline for the institutions and programs you list to receive the FAF.

Do not file this FAF *after March 15, 1979.*

It is not necessary to delay filing the FAF until the 1977 U.S. income tax return is filed. If the 1977 return has not been filed, estimate amounts you expect to report on the return.

WHAT PROCEDURES ARE FOLLOWED TO ENSURE ACCURACY?

It is important that you provide accurate and complete information on the FAF. Failure to do so may jeopardize your request for financial aid.

If you use the FAF to establish eligibility for federal student financial aid funds, you should know that *any person who intentionally makes false statements or misrepresentations on this form is subject to fine, or to imprisonment, or to both, under provisions of the United States Criminal Code.*

In order to ensure accurate reporting of data on the FAF, the CSS may request authorization to obtain an official copy of the parents' or student's 1977 U.S. income tax return from the Internal Revenue Service (IRS). Do not send any income tax returns with the FAF to the CSS. Your authorization and any tax returns obtained by using the authorization are confidential and are not sent to institutions and programs. Some institutions and programs may request that you send a copy of your income tax return to them. If so, send it directly to the requesting institution. In other cases, the CSS on behalf of institutions listed by you may seek verification of the information reported on your FAF.

WHAT IS MY CSS ESTIMATED CONTRIBUTION?

Your estimated contribution is the amount of money the CSS calculates you and your family are able to provide for the expenses of college or other education beyond high school. Each institution or program has final responsibility for determining your contribution. This figure may differ from the CSS estimated contribution.

The CSS estimate is provided as part of the Acknowledgment and is sent with explanatory material. If you want to receive the report of CSS Estimated Contribution, add $1.00 to the processing fee and check the appropriate box in Item 82.

WHAT IS THE FEE FOR FILING THE FAF?

The CSS processing fee is $4.50 for the first institution or program designated to receive a copy of the FAF and $2.25 for each additional one. If you are requesting the report of your CSS Estimated Contribution, you should include an additional fee of $1.00.

The fee covers the costs of analyzing the FAF and sending copies of the FAF and the analysis to institutions and programs. Please make your check or money order payable to the CSS. *Do not send cash.*

There is no charge for using the FAF to apply for the Basic Educational Opportunity Grant (BEOG) Program.

WHERE TO MAIL THE FAF

Mail your completed FAF to the appropriate CSS office listed below.

COLLEGE SCHOLARSHIP SERVICE Box 2700 Princeton, NJ 08540	OR	COLLEGE SCHOLARSHIP SERVICE Box 380 Berkeley, CA 94701

IF YOU LIVE IN:

Alabama . . . . . AL	New Hampshire NH	Alaska . . . . AK	Nebraska . . . . NE
Canal Zone . . CZ	New Jersey . . . NJ	American	Nevada . . . . . . NV
Connecticut . . CT	New York . . . . NY	Samoa . . . . . AS	New Mexico . NM
Delaware . . . . DE	North Carolina. NC	Arizona . . . . . . AZ	North Dakota ND
District of	Ohio . . . . OH	Arkansas . . . . . AR	Oklahoma . . . OK
Columbia . . DC	Pennsylvania . PA	California . . . . CA	Oregon . . . . . . OR
Florida . . . . FL	Puerto Rico . . PR	Colorado . . . . CO	South Dakota SD
Georgia . . . . . . GA	Rhode Island . RI	Guam . . . . . . GU	Texas . . . . TX
Indiana . . . . . . IN	South Carolina. SC	Hawaii . . . . HI	Trust Territory
Kentucky . . . . KY	Tennessee . . . TN	Idaho . . . . ID	(Marshall,
Louisiana . . . . LA	Vermont . . . . . VT	Illinois IL	Mariana, and
Maine . . . . ME	Virgin Islands VI	Iowa . . . . IA	Caroline Is.) TT
Maryland . . . . MD	Virginia . . . . . . VA	Kansas . . . . KS	Utah . . . . UT
Massachusetts MA	West Virginia . WV	Minnesota . . . MN	Washington . . WA
Michigan . . . . MI	Wisconsin . . . WI	Missouri . . . . MO	Wyoming . . . . WY
Mississippi . . . MS		Montana . . . . . MT	

If where you live is not listed above, send your FAF to the CSS office in Princeton, NJ.

WILL THE CSS SEND AN ACKNOWLEDGMENT?

If an institution or program is listed in Item 81, the CSS will send you an Acknowledgment when processing of your FAF has been completed. The Acknowledgment includes an Additional College Request form for you to submit if you later want copies of the FAF sent to institutions or programs not originally listed.

nancial Aid Form (FAF)
ademic Year 1978-79 ☐

STUDENT'S INFORMATION

	MONTH	DAY	YEAR	OPTIONAL

UDENT'S NAME — STUDENT'S LAST NAME / STUDENT'S FIRST NAME | MID. INIT. | **2** STUDENT'S SOCIAL SECURITY NUMBER | **3** STUDENT'S DATE OF BIRTH | **4** SEX: 1 ☐ M 2 ☐ F

UDENT'S RMANENT AILING DRESS — NUMBER, STREET, AND APARTMENT NUMBER

| CITY | STATE ABBREVIATION | ZIP CODE |

6 STUDENT'S STATE OF LEGAL RESIDENCE (See instructions.)

7 STUDENT'S MARITAL STATUS (Check only one box.)
Unmarried ☑1 Married ☐2 Separated ☐3
Date of marriage or separation: _____

8 IS STUDENT
• a U.S. citizen? Yes ☑1 No ☐2
• a permanent resident of the U.S. or trust territory? Yes ☑1 No ☐2

student's year in college or other education beyond high school during 1978-79: (Check only one box.)
FIRST (freshman) 1 ☐
SECOND (sophomore) 2 ☐
THIRD (junior) 3 ☐
FOURTH (senior) 4 ☐
FIFTH (undergraduate) 5 ☐
GRADUATE/PROFESSIONAL 6 ☑

Expected degree: _____
Expected date of graduation: _____

10 Name of institution student attended in 1977-78: _____

or what academic period(s) in 1978-79 does the student want financial assistance? (Check all oxes that apply.)
1 ☐ Academic year, 1978-79
2 ☑ Winter term, 1978-79
3 ☑ Fall term, 1978
5 ☑ Spring term, 1979
6 ☐ Summer term, 1979

12 During 1978-79, student plans to live: (Check only one box.)
1 ☑ with parents
2 ☐ on campus
3 ☐ off campus

If an entering first-time student student attended in 1978-79, enter your **secondary** school code number:

CODE NUMBER
9 5 6 8 3 2

udent ust answer estions 13, 14, and 15 for ch year.

13 Did (or will) student live with parents for more than two consecutive weeks during
1977? Yes ☑1 No ☐2
1978? Yes ☑1 No ☐2 1
1979? Yes ☑1 No ☐2

14 Was (or will) student (be) listed as an exemption on parents' U.S. income tax return for
1977? Yes ☑1 No ☐2
1978? Yes ☑1 No ☐2
1979? Yes ☑1 No ☐2

15 Did (or will) student receive assistance worth $600 or more from parents during
1977? Yes ☑1 No ☐2
1978? Yes ☑1 No ☐2
1979? Yes ☑1 No ☐2

16 Are both student's parents deceased?
Yes ☑1 No ☐2

PARENTS' CONFIDENTIAL STATEMENT

Parents' Annual Income and Expenses

2 Enter yearly amounts in boxes only.

TAXABLE INCOME BEFORE DEDUCTIONS	1976	1977	Estimated 1978
A. Wages, salaries, tips, and other compensation			
1. Father, stepfather, or male guardian	$	$	$
2. Mother, stepmother, or female guardian	$	$	$
B. Dividends	$	$	$
C. Interest income	$	$	$
D. Taxable income other than wages, dividends, and interest (Itemize and give dollar amounts in 80.)	$	$	$
Add 17A, 17B, 17C, and 17D	$	$	$
ADJUSTMENTS TO INCOME (lines 28 and 30 of IRS Form 1040)	$	$	$
ADJUSTED GROSS INCOME (Subtract 19 from 18.) (line 31 of IRS Form 1040 or line 10 of Form 1040A)	$	$	$
NONTAXABLE INCOME (See instructions.)			
A. Social security benefits	$	$	$
B. Other nontaxable income (veterans benefits, child support, welfare, etc.)	$	$	$
TOTAL INCOME (Add 20, 21A, and 21B.)	$	$	$
U.S. INCOME TAX PAID (line 47 of IRS Form 1040 or line 13 of IRS Form 1040A)		$	
IRS ITEMIZED DEDUCTIONS (line 39 of Schedule A, IRS Form 1040)		$	
STATE AND OTHER TAXES		$	
MEDICAL AND DENTAL EXPENSES NOT COVERED BY INSURANCE (See instructions.)		$	
CASUALTY OR THEFT LOSS(ES) (See instructions.)		$	
UNREIMBURSED ELEMENTARY AND HIGH SCHOOL TUITION AND FEES FOR DEPENDENT CHILDREN, excluding the student applicant		$	
OTHER UNUSUAL EXPENSES		$	

Parents' Assets and Indebtedness

3 Enter information in boxes only.

	Present Market Value	Unpaid Mortgage Principal or Debts
HOME, IF OWNED OR BEING PURCHASED YEAR PURCHASED 19 __ PURCHASE PRICE $	$	$
OTHER REAL ESTATE	$	$
INVESTMENTS (STOCKS, BONDS, AND OTHER SECURITIES)	$	$
BUSINESS (See instructions.)	$	$
FARM (See instructions.)	$	$
CASH, SAVINGS, AND CHECKING ACCOUNTS	$	
CONSUMER AND EDUCATIONAL INDEBTEDNESS		$
OTHER DEBTS OUTSTANDING (Do not include any debts entered above.)		$

Father, Stepfather, or Male Guardian

38 NAME _____ AGE _____
HOME ADDRESS _____
OCCUPATION _____
EMPLOYER _____ NUMBER OF YEARS _____
SOCIAL SECURITY NUMBER ▶ _____ STATE OF LEGAL RESIDENCE ▶ _____

Mother, Stepmother, or Female Guardian

39 NAME _____ AGE _____
HOME ADDRESS _____
OCCUPATION _____
EMPLOYER _____ NUMBER OF YEARS _____
SOCIAL SECURITY NUMBER ▶ _____ STATE OF LEGAL RESIDENCE ▶ _____

Parents' Additional Information

40 PARENTS' CURRENT MARITAL STATUS (Check only one box.)
1 ☐ Single 2 ☐ Married 3 ☐ Separated 4 ☐ Divorced 5 ☐ Mother living, father deceased 6 ☐ Father living, mother deceased

41 HAVE PARENTS FILED 1977 U.S. INCOME TAX RETURN? Yes ☐1 No ☐2

42 TOTAL NUMBER OF EXEMPTIONS claimed on parents' 1977 U.S. income tax return **1977** _____

43 TOTAL SIZE OF PARENTS' HOUSEHOLD (Include the student named on this form **if a member of parents' household,** parents, other dependent children, and other dependents. See instructions.) **1978-79** _____

44 IF STUDENT APPLICANT IS NOT INCLUDED IN 43, CHECK HERE ☐

45 NUMBER IN COLLEGE Of the number entered in item 43, how many will be enrolled in college or other education beyond high school at least half-time during the 1978-79 academic year? **1978-79** _____

46 IF STUDENT APPLICANT IS NOT INCLUDED IN 45, CHECK HERE ☐

47 PROVIDE BELOW INFORMATION FOR **ALL CHILDREN AND OTHER DEPENDENTS** ENTERED IN 43.

A. Name (If you need additional space, use 80.)	B. Age	C. Name of institution to be attended in 1978-79	D. Year in school in 1978-79	E. Tuition and fees	F. Enrolled: Full-time	F. Enrolled: Half-time or more
1. STUDENT APPLICANT						
2.				$		
3.				$		
4.				$		
5.				$		

Divorced/Separated Parents

(To be completed by parent or guardian who has filed this FAF)

48 A. OTHER PARENT'S NAME _____
HOME ADDRESS _____
OCCUPATION/EMPLOYER _____

B. Date of divorce or separation: MONTH _____ YEAR _____

C. Who claimed student as a tax dependent? _____

D. Amount of monthly child support received for all children: $ _____

E. According to court order, when will (did) support for student end? MONTH _____ YEAR _____

F. Is there any agreement specifying a contribution for student's education? Yes ☐ No ☐ ..... If yes, how much per year? $ _____

Student's Information (continued) — *to be completed by all students*

Student's Income and Expenses

Enter information in boxes only. Do not enter monthly amounts.	Calendar Year 1977	Summer 1978 3 months	Estimated Academic Year 1978-79 9 months
49 STUDENT'S WAGES, SALARIES, TIPS, etc. (before taxes and deductions) (Do not include work-study earnings.)	$	$	$
50 SPOUSE'S WAGES, SALARIES, TIPS, etc. (before taxes and deductions) (Do not include work-study earnings.)	$	$	$
(51) OTHER TAXABLE INCOME (dividends, interest, etc.)	$	$	$
52 ADJUSTED GROSS INCOME (line 31 of IRS Form 1040 or line 10 of IRS Form 1040A). (Do not include work-study earnings. See instructions.)	$		
(53) NONTAXABLE INCOME AND BENEFITS. (See instructions. Do not include educational benefits reported in 63-66.)	$	$	$
54 FINANCIAL ASSISTANCE FROM STUDENT'S PARENTS		$	$
55 FINANCIAL ASSISTANCE FROM SPOUSE'S PARENTS		$	$
(56) GRANTS, SCHOLARSHIPS, EDUCATIONAL LOANS, WORK-STUDY. (Include only aid actually awarded.)		$	$
57 U.S. INCOME TAX PAID (line 47 of IRS Form 1040 or line 13 of IRS Form 1040A)	$		
(58) IRS ITEMIZED DEDUCTIONS (line 39 of Schedule A, IRS Form 1040)	$		
(59) MEDICAL AND DENTAL EXPENSES NOT COVERED BY INSURANCE (See instructions.)	$	$	$
(60) CASUALTY OR THEFT LOSS(ES) (See instructions.)	$	$	$
61 UNREIMBURSED ELEMENTARY AND HIGH SCHOOL TUITION AND FEES FOR DEPENDENT CHILDREN	$	$	$
(62) OTHER UNUSUAL EXPENSES	$	$	$

Student's Educational Benefits

	Calendar Year 1977	July 1, 1978-June 30, 1979
63 AMOUNT OF SOCIAL SECURITY BENEFITS to be received **per month**	$	$
64 NUMBER OF MONTHS social security benefits to be received		
65 AMOUNT OF VETERANS EDUCATIONAL BENEFITS to be received **per month**		$
66 NUMBER OF MONTHS veterans educational benefits to be received		

Student's Assets and Indebtedness

		Present Market Value	Unpaid Mortgage Principal or Debts
67 CASH, SAVINGS, AND CHECKING ACCOUNTS			$
68 HOME, IF OWNED OR BEING PURCHASED **4** YEAR PURCHASED 19 PURCHASE PRICE $		$	$
(69) INVESTMENTS (STOCKS, BONDS, AND OTHER SECURITIES) AND OTHER REAL ESTATE		$	$
70 BUSINESS (See instructions.)		$	$
71 FARM (See instructions.)		$	$
72 CONSUMER AND EDUCATIONAL INDEBTEDNESS			$
(73) OTHER DEBTS OUTSTANDING (Do not include any debts entered above.)			$

Student's Additional Information

74 TOTAL NUMBER OF EXEMPTIONS claimed on student's (and spouse's) 1977 U.S. income tax return **1977**	
75 TOTAL SIZE OF STUDENT'S HOUSEHOLD (Include the student named on this form, spouse, dependent children, and other dependents. See instructions.) **1978-79**	
76 NUMBER IN COLLEGE. Of the number entered in item 75, how many will be enrolled in college or other education beyond high school at least half-time during the 1978-79 academic year? **1978-79**	

77 STUDENT'S —	78 SPOUSE'S —
Occupation:	Occupation:
Employer:	Employer:

79 PROVIDE BELOW INFORMATION FOR **SPOUSE, CHILDREN, AND OTHER DEPENDENTS** ENTERED IN 75.

A. Name	(If you need additional space, use 80.)	B. Age	C. Name of institution to be attended in 1978-79	D. Year in school in 1978-79	E. Tuition and fees	F. Enrolled: Full-time	Half-time or more
1.					$		
2.					$		
3.					$		

---

80 Use this space to explain all circled items and any unusual circumstances.

If more space is needed, attach additional sheets of paper.

Institutions and Programs to Receive This FAF

81 If you are applying for financial aid administered by institutions, states, and other programs and want them to rece copies of this FAF, enter their complete names, addresses, and CSS code numbers. Obtain code numbers from CSS Code List. If you are unable to obtain a code number, leave the CSS code number box blank.

Do not enter the BEOG Program in this item. If you are applying ONLY to the BEOG Program, leave this item and blank and complete 83 and 84.

NAME	CITY	STATE	CSS CODE N

82 Check the box next to the number of institutions and programs entered in 81.

1 ☐ $4.50   2 ☐ $6.75   3 ☐ $9.00   4 ☐ $11.25   5 ☐ $13.50   6 ☐ $15.75

■ If you wish to receive a report of your **CSS Estimated Contribution**, check here and add $1 to the amount checked above .... ☐ $1.0

■ Mail this FAF with check or money order for appropriate amount to the CSS.

Basic Educational Opportunity Grant Program

83 In order to be considered for BEOG assistance, do you authorize information from this FAF to be released to the BEOG Program? (There is no charge for applying to the BEOG Program.) Yes ☐ 1 No ☐

If yes, enter your first two institutional choices, so that the BEOG Program can notify these institutions of your BEOG status.

NAME	CITY	STATE	CSS CODE N

84 Do you authorize the BEOG Program to release the appropriate information provided on this form (includin any new information or corrections for the 1978-79 academic year) to the agency administering financial ai programs in your state of legal residence for the purpose of calculating state awards, verifying data provide on state student aid applications, and conducting research? Yes ☐ 1 No ☐

Certification and Authorization

I (We) declare that the information reported is true, correct, and complete. I (We) authorize the use of this form the CSS as described in the FAF instructions. I (We) further authorize the CSS to transmit the information on form to state student aid programs, when an institution or a program is listed in 81, for the purpose of assisting the stud in being considered for financial aid. I (We) agree that, to verify information reported in this form, I (we) will on requ provide to the CSS or any of the authorized recipients, including the BEOG Program, an official photostatic copy of my (w 1977 state or U.S. income tax return. I (We) further agree to provide, if requested, any other official documenta necessary to verify information reported.

Student's Signature _____

Spouse's Signature _____

Signature(s) of Both Parents (or Guardian)

Student's Telephone: ( ) _____ AREA NUMBER

Date Completed: | MONTH | DAY | YEA

BASIC EDUCATIONAL OPPORTUNITY GRANT PROGRAM

GENERAL INFORMATION

The Basic Educational Opportunity Grant (BEOG) Program is a Federal student aid program designed to provide financial assistance, in the form of a grant (which need not be repaid) to those who need it to attend colleges and other institutions offering education beyond high school. The amount of the BEOG is determined according to your own and your family's financial resources. It is estimated that grants will range from $200 to $1,600 during the 1978-79 academic year.

This form may be used to apply for a BEOG and/or for financial assistance from institutions, states, and other programs. As a result of completing this form, you may be found eligible to receive BEOG assistance for any period of enrollment beginning July 1, 1978, through June 30, 1979.

To use this form to apply to the BEOG Program, you must check "Yes" in Item 83 and file the FAF *after January 1, 1978*. The CSS will forward the necessary information to the BEOG Program at no cost to you. The deadline for receipt of this form for purposes of applying to the BEOG Program is *March 15, 1979*. If you want, in addition, to have the CSS send copies of this FAF to institutions and programs, you must enter them in Item 81 and enclose the appropriate fee.

STUDENT ELIGIBILITY

You will be eligible for a Basic Grant if you meet *all* of the following criteria:

1. You have established your financial need for a BEOG by means of this form.

2. You will be enrolled (at least half-time) in an undergraduate course of study in an eligible program at one of over 6,000 institutions approved for participation in the BEOG Program.

3. You will not have previously received a Bachelor's degree from any institution.

4. You are a U.S. citizen, or you are in the United States for other than a temporary purpose and intend to become a permanent resident, or are a permanent resident of the Trust Territory of the Pacific Islands.

5. You will have received no more than four full years of BEOG payments. Exception: you may receive BEOG assistance for five years only when the institution either: (a) designed the program of study leading to a Bachelor's degree to be five years in length, or (b) required your enrollment in a remedial course of study which meant you were unable to complete the regular program in four academic years.

Within six weeks after you mail this form to the CSS, you will receive a Student Eligibility Report (SER) from the BEOG Program. The SER is the official notification of your eligibility for a BEOG and must be presented to the school you will attend to determine the amount of your grant. When you receive the SER, carefully read and follow the instructions it contains.

BEOG SPECIAL CIRCUMSTANCES

If you experience a dramatic change in income from 1977 to 1978, you may be eligible to apply for a BEOG based on estimated 1978 income rather than actual 1977 income. For further details regarding your eligibility to apply for a BEOG in this manner, contact your high school guidance counselor or financial aid administrator.

ADDITIONAL INFORMATION

If you would like to receive additional information on the BEOG Program, as well as general information on student financial aid, please write to: BEOG, Box 84, Washington, DC 20044. Ask for a copy of the *Student Guide*.

NOTICE TO APPLICANTS

INFORMATION COLLECTED ON THIS FORM FOR BASIC GRANT PURPOSES

Subsection (e)(3) of the Privacy Act of 1974 (5 U.S.C. 552a(e)(3)) requires that an agency inform each individual whom it asks to supply information: (1) the authority (whether granted by statute, or by executive order of the President) which authorizes the solicitation of the information and whether disclosure of such information is mandatory or voluntary; (2) the principal purpose or purposes for which the information is intended to be used; (3) the routine uses which may be made of the information as published in the Federal Register; and (4) the effects, if any, of not providing all or any part of the requested information.

1. The authority for collecting the requested information is section 411(b)(2) of Title IV – A – 1 of the Higher Education Act of 1965, as amended (20 U.S.C. 1070a(b)(2)). Applicants are advised that, except as noted in paragraph 4, the disclosure of the requested information is mandatory.

2. This information is being collected in order to calculate a student's eligibility index under the BEOG. The eligibility index is one of the three factors used in determining the amount, if any, of the applicant's BEOG.

3. The "routine uses," as defined in 5 U.S.C. 552a(a)(7), which may be made of the information collected are: An applicant's name, address, social security number, date of birth and eligibility index will be provided to the institution of higher education which the applicant indicates he is attending or will attend and to the State scholarship agency of the applicant's state of legal residence if such an agency has an agreement with the Commissioner of Education permitting it to secure such information. Such information will be used by the State agency in coordinating its program of student financial aid with the BEOG Program. Furthermore, on request, information may be provided to members of Congress who inquire on behalf of a student who is a constituent or, where appropriate, on behalf of the parents of the student. In addition, the routine uses listed in Appendix B of 45 CFR 5B may be utilized.

4. Applicants must provide information for all of the following items in order to have their application for a BEOG award processed: Items 1-3, 5, 7, 8, 13-15, 83, and the Certification and Authorization section. In addition, if the applicant answers "Yes" for *any* question for *any* year in Items 13-15, then Items 16, 17A1 (1977), 17A2 (1977), 20 (1977), 21A (1977), 21B (1977), 23, 24, 26-28, 30-35, 40, 42, 43, 45, and 65-71 must be completed. If the applicant answers "No" to *all* years and *all* questions in Items 13-15, then Items 49 (1977), 50 (1977), 52 (1977), 53 (1977), 57-61 (1977), 63-64 (1977), 65-71, and 74-76 must be completed.

Students need not complete Items 6, 9, 38 (age), 39 (age), 63 (1978-79), 64 (1978-79), 83 (institution choices), and 84; however, answering these items will facilitate the administration of state student assistance programs. Failure to answer Item 84 will be considered a No response to that item.

Responses to all other items are voluntary with regard to the BEOG Program.

USE OF SOCIAL SECURITY NUMBER

Section 7(b) of the Privacy Act of 1974 (5 U.S.C. 522a) requires that when any Federal, State, or local government agency requests an individual to disclose his social security account number, that individual must also be advised whether that disclosure is mandatory or voluntary, by what statutory or other authority the number is solicited, and what uses will be made of it. Accordingly, applicants are advised that disclosure of their social security account number (SSAN) is required as a condition for participation in the BEOG, in view of the practical administrative difficulties which the program would encounter in maintaining adequate program records without the continued use of the SSAN.

The SSAN will be used to verify the identity of the applicant, and as an account number (identifier) throughout the life of the grant in order to record necessary data accurately. As an identifier, the SSAN is used in such Program activities as: determining Program eligibility; certifying school attendance and student status; making grant payments under the alternative disbursement system; and verifying grant payments.

Authority for requiring the disclosure of an applicant's SSAN is grounded on section 7(a)(2) of the Privacy Act, which provides that an agency may continue to require disclosure of an individual's SSAN as a condition for the granting of a right, benefit, or privilege provided by law where the agency required this disclosure under statute or regulations prior to January 1, 1975, in order to verify the identity of an individual.

The Office of Education has, for several years, consistently required the disclosure of SSAN numbers on application forms and other necessary BEOG documents. (See section 411(b)(2) of Title IV – A – 1 of the Higher Education Act of 1965, as amended (20 U.S.C. 10701(b)(2).)

In addition, it should be noted that the social security account number of a parent of the applicant is also requested. Parents are advised that disclosure of their SSAN is voluntary and failure to provide it will not affect the applicant's eligibility for a BEOG award. Parent's SSAN will be recorded only on the application form itself and will not be maintained in any other system of records. Its use will be restricted to a sample of cases which may be used for further verification of information reported on the application by the applicant and/or parent(s).

If you are not applying to the BEOG Program, provision of your SSAN is optional; however, because many of those who complete the FAF have similar names, the SSAN is most helpful, and often critical, in assuring proper identification of an individual student by the CSS and by institutions and programs using the FAF. You are, therefore, strongly encouraged to include your SSAN if available.

21076 • UU97P6372 • 218398 • Printed in U.S.A.

Financial Aid Form
Academic Year 1978-79

TO BE COMPLETED BY FARM OR RANCH OWNERS, OPERATORS, OR FARM TENANTS

FARM SUPPLEMENT

INSTRUCTIONS

- Complete this supplement before continuing with the FAF. If you own more than one farm, submit a copy of the Farm Supplement for each.

- When completing this supplement, refer to your current and past IRS tax returns, Schedules F and D (1040). **For any year that tax forms have not been completed, estimate as accurately as possible.**

- In the case of partnerships or corporations, enter your percentage of ownership on **LINE 1E** and, where amounts are not readily separable, indicate total amounts under Income and Expenses and report your share of net farm profit on **LINE 9.**

- Do not submit balance sheets, profit and loss statements, or tax returns in place of the Farm Supplement.

- **LINES 2A, 2B,** and **3:** If farm income is reported on the accrual basis, the required information can be found on IRS Schedule F (1040). In this case, disregard **LINES 2A** and **2B** and begin your entries with gross profit on **LINE 3.**

- **LINE 7:** Report all gains or losses from the sales or exchanges of livestock and farm machinery at their full amount. Do not include other property sales or exchanges reported on IRS Schedule D (1040).

- If your home is on the farm, enter its value and amount of mortgage in **30** on the FAF. Do not enter home value or mortgage on this supplement.

STUDENT'S INFORMATION

STUDENT'S NAME

STUDENT'S LAST NAME | STUDENT'S FIRST NAME | MID. INIT. | STUDENT'S SOCIAL SECURITY NUMBER | STUDENT'S DATE OF BIRTH (MONTH DAY YEAR) | OPTIONAL 1 ☐ M 2 ☐ F | SEX

STUDENT'S ADDRESS

STREET ADDRESS | CITY | STATE | ZIP CODE

FARM INFORMATION

1A. LOCATION OF FARM — TOWNSHIP / COUNTY / STATE

B. YEAR PURCHASED 19___

C. FARM IS
- ☐ PARTNERSHIP
- ☐ CORPORATION
- ☐ SOLE OWNERSHIP

E. PERCENTAGE OF OWNERSHIP _____ %

G. TOTAL ACRES OWNED _____

Estimated present market value per acre $_____

D. RESIDENCE INFORMATION

1. Do you live on the farm? ☐ NO ☐ YES

2. Your family dwelling is ☐ OWNED ☐ RENTED ☐ RENT-FREE

F. DESCRIBE PRINCIPAL PRODUCTS.

H. NUMBER OF ACRES

	OWNED	RENTED FROM OTHERS	RENTED TO OTHERS
Tillable: PRODUCTIVE ORCHARDS			
TRUCK CROPS			
OTHER			
Nontillable pasture			
Woodland and waste			
Agricultural reserve			
TOTAL			

INCOME AND EXPENSES

The IRS line references below are for 1976. For 1977, use the corresponding lines from IRS Schedules F or D.

	1976 (Jan. 1-Dec. 31)	1977 (Jan. 1-Dec. 31)	Estimated 1978 (Jan. 1-Dec. 31)
2 FARM INCOME			
A. PROFIT (OR LOSS) ON SALES OF PURCHASED LIVESTOCK AND OTHER ITEMS PURCHASED FOR RESALE. From IRS Schedule F (1040), Part I, line 4	$	$	
B. SALES OF MARKET LIVESTOCK, PRODUCE RAISED, AND OTHER FARM INCOME, including crop sales and government payments. From IRS Schedule F (1040), Part I, line 27			
3 GROSS PROFIT (Add 2A and 2B.) From IRS Schedule F (1040), Part I, line 28	$	$	
4 FARM DEDUCTIONS			
A. FARM DEDUCTIONS. From IRS Schedule F (1040), Part II, line 51			
B. DEPRECIATION. From IRS Schedule F (1040), Part II, line 52			
5 TOTAL DEDUCTIONS (Add 4A and 4B.) From IRS Schedule F (1040), Part II, line 53	$	$	
6 NET FARM PROFIT (OR LOSS) (Subtract 5 from 3.) From IRS Schedule F (1040), Part II, line 54			
7 CAPITAL GAINS (OR LOSSES) from the sales or exchanges of livestock and farm machinery. From IRS Schedule D (1040)			Estimated 1978
8 TOTAL NET FARM PROFIT (Add 6 and 7.)	$	$	$
9 YOUR SHARE OF NET FARM PROFIT Enter amounts for 1977 and 1978 (estimated) in 17D on the FAF.	$	$	$

ASSETS AND INDEBTEDNESS

	As of December 31, 1976	As of December 31, 197_
10 ASSETS (Farm only)		
A. LAND AND BUILDINGS excluding farm home (present market value)	$	$
B. FARM BANK ACCOUNTS		
C. ACCOUNTS RECEIVABLE		
D. LIVESTOCK (fair market value): Type ___ Number ___ Type ___ Number ___		
E. GRAIN, HAY, AND OTHER PRODUCTS		
F. MACHINERY AND OTHER FARM ASSETS (fair market value)		
11 TOTAL ASSETS (Add 10A through 10F.)		
12 MULTIPLY TOTAL ASSETS BY PERCENTAGE OF OWNERSHIP Enter amount for 1977 on the FAF in 34, market value.	$	$
13 INDEBTEDNESS (Farm only)		
A. MORTGAGE ON FARM excluding farm home		
B. DEBTS ON FARM MACHINERY AND EQUIPMENT		
C. OTHER FARM DEBTS		
14 TOTAL INDEBTEDNESS (Add 13A through 13C.)		
15 MULTIPLY TOTAL INDEBTEDNESS BY PERCENTAGE OF OWNERSHIP Enter amount for 1977 on the FAF in 34, debts.	$	$

SIGNATURE

FATHER OR MALE GUARDIAN'S SIGNATURE | DATE

MOTHER OR FEMALE GUARDIAN'S SIGNATURE | DATE

21076 • E77P500 • 218411

Financial Aid Form
Academic Year 1978-79

TO BE COMPLETED BY
OWNERS OF BUSINESSES

BUSINESS SUPPLEMENT

STUDENT'S INFORMATION

STUDENT'S NAME

| STUDENT'S LAST NAME | STUDENT'S FIRST NAME | MID. INIT. | STUDENT'S SOCIAL SECURITY NUMBER | STUDENT'S DATE OF BIRTH (MONTH DAY YEAR) | OPTIONAL | SEX |

1 ☐ M 2 ☐ F

STUDENT'S ADDRESS

| STREET ADDRESS | CITY | STATE | ZIP CODE |

BUSINESS INFORMATION

1A. NAME OF BUSINESS

B. DATE BUSINESS COMMENCED

C. BUSINESS ADDRESS — STREET — CITY — STATE

D. TYPE OF BUSINESS
- ☐ SOLE PROPRIETOR
- ☐ PARTNERSHIP
- ☐ CORPORATION

E. PERCENTAGE OF OWNERSHIP _____ %

F. DESCRIBE PRODUCT OR SERVICE.

G. IF PARTNERSHIP, GIVE PARTNER'S NAME(S).

H. NUMBER OF EMPLOYEES

INCOME AND EXPENSES

	1976 (Jan. 1-Dec. 31)	1977 (Jan. 1-Dec. 31)	Estimated 1978 (Jan. 1-Dec. 31)
2 BUSINESS INCOME			
A. GROSS RECEIPTS OR SALES LESS RETURNS AND ALLOWANCES	$	$	
B. COST OF GOODS SOLD and/or OPERATIONS (Do not include expenses listed under 4 below.)			
C. GROSS PROFIT (Subtract 2B from 2A.)			
D. OTHER BUSINESS INCOME			
3 TOTAL INCOME (Add 2C and 2D.)	$	$	
4 BUSINESS DEDUCTIONS			
A. DEPRECIATION			
B. RENT ON BUSINESS PROPERTY			
C. SALARIES AND WAGES NOT INCLUDED IN 2B ABOVE (Do not include any paid to yourself.)			
D. 1. **PARTNERSHIP ONLY.** YOUR SALARY, if any (Enter amount here and in 17A on the FAF.)			
D. 2. **CORPORATION ONLY.** YOUR SALARY, if any (Enter amount here and in 17A on the FAF.)			
OTHER BUSINESS EXPENSES:			
E.			
F.			
G.			
H.			
5 TOTAL DEDUCTIONS (Add 4A through 4H.)	$	$	Estimated 1978
6 NET PROFIT (OR LOSS) — Sole Proprietor or ORDINARY INCOME — Partnership or TAXABLE INCOME — Corporation (Subtract 5 from 3.) From IRS Schedule C(1040) or Form 1065 or Form 1120.	$	$	$
7 YOUR SHARE OF LINE 6 (If you are a sole proprietor, line 7 should equal line 6.)	$	$	$

If your business is **sole proprietorship or partnership,** include these amounts in 17D on the FAF.

If your business is a **corporation,** enter these amounts in the appropriate item in 17 on the FAF. Explain in 80 on the FAF the item number (17A, 17B, 17C, or 17D) where income is entered.

ASSETS AND INDEBTEDNESS

	As of December 31, 1976	As of December 31, 1977
8 CURRENT ASSETS (Business only)		
A. CASH (Business accounts only)	$	$
B. OTHER CURRENT ASSETS		
C. SUBTOTAL (Add 8A and 8B.)		
D. RESERVE FOR BAD DEBTS		
E. TOTAL CURRENT ASSETS (Subtract 8D from 8C.)		
9 FIXED ASSETS (Business only)		
A. LAND AND BUILDINGS (present market value)		
B. EQUIPMENT AND OTHER FIXED ASSETS (fair market value)		
C. TOTAL FIXED ASSETS (Add 9A and 9B.)		
10 TOTAL ASSETS (Add 8E and 9C.)		
11 MULTIPLY TOTAL ASSETS BY PERCENTAGE OF OWNERSHIP Enter amount for 1977 on the FAF in 33, market value.	$	$
12 INDEBTEDNESS (Business only)		
A. MORTGAGE ON LAND AND BUILDINGS		
B. OTHER INDEBTEDNESS		
13 TOTAL INDEBTEDNESS (Add 12A and 12B.)		
14 MULTIPLY TOTAL INDEBTEDNESS BY PERCENTAGE OF OWNERSHIP Enter amount for 1977 on the FAF in 33, debts.	$	$

FATHER OR MALE GUARDIAN'S SIGNATURE	DATE
MOTHER OR FEMALE GUARDIAN'S SIGNATURE	DATE

To avoid delays in processing, it is important that you complete all items on the FAF according to the following instructions:

- **Please type or print all entries in black or dark ink; do not use a pencil.**
- **Enter each response in the proper area. Do not make entries outside boxes or enter more than one set of figures in a box.**
- **Enter amounts in dollars; omit cents. Do not use commas between dollar values. For example, if wages, salaries, tips, and other compensation are $5,398.24, enter $5398.**
- **Do not leave dollar items blank. Enter a zero (0) where appropriate. Do not use such words as "unknown," "none," or "same."**
- **Use Item 80 to explain all circled items and any unusual circumstances. Attach additional sheets of paper if more space is needed. On any additional sheets, be certain to give the student's complete identification information and the CSS code numbers of the institutions and programs to receive the FAF.**

Certain sections of the FAF are reproduced below to assist you in completing the form. Keep these instructions and the worksheets for your records.

STUDENT'S INFORMATION

ITEM 1. Enter student's complete name, giving last name, first name, and middle initial.

ITEM 2. Enter student's social security number. Student's social security number is required if student is applying for a Basic Educational Opportunity Grant (BEOG).

ITEM 3. Enter student's date of birth, using numbers for month, day, and year.

ITEM 4. Indicate student's sex.

ITEM 5. Enter the address where the student can be certain of receiving notification of the processing of this form. Use the state abbreviations on the front cover.

ITEM 6. Enter the abbreviation for the student's state of legal residence. Use the state abbreviations on the front cover.

ITEM 7. Indicate student's current marital status. If married or separated, enter the date of marriage or separation. If student intends to marry before July 1, 1979, enter date of intended marriage.

ITEM 8. Indicate student's U.S. citizenship status. If student is not a U.S. citizen or a permanent resident of the United States or the Trust Territory of the Pacific Islands, enter student's visa number in Item 80. If student is not a U.S. citizen, see the back cover for BEOG eligibility criteria.

ITEM 9. Indicate student's year in college or other education beyond high school during 1978-79. Also, enter student's present degree objective and expected date of graduation. "Fifth (undergraduate)" means the fifth year of an undergraduate curriculum that normally requires five years for completion. If "fifth" is indicated, see the back cover for BEOG eligibility criteria.

ITEM 10. Enter the name of the institution, if any, that student attended in 1977-78. If the student is an entering, first-time student in 1978-79, enter the student's secondary school code number. The code number may be obtained from the guidance office of the student's high school.

ITEM 11. Indicate the academic period(s) for which the student is seeking financial assistance. Check all boxes that apply.

ITEM 12. Indicate where the student plans to live during 1978-79. "On campus" means residence facilities operated by or for the institution; "off-campus" means residence facilities not operated by or for the institution, but not including the parents' home. If student's choice of institution has not been made, the student should indicate his or her plans for the first institution listed in Item 81.

ITEMS 13-15. For purposes of this form, the term "parents" is generally defined to be the student's mother and/or father. Items 13-15 should be completed with regard to student's mother or father.

If you answer "Yes" for any question for any year, the parents' confidential statement (Items 17-48) must be completed.

If you answer "No" to every question for every year with regard to student's mother and father, the parents' confidential statement (Items 17-48) need not be completed; however, some institutions or programs to which you are applying may require this information. You should follow any specific instructions you receive from the institution or program.

If some person other than a parent (or spouse) provided or will provide more than one-half of the student's support during 1978, Items 13-15 should be completed with that person considered the "parent." If you answer "Yes" to any questions for any year with regard to the "parent," Items 17-48 must be completed by that person. In no case would a spouse be considered the student's "parent."

ITEM 16. Indicate whether both of student's parents are deceased.

Note: Funds received by the student or parents as an award under the Distribution of Judgment Funds Act or the Alaska Native Claims Settlement Act should NOT be reported as an asset if: (a) it may not be sold or have loans placed against it without consent of the Secretary of Interior, or (b) the property is held in trust by the U.S. Government.

Note: If student or parents are residents of Puerto Rico, the Virgin Islands, Guam, American Samoa, or the Trust Territory of the Pacific Islands and filed a 1977 income tax return with its Government, enter information corresponding to that requested in any item referring to the U.S. income tax return.

PARENTS' CONFIDENTIAL STATEMENT

If student's parents are separated or divorced, provide information for the parent who has or had custody of the student. If no custody was awarded, or if parents have or had equal custody of the student, provide information for the parent with whom the student resided for the greater portion of the 12-month period preceding the date of completing this form.

If parents are divorced, or if parent is widowed, and the parent has remarried, financial information of student's stepparent may need to be reported. Student's stepparent's information should be reported (together with parent's information) if either (a) student did or will live with stepparent (and parent) for six weeks or more during 1977, 1978, or 1979; or (b) student did or will receive $600 or more in financial assistance from stepparent in 1977, 1978, or 1979.

PARENTS' ANNUAL INCOME AND EXPENSES

Enter yearly amounts in boxes only.	1976	1977	Estimated 1978
17 TAXABLE INCOME BEFORE DEDUCTIONS			
A. Wages, salaries, tips, and other compensation			
1. Father, stepfather, or male guardian	$	$	$
2. Mother, stepmother, or female guardian	$	$	$
B. Dividends	$	$	$
C. Interest income	$	$	$
(D). Taxable income other than wages, dividends, and interest (Itemize and give dollar amounts in 80.)	$	$	$
18 Add 17A, 17B, 17C, and 17D	$	$	$
(19) ADJUSTMENTS TO INCOME (lines 28 and 30 of IRS Form 1040)	$	$	$
20 ADJUSTED GROSS INCOME (Subtract 19 from 18) (line 31 of IRS Form 1040 or line 10 of Form 1040A)	$	$	$
21 NONTAXABLE INCOME (See instructions.) A. Social security benefits	$	$	$
(B). Other nontaxable income (veterans benefits, child support, welfare, etc.)	$	$	$
22 TOTAL INCOME (Add 20, 21A, and 21B.)	$	$	$
23 U.S. INCOME TAX PAID (line 47 of IRS Form 1040 or line 13 of IRS Form 1040A)		$	
(24) IRS ITEMIZED DEDUCTIONS (line 39 of Schedule A, IRS Form 1040)		$	
(25) STATE AND OTHER TAXES		$	
(26) MEDICAL AND DENTAL EXPENSES NOT COVERED BY INSURANCE (See instructions.)		$	
(27) CASUALTY OR THEFT LOSS(ES) (See instructions.)		$	
28 UNREIMBURSED ELEMENTARY AND HIGH SCHOOL TUITION AND FEES FOR DEPENDENT CHILDREN, excluding the student applicant		$	
(29) OTHER UNUSUAL EXPENSES		$	

Enter total annual amounts only. Whenever an individual entry is from more than one source, itemize and give dollar amounts in Item 80. If parents' 1977 U.S. income tax return has not been filed, estimate amounts that parents expect to report on their tax return. The IRS references on the FAF are for the 1977 U.S. income tax return. For 1978 provide best estimates.

In completing Items 17-20 and 23-27, if parents are married and file separate U.S. income tax returns, add the figures from both returns and report the total.

If parents did not and will not file a 1977 U.S. income tax return, enter zeros for Items 17-20, 23, and 24. Enter any untaxed earned income in Item 21B.

ITEM 17A. Enter the amount of "wages, salaries, tips, and other employee compensation" reported on line 8 of parents' 1977 U.S. income tax Form 1040, or line 7 of Form 1040A for: (1) father (or stepfather or male guardian) and (2) mother (or stepmother or female guardian).

ITEM 17B. Enter the amount of "dividends" reported on line 10c of parents' 1977 U.S. income tax Form 1040, or line 8c of Form 1040A.

ITEM 17C. Enter the amount of "interest income" reported on line 9 of parents' 1977 U.S. income tax Form 1040 or 1040A.

ITEM (17D). Enter the amount of income other than wages, dividends, and interest reported on lines 11-20 of parents' 1977 U.S. income tax Form 1040. Itemize and give dollar amounts in Item 80. If parents own a business or farm, be certain to include the net profit (if a sole ownership) or ordinary income (if a partnership) in this item.

ITEM 18. Enter the total of Items 17A1, 17A2, 17B, 17C, and 17D.

ITEM (19). Enter the amount of "adjustments to income" reported on lines 28 and 30 of parents' 1977 U.S. income tax Form 1040. Enter only IRS allowable amounts for forfeited interest, moving expense, employee business expense, payments to a Keogh or an individual retirement plan, alimony paid, and disability income exclusion (sick pay). Itemize and give dollar amounts in Item 80.

Parents' Annual Income and Expenses (continued)

ITEM 20. Enter the amount of "adjusted gross income" reported on line 31 of parents' 1977 U.S. income tax Form 1040, or line 10 of Form 1040A. Amount should equal Item 18 minus Item 19.

ITEM 21A. Enter the total amount of social security benefits received by or for all household members reported in Item 43, *including the student.*

ITEM 21B. Enter the total of all other nontaxable income. Include welfare benefits, child support, unemployment compensation, and earned income that is *not* reported in Item 17.

Also include all veterans benefits *except educational* benefits received by the student or other members of the household.

In addition, include any other income which is not subject to income tax, such as interest on tax-free bonds, untaxed portions of pensions and capital gains, and housing and subsistence allowances (for military, clergy, and faculty).

Do not include amounts received from student aid programs (educational loans, work-study earnings, grants, or scholarships), veterans educational benefits (GI Bill or War Orphans' and Widows' Education Assistance), or any "adjustments to income" reported in Item 19. *Do not* include any income reported in Item 17.

ITEM 22. If the amount entered for 1977 is different by $2,000 or more than that entered for 1976, complete the shaded 1976 column for Items 17-21. Also, if the amount entered for 1978 is different by $2,000 or more from that entered for 1977, explain in Item 80.

ITEM 23. Enter parents' U.S. income tax paid (or estimated to be paid) as reported on line 47 of 1977 U.S. income tax Form 1040, or line 13 of Form 1040A. Do not copy from a W-2 Form tax withheld.

ITEM 24. If parents itemize deductions on their 1977 U.S. income tax return, enter the amount of "total deductions" reported on line 39 of Schedule A, Form 1040. If parents do not itemize deductions, enter a zero.

ITEM 25. If parents itemize deductions on their 1977 U.S. income tax return, enter the amount of state and other taxes reported on line 17 of Schedule A, Form 1040. If parents take a standard deduction or will not file a 1977 return, enter the total of state and local income, real estate, gasoline, sales, personal property, and other taxes. Do not include U.S. income tax.

ITEM 26. If parents itemize deductions on their 1977 U.S. income tax return, enter the total of medicine, drugs, and other medical and dental expenses reported on lines 2 and 6 of Schedule A, Form 1040. If parents take a standard deduction or will not file a 1977 return, enter the amount of medical and dental expenses for parents' household for 1977 which were *not* covered by insurance. Do not include the cost of medical and dental insurance premiums.

ITEM 27. If parents itemize deductions on their 1977 U.S. income tax return, enter the amount of casualty or theft loss(es) reported on line 29 of Schedule A, Form 1040. If parents take a standard deduction or will not file a 1977 return, determine the amount of each loss not covered by insurance, due to theft or damage by fire, storm, or accident. Subtract $100 from the amount of each loss; add the net amount of each of these losses and enter the total.

ITEM 28. Enter the amount of elementary, junior high, and senior high school tuition and fees parents paid in 1977 for all dependent children (other than the student) included in Item 43. Do not report any amounts which were paid by scholarships or other forms of student aid.

ITEM 29. Enter the total amount of other unusual expenses such as payments for child support, funerals, legal fees, and water, street, and sewer assessments. Itemize and give dollar amounts in Item 80.

ITEM 32. Enter the present market value of parents' investments (including stocks, bonds, and other securities). Also, enter unpaid debts on parents' investments. Report business or farm assets and debts only in Item 33 or 34.

ITEM 33. If parents own all or part of a business, enter the present market value of business. Also, enter the present mortgage and related debts for which the business assets are used as collateral. Do not include value of home even if part of business property; report value of home only in Item 30. If parents are not the sole owners of the business, enter only the amount of their share of the total business market value and debt.

BUSINESS WORK SHEET

A. Percentage of ownership . . . . _____%

B. Current assets (cash and other current assets less reserve for bad debts) . . . . $_____

C. Fixed assets (present market value of land, buildings, equipment, and other fixed assets) . . . . . . $_____

D. Total assets (Add B and C.) . . . . $_____

E. Multiply total assets by percentage of ownership. (Enter amount in Item 33, market value.) . . . . $_____

F. Total indebtedness (mortgage on land and buildings and other business indebtedness) . . . . . . $_____

G. Multiply total indebtedness by percentage of ownership. (Enter amount in Item 33, debts.) . . . . $_____

ITEM 34. If parents own all or part of a farm, enter the present market value of farm. Also, enter the present mortgage and related debts for which the farm assets are used as collateral. Do not include value of home even if part of farm property; report value of home only in Item 30. If parents are not the sole owners of the farm, enter only the amount of their share of the total farm market value and debt.

FARM WORK SHEET

A. Percentage of ownership . . . . _____%

B. Total assets (present market value of land and buildings, excluding farm home; bank accounts and accounts receivable; livestock, grain, hay, and other products; machinery and other assets) . . . . . . $_____

C. Multiply total assets by percentage of ownership. (Enter amount in Item 34, market value.) . . . . $_____

D. Total indebtedness (mortgage on farm, excluding farm home; debts on machinery and equipment; other debts) . . . . $_____

E. Multiply total indebtedness by percentage of ownership. (Enter amount in Item 34, debts.) . . . . $_____

ITEM 35. Enter the present amount of parents' cash, savings, and checking accounts.

ITEM 36. Enter the present amount of parents' consumer indebtedness (such as debts for purchase of automobiles, appliances, and other consumer durables; and retail store and bank charge accounts), and educational indebtedness of parents or other family members, except the student. Enter student's educational indebtedness in Item 72.

ITEM 37. Do not include any expenses already entered in Items 23-29 or any debt entered in Items 30-34 and 36. *Include only debt outstanding from 1976 or before.* Include such past debts as medical and dental expenses; remaining business indebtedness if business dissolved; funeral expenses; legal fees; unreimbursed job-related moving expenses; natural disasters not covered by insurance; liens; and living expenses if business failure, prolonged illness, or unemployment has depleted assets and forced indebtedness. *Do not include any other type of debt outstanding.*

PARENTS' ASSETS AND INDEBTEDNESS

Enter information in boxes only.

	Present Market Value	Unpaid Mortgage Principal or Debts
30 HOME, IF OWNED OR BEING PURCHASED — YEAR PURCHASED 19___ PURCHASE PRICE $_____	$	$
31 OTHER REAL ESTATE	$	$
32 INVESTMENTS (STOCKS, BONDS, AND OTHER SECURITIES)	$	$
33 BUSINESS (See instructions.)	$	$
34 FARM (See instructions.)	$	$
35 CASH, SAVINGS, AND CHECKING ACCOUNTS	$	
36 CONSUMER AND EDUCATIONAL INDEBTEDNESS		$
37 OTHER DEBTS OUTSTANDING (Do not include any debts entered above.)		$

In completing Items 30-34, enter the present market value of each asset listed. Do not use such valuations as assessed value, insured value, and taxed value. Do not report personal or consumer debts that are not related to the assets listed.

Do not report any asset or debt more than once.

ITEM 30. Enter the present market value of parents' home. Also, enter unpaid mortgage principal and related debts on parents' home.

ITEM 31. Enter the present market value of parents' other real estate. Also, enter unpaid mortgage principal and debts on parents' other real estate. Report business or farm assets and debts only in Item 33 or 34.

PARENTS' INFORMATION

ITEM 38. Enter appropriate information for father, stepfather, or male guardian.

ITEM 39. Enter appropriate information for mother, stepmother, or female guardian.

ITEM 40. Indicate parents' *current* marital status. Check only one box.

ITEM 41. Indicate whether parents have filed their 1977 U.S. income tax return. If parents did not or will not file a 1977 return, check "No."

ITEM 42. Enter the number of exemptions reported on line 7 of parents' 1977 U.S. income tax Form 1040, or line 6 of Form 1040A. If parents did not and will not file a 1977 return, enter zero.

ITEM 43. Enter the total number of persons for whom parents will provide more than one-half support between July 1, 1978, and June 30, 1979. Include the student *if a member of parents' household,* parents, parents' dependent children, and other dependents (persons who live with parents and receive more than one-half their support from the parents). Do not leave blank and do not enter zero. List children and other dependents in Item 47.

ITEM 44. Indicate whether student is included in number reported in Item 43.

ITEM 45. Enter the appropriate number of persons reported in Item 43 who will be enrolled in a college, university, vocational or technical school, or other education beyond high school, on at least a half-time basis, during the 1978-79 academic year.

ITEM 46. Indicate whether student is included in number reported in Item 45.

ITEM 47. Enter appropriate information for student and all children and other dependents included in the number entered in Item 43. Do not list parents.

ITEM 48. If student's parents are separated or divorced, enter appropriate information regarding the other parent.

STUDENT'S INFORMATION (continued)

Dependent students who are not married or who have no dependents of their own should complete only the following: Items 49-56 for summer 1978 and academic year 1978-79; Items 63-66; Item 67 (and Items 68-73, if applicable); and Items 80 and following.

Other students should complete all items.

STUDENT'S INCOME AND EXPENSES

Enter information in boxes only. Do not enter monthly amounts.	Calendar Year 1977	Summer 1978 3 months	Estimated Academic Year 1978-79 9 months
49 STUDENT'S WAGES, SALARIES, TIPS, etc. (before taxes and deductions) (Do not include work-study earnings.)	$	$	$
50 SPOUSE'S WAGES, SALARIES, TIPS, etc. (before taxes and deductions) (Do not include work-study earnings.)	$	$	$
51 OTHER TAXABLE INCOME (dividends, interest, etc.)	$	$	$
52 ADJUSTED GROSS INCOME (line 31 of IRS Form 1040 or line 10 of IRS Form 1040A). (Do not include work-study earnings. See instructions.)	$		
53 NONTAXABLE INCOME AND BENEFITS. (See instructions. Do not include educational benefits reported in 63-66.)	$	$	$
54 FINANCIAL ASSISTANCE FROM STUDENT'S PARENTS		$	$
55 FINANCIAL ASSISTANCE FROM SPOUSE'S PARENTS		$	$
56 GRANTS, SCHOLARSHIPS, EDUCATIONAL LOANS, WORK-STUDY (Include only aid actually awarded.)		$	$
57 U.S. INCOME TAX PAID (line 47 of IRS Form 1040 or line 13 of IRS Form 1040A)	$		
58 IRS ITEMIZED DEDUCTIONS (line 39 of Schedule A, IRS Form 1040)	$		
59 MEDICAL AND DENTAL EXPENSES NOT COVERED BY INSURANCE (See instructions.)	$	$	$
60 CASUALTY OR THEFT LOSS(ES) (See instructions.)	$		
61 UNREIMBURSED ELEMENTARY AND HIGH SCHOOL TUITION AND FEES FOR DEPENDENT CHILDREN	$	$	$
62 OTHER UNUSUAL EXPENSES	$	$	$

Enter total amounts according to the column headings. Whenever an individual entry is from more than one source, itemize and give dollar amounts in Item 80. If student's 1977 U.S. income tax return has not been filed, estimate amounts that student expects to report on the tax return. The IRS references on the FAF are for the 1977 U.S. income tax return. For summer 1978 and academic year 1978-79, provide best estimates.

If student is married, Items 51-62 apply to both student and student's spouse. If student is separated or divorced, provide only that information which applies to the student.

In completing Items 49-52 and 57-60, if student is married and student and spouse file separate U.S. income tax returns, add the figures from both returns and report the total.

If student did not and will not file a 1977 U.S. income tax return, enter zeros for Items 49-52, 57, and 58. Enter untaxed earned income in Item 53.

ITEM 49. Enter the amount of student's "wages, salaries, tips, and other employee compensation" included in line 8 of student's 1977 U.S. income tax Form 1040, or line 7 of Form 1040A. Do not include any income received as a result of employment provided by student aid programs.

ITEM 50. Enter the amount of spouse's "wages, salaries, tips, and other employee compensation" included in line 8 of student's 1977 U.S. income tax Form 1040, or line 7 of Form 1040A. Do not include any income received as a result of employment provided by student aid programs.

ITEM 51. Enter all other taxable income, including "dividends" (line 10c of student's U.S. income tax Form 1040, or line 8c of Form 1040A); "interest income" (line 9 of Form 1040 or 1040A); and income other than wages, dividends, and interest (lines 11-20 of Form 1040). Itemize and give dollar amounts in Item 80. If student owns a business or farm, be certain to include the net profit (if a sole ownership) or ordinary income (if a partnership) in this item.

ITEM 52. Enter the amount of "adjusted gross income" reported on line 31 of student's

1977 U.S. income tax Form 1040, or line 10 of Form 1040A. Do not include any income received as a result of employment provided by student aid programs.

ITEM 53. Enter all nontaxable income and benefits *except social security educational benefits and veterans educational benefits reported in Items 63-66.*

Include the total amount of social security benefits received by or for all household members reported in Item 75, *excluding the student.*

Also, include all veterans benefits received by members of the household, *except* those *educational* benefits received by the student or other members of the household.

Include the total of all other nontaxable income. Include welfare benefits, child support, unemployment compensation, and earned income that is *not* reported in Items 49-52.

In addition, include any other income which was not subject to income tax, such as interest on tax-free bonds, untaxed portions of pensions and capital gains, and housing and subsistence allowances (for military, clergy, and faculty).

Do not include amounts received from student aid programs (educational loans, work-study earnings, grants, or scholarships), social security educational benefits for the student, or veterans educational benefits (GI Bill or War Orphans' and Widows' Education Assistance). *Do not* include any income reported in Items 49-52.

ITEM 54. Enter the total amount of assistance estimated to be available from student's parents, including cash, gifts, and expenses paid by student's parents (such as food, clothing, and insurance).

ITEM 55. Enter the total amount of assistance estimated to be available from spouse's parents, including cash, gifts, and expenses paid by spouse's parents (such as food, clothing, and insurance).

ITEM 56. Enter the total amount of grants, scholarships, educational loans, and earnings from student employment, including work-study, which has *actually been awarded.* Do not include any student aid for which you are now applying.

ITEM 57. Enter U.S. income tax paid (or estimated to be paid) as reported on line 47 of student's 1977 U.S. income tax Form 1040, or line 13 of Form 1040A. Do not copy from a W-2 Form tax withheld.

ITEM 58. If student itemizes deductions on the 1977 U.S. income tax return, enter the amount of "total deductions" reported on line 39 of Schedule A, Form 1040A. If student does not itemize, enter a zero.

ITEM 59. If student itemizes deductions on the 1977 U.S. income tax return, enter the total of medicine, drugs, and other medical and dental expenses reported on lines 2 and 6 of Schedule A, Form 1040. If student takes a standard deduction or will not file a 1977 return, enter the amount of medical and dental expenses for student's household for 1977 which were not covered by insurance. Do not include the cost of medical and dental insurance premiums.

ITEM 60. If student itemizes deductions on the 1977 U.S. income tax return, enter the amount of casualty or theft loss(es) reported on line 29 of Schedule A, Form 1040. If student takes a standard deduction or will not file a 1977 return, determine the amount of each loss not covered by insurance, due to theft or damage by fire, storm, or accident. Subtract $100 from the amount of each loss; add the net amounts of each of the losses and enter the total.

ITEM 61. Enter the amount of elementary, junior high, and senior high school tuition and fees that student paid in 1977 for dependent children included in Item 75. Do not report any amounts which were paid by scholarships or other forms of student aid.

ITEM 62. Enter the total amount of expenses for housing, food, transportation, child care, taxes, etc., which are considered extraordinary. Also include the total amount of other unusual expenses such as payments for child support, funerals, legal fees, and water, street, and sewer assessments. Itemize and give dollar amounts in Item 80.

STUDENT'S EDUCATIONAL BENEFITS

	Calendar Year 1977	July 1, 1978- June 30, 1979
63 AMOUNT OF SOCIAL SECURITY BENEFITS to be received **per month**	$	$
64 NUMBER OF MONTHS social security benefits to be received		
65 AMOUNT OF VETERANS EDUCATIONAL BENEFITS to be received **per month**		$
66 NUMBER OF MONTHS veterans educational benefits to be received		

ITEM 63. Enter the amount of social security educational benefits per month the student received during calendar year 1977 *and* expects to receive between July 1, 1978, and June 30, 1979. Include only amounts that student (not other members of the student's household) will receive if he or she is between 18 and 22 years of age and enrolled in an educational institution.

ITEM 64. Enter the number of months that benefits reported in Item 63 were received during calendar year 1977 *and* are to be received between July 1, 1978, and June 30, 1979.

ITEM 65. Enter the amount of veterans educational benefits per month the student expects to receive between July 1, 1978, and June 30, 1979. Include only amounts that student (not other members of the student's household) will receive from the GI Bill or War Orphans' and Widows' Education Assistance Program. If you are unsure of these amounts, contact your local Veterans Administration office.

ITEM 66. Enter the number of months between July 1, 1978, and June 30, 1979, that benefits reported in Item 65 are to be received.

STUDENT'S ASSETS AND INDEBTEDNESS

			Present Market Value	Unpaid Mortgage Principal or Debts
67	CASH, SAVINGS, AND CHECKING ACCOUNTS		$	
68	HOME, IF OWNED OR BEING PURCHASED YEAR PURCHASED **19** PURCHASE PRICE $ . . .		$	$
69	INVESTMENTS (STOCKS, BONDS, AND OTHER SECURITIES) AND OTHER REAL ESTATE		$	$
70	BUSINESS (See instructions.)		$	$
71	FARM (See instructions.)		$	$
72	CONSUMER AND EDUCATIONAL INDEBTEDNESS			$
73	OTHER DEBTS OUTSTANDING (Do not include any debts entered above.)			$

If student is married, Items 67-77 apply to both student and student's spouse. If student is separated or divorced, provide only that information which applies to the student.

In completing Items 68-71, enter the present market value of each asset listed. Do not use such valuations as assessed value, insured value, and taxed value. Do not report personal or consumer debts that are not related to the assets listed. *Do not report parents' assets.*

Do not report any asset or debt more than once.

ITEM 67. Enter the present amount of student's cash, savings, and checking accounts. Do not include any amounts received through educational loans, grants, or scholarships.

ITEM 68. Enter the present market value of student's home. Also, enter unpaid mortgage principal and related debts on student's home.

ITEM 69. Enter the total present market value of student's investments (endowments, trusts, stocks, bonds, and other securities) and other real estate. Also, enter total debts and unpaid mortgage principal on student's investments and other real estate. Report business or farm assets and debts only in Item 70 or 71.

ITEM 70. If student owns all or part of a business, enter the present market value of business (including land, buildings, machinery, equipment, inventories, etc.). Also, enter the present mortgage and related debts for which the business assets are used as collateral. Do not include value of home even if part of business property; report value of home only in Item 68. If student is not the sole owner of the business, enter only the amount of his or her share of the total business market value and debt.

ITEM 71. If student owns all or part of a farm, enter the present market value of farm (including land, buildings, machinery, equipment, animals, inventories, etc.). Also, enter the present mortgage and related debts for which the farm assets are used as collateral. Do not include value of home even if part of farm property; report value of home only in Item 68. If student is not the sole owner of the farm, enter only the amount of his or her share of the total farm market value and debt.

ITEM 72. Enter the present amount of student's consumer indebtedness (such as debts for purchase of automobiles, appliances, and other consumer durables; and retail store and bank charge accounts), and educational indebtedness of student or other family members.

ITEM 73. Do not include any expenses already entered in Items 57-62 or any debt entered in Items 68-72. *Include only debt outstanding from 1976 or before.* Include such past debts as medical and dental expenses; remaining business indebtedness if business dissolved; funeral expenses; legal fees; unreimbursed job-related moving expenses; natural disasters not covered by insurance; liens; and living expenses if business failure, prolonged illness, or unemployment has depleted assets and forced indebtedness. *Do not include any other type of debt outstanding.*

STUDENT'S ADDITIONAL INFORMATION

ITEM 74. Enter the number of exemptions reported on line 7 of student's 1977 U.S. income tax Form 1040, or line 6 of Form 1040A. If student did not and will not file a 1977 return, enter zero.

ITEM 75. Enter the total number of persons for whom the student (and/or student's spouse) will provide more than one-half support between July 1, 1978, and June 30, 1979. Include the student, student's spouse, dependent children, and other dependents (persons who live with the student and receive more than one-half their support from the student): Do not leave blank and do not enter zero. List spouse, children, and other dependents in Item 79.

ITEM 76. Enter the appropriate number of persons (including the student) reported in Item 75 who will be enrolled in a college, university, vocational or technical school, or other education beyond high school, on at least a half-time basis, during the 1978-79 academic year.

ITEM 77. Enter the appropriate information for the student.

ITEM 78. Enter the appropriate information for the student's spouse.

ITEM 79. Enter appropriate information for spouse, dependent children, and other dependents included in the number entered in Item 75. Do not list the student.

EXPLANATIONS AND UNUSUAL CIRCUMSTANCES

ITEM 80. Explain all circled items and any unusual circumstances. If more space is needed, attach additional sheets of paper.

INSTITUTIONS AND PROGRAMS TO RECEIVE THIS FAF

ITEM 81. If you are applying for financial aid administered by institutions, states, and other programs and want them to receive copies of this FAF, enter their complete names, addresses, and CSS code numbers. Obtain code numbers from the CSS Code List. If you are unable to obtain a code number, leave the CSS code number box blank.

Do not enter the BEOG Program in this item. If you are applying ONLY to the BEOG Program, leave this item and Item 82 blank and complete Items 83 and 84.

ITEM 82. Check the box next to the number of institutions and programs entered in Item 81. Also, if you wish to receive a report of your CSS Estimated Contribution, check the appropriate box. Be certain to enclose a check or money order for the appropriate amount when you mail the FAF to the CSS.

BASIC EDUCATIONAL OPPORTUNITY GRANT PROGRAM

ITEM 83. The FAF may be used to apply for the BEOG Program. Indicate whether you authorize the CSS to release information from the FAF to the Program. There is no charge for applying to the BEOG Program. If you authorize this release, you may list your first two institutional choices, so that the Program can notify these institutions of your BEOG status. Enter complete names, addresses, and CSS code numbers of institutions. Obtain code numbers from the CSS Code List. If you are unable to obtain a code number, leave the CSS code number box blank.

ITEM 84. Indicate whether you authorize the BEOG Program to release appropriate information from the FAF (including any new information or corrections for the 1978-79 academic year) to the agency administering financial aid programs in your state of legal residence for the purpose of calculating state awards, verifying data provided on state student aid applications, and conducting research.

(Note: Failure to provide this authorization may result in a delay or denial of aid from your state, but will have no effect on your consideration for a BEOG award.)

CERTIFICATION AND AUTHORIZATION

All persons providing information on the FAF should sign the Certification and Authorization section. Also, enter the date the FAF is completed.

In addition, enter the telephone number where the student may be reached in the event institutions or programs receiving the FAF need to obtain additional information or clarification.

To assist in the determination of financial need, those signing the Certification and Authorization section authorize the recipients of the FAF to discuss information contained on the form with the student.

FAMILY FINANCIAL STATEMENT (FFS) 1978-79

THE AMERICAN COLLEGE TESTING PROGRAM

R

- DO NOT complete this form prior to January 1, 1978.
- This form is obsolete after April 15, 1979, and may not be used to apply for a Basic Educational Opportunity Grant (BEOG) after March 15, 1979.
- Please read the instructions carefully as you complete this form.

WARNING: If you use this form to establish your eligibility for federal student aid funds, you should know that any person who makes false statements or misrepresentations on this form is subject to a fine or to imprisonment, or both, under provisions of the United States Criminal Code.

A. STUDENT'S INFORMATION

1 STUDENT'S NAME

Last Name | First Name | MI

2,3 STUDENT'S PERMANENT MAILING ADDRESS (Continued in items 4 and 5)

House Number, Street Name, etc.

City (Do Not Enter State in This Area)

4 STATE CODE

SEE INSTRUCTIONS FOR STATE CODE LISTING

5 ZIP CODE

6 STUDENT'S SOCIAL SECURITY NUMBER

7 STUDENT'S DATE OF BIRTH

Month	Day	Year

8 SEX

○ Male ○ Female

9 Is Student a U.S. Veteran?

○ Yes

10 Student's U.S. Citizenship Status

○ U.S. citizen
○ In the U.S. for other than a temporary purpose and intend to become a permanent resident, or a permanent resident of the Trust Territories of the Pacific Islands.

11 Student's Present Marital Status

○ Unmarried
○ Married
○ Separated

12 Student's Educational Level Fall, 1978

Undergraduate
○ 1st Year
○ 2nd Year
○ 3rd Year
○ 4th Year
○ 5th Year or more

Graduate
○ 1st Year
○ 2nd Year
○ 3rd Year

13 Student's Class Level Fall, 1978

Undergraduate
○ Freshman
○ Sophomore
○ Junior
○ Senior or 5th Year
○ Graduate or Professional Student
○ Other

PAGE 1

OFFICE USE ONLY

---

14 Did (or Will) Parents Claim the Student as a U.S. Income Tax Exemption During:

5

	1977?	1978?	1979?
	○ Yes	○ Yes	○ Yes
	○ No	○ No	○ No

15 Did (or Will) Student Live with Parents More Than Two Consecutive Weeks During:

	1977?	1978?	1979?
	○ Yes	○ Yes	○ Yes
	○ No	○ No	○ No

16 Did (or Will) Student Receive Assistance Worth $600 or More from Parents During:

	1977?	1978?	1979?
	○ Yes	○ Yes	○ Yes
	○ No	○ No	○ No

STOP ⬆ **IF:** ANY QUESTION FOR **ANY YEAR** IN SECTION B IS ANSWERED **YES**, SKIP SECTION C, AND COMPLETE PAGES 3 AND 4. EXCEPTION: IF STUDENT IS MARRIED OR HAS PERSONS DEPENDENT ON HIM/HER, COMPLETE SECTION C AND PAGES 3 AND 4.

OR: IF **ALL** QUESTIONS FOR **ALL** YEARS IN SECTION B ARE ANSWERED **NO**, COMPLETE SECTION C AND PAGE 4, SKIP PAGE 3

C. STUDENT'S (AND SPOUSE'S) FINANCIAL STATEMENT

1977 ACTUAL INCOME AND EXPENSES

- **17** 1977 Nontaxable Income
- **18** 1977 U.S. Tax Return Figures Are: ○ From Completed Return ○ Estimated ○ Will Not File Return for 1977
- **19** 1977 Total Tax Exemptions
- **20** 1977 Adjusted Gross Income
- **21** Student's 1977 Employment Earnings
- **22** Spouse's 1977 Employment Earnings
- **23** 1977 U.S. Income Tax Paid
- **24** 1977 Total Itemized Deductions
- **25** 1977 Medical & Dental Expenses
- **26** 1977 Casualty & Theft Losses
- **27** Unreimbursed Elem. & H.S. Tuition

STUDENT'S/ SPOUSE'S ASSETS AND DEBTS

- **28** Total Cash, Savings, & Checking Accounts
- **29** Consumer Debts
- **30,31** Home — **6** — Present Market Value — Unpaid Mortgage & Related Debts
- **32,33** Investments & Other Real Estate — Present Market Value — Unpaid Mortgage & Related Debts
- **34,35,36** Business or Farm (Your Portion Only) — Present Market Value — Unpaid Mortgage & Related Debts — These Assets/Debts Are Primarily from a: ○ Business ○ Farm

1978-79 STUDENT'S/ SPOUSE'S INFORMATION (July 1, 1978 through June 30, 1979)

- **37** Nontaxable Income (See Instruction)
- **38,39** Student's Est. Earnings — Summer 1978 — Academic Year 1978-79
- **40,41** Spouse's Est. Earnings — Summer 1978 — Academic Year 1978-79
- **42** Other Taxable Income
- **43** Assistance From Student's & Spouse's Parents
- **44** Total Size of Student's Household — Include student, spouse, student's dependent children, and others who depend on student (and/or spouse) for more than half their support (See instruction)
- **45** Household Members in Education Beyond High School in 78-79 — Of the number entered in item 44, how many will attend a college, university, or other institution beyond high school at least half time during 1978-79?

A
G
E

2

D. STUDENT'S INFORMATION

46,47 Student's Estimated Earnings
- Summer 1978
- Academic Year 78-79

48 78-79 Nontaxable Income (Not S.S. or V.A. Benefits)

49 Student's Present Savings & Other Assets

E. PARENTS' INFORMATION

50 Parents' Current Marital Status
- ○ Single
- ○ Married
- ○ Divorced
- ○ Separated
- ○ Mother Living, Father Deceased
- ○ Father Living, Mother Deceased
- ○ Both Deceased

51,52 Main Earner's
- Age
- Occupation Code (See List)

53 State Code (See Instruction)

54 Total Size of Parents' Household

Include the student, parents, parents' dependent children, and others for whom parents will provide at least half support during 1978-79. (See Instruction)

55 Parents' Household Members in Education Beyond High School in 78-79

Of the number entered in item 54, how many will attend a college, university, or other institution beyond high school at least half time during 1978-79?

56 1976 Adjusted Gross Income

57 1976 Nontaxable Income

58 See Instruction 58

F. PARENTS' FINANCIAL STATEMENT

59 1977 Nontaxable Income (See Instruction)

60 1977 U.S. Tax Return Figures Are:
- ○ From Completed Return
- ○ Estimated
- ○ Will Not File Return for 1977

61 1977 Total Tax Exemptions

62 1977 Adjusted Gross Income

63 Father's 1977 Employment Earnings (See Instruction)

64 Mother's 1977 Employment Earnings (See Instruction)

65 1977 Total U.S. Income Tax Paid

66 1977 Total Itemized Deductions

67 1977 Medical & Dental Expenses

68 1977 Casualty & Theft Losses

69 1977 Unreimbursed Elementary & High School Tuition

70 Total Cash, Savings, & Checking Accounts

71 Consumer Debts

72,73 Home
- Present Market Value
- Unpaid Mortgage & Related Debts

74,75 Investments & Other Real Estate
- Present Market Value
- Unpaid Mortgage & Related Debts

76,77,78 Business or Farm (Parents' Portion Only)
- Present Market Value
- Unpaid Mortgage & Related Debts

These Assets/Debts Are Primarily from a.
- ○ Business
- ○ Farm

79,80 Parents' Estimated Income for 1978
- Adjusted Gross Income
- Nontaxable Income

P
A
G
E
3

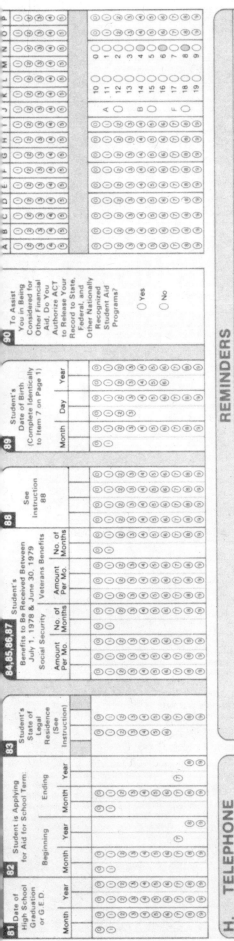

81 Date of High School Graduation or G.E.D. — Month, Year

82 Student is Applying for Aid for School Term. — Beginning: Month, Year; Ending: Month, Year

83 Student's State of Legal Residence (See Instruction)

84, 85, 86, 87 Student's Benefits to Be Received Between July 1, 1978 & June 30, 1979

Social Security		Veterans Benefits	
Amount Per Mo.	No. of Months	Amount Per Mo.	No. of Months

See Instruction 88

88

89 Student's Date of Birth (Complete Identically to Item 7 on Page 1) — Month, Day, Year

90 To Assist You in Being Considered for Other Financial Aid, Do You Authorize ACT to Release Your Record to State, Federal, and Other Nationally Recognized Student Aid Programs?

○ Yes
○ No

REMINDERS

1. Please check again to make sure that every item has been completed, and that a zero has been entered for those items which do not apply to you or your parents. Zeros do not have to be entered in sections that you have been instructed to skip.

2. Be sure that this form has been completed using a soft lead pencil, not ink. Erase any stray marks on the form.

3. ERASURES—If you have blackened, then erased, any oval in any item, be sure that the oval for the correct figure (or a zero oval) has been blackened in that column of the item. If this is not done, the erased oval may be read as your entry.

4. You are encouraged to apply to the Basic Educational Opportunity Grant (BEOG) Program by answering "yes" to item 92 below. See the instructions for eligibility requirements. There is no additional charge for applying to the BEOG Program.

5. Please check again to make sure that your name and mailing address are correctly entered in Section A, items 1 through 5, so that the results of processing this form can be mailed to you.

H. TELEPHONE

Telephone Number Where You May Be Reached (Optional)

Area Code | Number

I. REPORT REQUEST, AUTHORIZATIONS, CERTIFICATION, AND SIGNATURES

91 List ACT Codes of Colleges, Schools, and Agencies to Receive This Report (See Enclosed ACT Code Listing)

1st Report | 2nd Report | 3rd Report

FEE

92 NUMBER OF CODES TO RECEIVE REPORTS

One Code Fee = $4.00
Two Codes Fee = $6.00
Three Codes Fee = $8.00

MAKE CHECK PAYABLE TO ACT. DO NOT SEND CASH.

Do you authorize appropriate information from this FFS to be released to the BEOG Program in order to be considered for BEOG assistance?
○ Yes ○ No

93 Do you authorize the BEOG Program to release this form application provided on this form (including any new information or corrections for the 1978-79 academic year) to the agency administering financial aid in your state of legal residence or purpose of enabling the state's aid-granting authorities verifying data provided on state and applications, and conducting research? (NOTE: Failure to provide this authorization may result in delay or denial of aid from your state but will have no effect on your BEOG award.)
○ Yes ○ No

94 Are you using this FFS only to apply for the BEOG program? (Carefully read instructions before answering)
○ Yes ○ No

95 I (we) certify that the information contained in this Family Financial Statement is correct and complete to the best of my (our) knowledge. I (we) authorize The American College Testing Program to transmit the information to the college(s), school(s), or agency(ies) I (we) indicated, and I (we) agree to release copies of my (our) U.S. or State income tax Returns upon request to ACT to the BEOG Program (if item 92 is answered "yes"), or the other parties named herein. I (we) authorize the recipients named herein to disclose the information on this form with the student. BLACKEN OVAL FOR EACH PERSON SIGNING.

○ Student's Signature

○ Student's Spouse's Signature

○ Father or Male Guardian

○ Mother or Female Guardian

Name of Parent (Please Print)

Parent's Address (House Number and Street)

City _____ State _____ Zip Code _____

Parent's Social Security No

96 Date Signed ○ 1978 ○ 1979

Month	Day
Jan.	
Feb.	
March	
April	
May	
June	
July	
Aug	
Sept.	
Oct.	
Nov	
Dec.	

R

ACT STUDENT DATA FORM 1978-79

Please Print Using Black Ink.

MAIL THIS COMPLETED FORM TO ACT WITH YOUR 1978-79 FAMILY FINANCIAL STATEMENT

STUDENT INFORMATION

NAME _____
last   first   middle

PERMANENT
MAILING _____
ADDRESS number   street   apt. no.
_____
city   state   zip code

PHONE (_____) _____

SOCIAL SECURITY
NUMBER (optional) _____

BIRTH
DATE _____

MAJOR AREA OF STUDY _____

DURING 1978-79, STUDENT WILL BE A
☐ Full-time student   ☐ Half-time student   ☐ Less than half-time student

INDICATE FINANCIAL AID PREFERENCE (enter 1 for first choice, etc.)
___ Grant   ___ Long-term loan   ___ Part-time work
___ Academic scholarship
___ Activity scholarship (name activity) _____
___ Other (specify) _____

COLLEGES, SCHOOLS, OR AGENCIES TO RECEIVE THIS FORM (list those coded in item 91 of the FFS)

ACT Code Number			Name of College/School/Agency	City	State	Have you attended this school before? If yes, list dates of attendance and student ID number.	During 1978-79, where will you live?		
							With Parents	On Campus	Off Campus
			1.						
			2.						
			3.						

PARENTAL INFORMATION

FATHER/STEPFATHER
GUARDIAN _____
name   age
address _____
city _____ state _____
zip code _____ (_____) _____ phone

OCCUPATION
(or previous, if retired) _____

EMPLOYER _____
name   city   state
NO. OF YRS. WITH _____

MOTHER/STEPMOTHER
GUARDIAN _____
name   age
address _____
city _____ state _____
zip code _____ (_____) _____ phone

OCCUPATION
(or previous, if retired) _____

EMPLOYER _____
name   city   state
NO. OF YRS. WITH _____

NAMES AND AGES OF PARENTS' DEPENDENTS	1. Name	Age	3. Name	Age	5. Name	Age
	2. Name	Age	4. Name	Age	6. Name	Age

STUDENT'S ESTIMATED RESOURCES

INCOME AVAILABLE TO MEET EXPENSES
DURING TERM(S) FINANCIAL AID IS DESIRED

8

Personal funds (cash, savings, etc.)	$
Private loans	$
Total summer earnings: $ _____ ; amount available for school	$
Earnings while in school (exclude College Work-Study)	$
Parental support	$
Spouse's support	$
Scholarship received (name source)	$
Veterans benefits/War Orphans benefits	$
Welfare benefits	$
Social Security benefits	$
Alimony	$
Other income (name source)	$
TOTAL INCOME	$

MARRIED STUDENTS (OR SINGLE WITH DEPENDENTS)

NUMBER OF DEPENDENTS _____ **AGES** ☐☐☐☐☐

SPOUSE'S NAME _____

SOCIAL SECURITY NO. (optional) _____ **AGE** _____

ADDRESS (if different from yours) _____
_____ **PHONE** (_____)
city   state   zip code

SPOUSE'S OCCUPATION _____

SPOUSE'S EMPLOYER _____

DATE OF EMPLOYMENT _____ **PRESENT MONTHLY GROSS EARNINGS** $ _____

SPOUSE'S MONTHLY GROSS EARNINGS AT TIME AWARD WILL BE USED $ _____

WILL SPOUSE BE A STUDENT DURING 1978-79? ☐ Yes ☐ No

IF YES, AT WHICH SCHOOL OR COLLEGE? _____

WILL SPOUSE APPLY FOR FINANCIAL AID FOR 1978-79? ☐ Yes ☐ No

If you have entered any amount in item 27 or 69 (Elementary and High School Tuition) or item 58 or 88 (Unusual Debts) on the FFS, please explain those entries in this space. Also, if you feel that there are unusual circumstances which significantly affect your family's financial status, they may be explained here. If you need more space, continue on the back of this page.

Copies of this form will be sent to the schools and programs listed. Information provided on this form will not affect the analysis done by ACT but will assist the school financial aid administrator in considering you for assistance.

INSTRUCTIONS *for completing the*
FAMILY FINANCIAL STATEMENT *(FFS) 1978-79*

DO NOT COMPLETE THE FAMILY FINANCIAL STATEMENT PRIOR TO JANUARY 1, 1978. SAVE THESE INSTRUCTIONS FOR FUTURE REFERENCE.

GENERAL INFORMATION

You are completing this Family Financial Statement as part of the process of seeking financial assistance to attend a college, university, vocational or technical school, or other institution offering education beyond high school. This form may be used to apply for a Basic Educational Opportunity Grant (BEOG) and/or for financial assistance from institutions, your state, and other scholarship programs. As a result of completing this form, you may be found eligible to receive financial assistance for any period of enrollment between June 1, 1978 (July 1, 1978 for the BEOG) and June 30, 1979. The completed FFS must be received at ACT by **April 15, 1979**; if you wish to be considered for a BEOG, it must be received by **March 15, 1979**. Schools and scholarship programs normally have much earlier deadlines for financial aid application.

If you indicate in item 92 that you wish to apply for a BEOG, ACT will forward the necessary information to the BEOG Program at no cost to you. If you wish to have ACT need analysis reports sent to the institutions and programs coded in item 91, you must enclose the appropriate fee.

BASIC EDUCATIONAL OPPORTUNITY GRANT

The Basic Educational Opportunity Grant (BEOG) Program is a federal student aid program designed to provide financial assistance in the form of a grant (which need not be repaid) to those who need it to attend colleges and other institutions offering education beyond high school. The amount of the grant is determined according to your own and your family's financial resources. It is estimated that grants will range from $200 to $1,600 during the 1978-79 academic year.

BEOG Eligibility Criteria

You will be eligible for a Basic Grant if you meet **all** of the following criteria:

1. You have established your financial need for a BEOG by means of this form.

2. You will be enrolled (at least half time) in an undergraduate course of study in an eligible program at one of more than 6,000 institutions approved for participation in the BEOG Program.

3. You will not have previously received a Bachelor's degree from any institution.

4. You are a U.S. citizen, or you are in the United States for other than a temporary purpose and intend to become a permanent resident.

5. You will have received no more than four full years of BEOG payments. Exception: You may receive BEOG assistance for five years when the institution either (a) designed the program of study leading to a Bachelor's degree to be five years in length, or (b) required your enrollment in a remedial course of study which prevented you from completing the regular program in four academic years.

BEOG Notification

Within 6 weeks after you mail this form to ACT, you will receive a Student Eligibility Report (SER) from the BEOG Program. The SER is the official notification of your eligibility for a BEOG and must be reviewed by the school you will attend to determine the amount of your grant. When you receive the SER, carefully read and follow the instructions it contains. If you have designated schools or programs to receive an ACT need analysis report and have enclosed the appropriate fee, you will **also** receive a Student Financial Aid Report (SFAR) from ACT confirming that reports have been sent to the schools or programs you have listed.

BEOG Special Circumstances

If you experience a dramatic change in income from 1977 to 1978, you may be eligible to apply for a Basic Grant based on estimated 1978 income, rather than actual 1977 income. For further details regarding your eligibility to apply for a grant in this manner, contact your high school guidance counselor or financial aid officer.

OTHER FORMS OF FINANCIAL AID

Financial assistance for education beyond high school is available from a wide variety of sources in addition to the BEOG Program. You may use this Family Financial Statement to apply for further assistance from the institutions, state agencies, and scholarship programs listed in the enclosed ACT Financial Aid Code Listing. Contact the scholarship agencies and the financial aid offices at the schools you are considering about application procedures and deadlines.

If you would like to receive additional information on the BEOG Program, as well as general information on student financial aid, please write to: BEOG, P.O. Box 84, Washington, D.C. 20044. Ask for a copy of the "Student Guide."

HOW TO COMPLETE THIS FORM

- By blackening the ovals, you are preparing your own computer input. Take care; the results will be accurate only if your entries are accurate.

- Use a soft (No. 2) lead pencil. EXAMPLES: ⇒

- Read each instruction carefully before you complete an item. This will help avoid mistakes, delays, and additional cost to you.

- Complete each item as instructed.

- If an item contains boxes and columns of ovals, print your response in the boxes and completely blacken the corresponding ovals. In items 2 and 3 (street address and city), leave one box blank between parts of your address and blacken the space rectangle (▯) below each blank box. See example at right.

- Round amounts to whole dollars. (E.g., enter $8,450.45 as
  0 8 4 5 0 .) Enter figures so they end in the right-hand box of the item.

- If an item has several responses, blacken the oval beside the correct response.

- If an item does not apply to you or your parents, print a zero (0) in the right-hand box of that item and blacken the corresponding zero oval.

- Erasures: If you blacken, then erase, any oval in any item, be sure that the oval for the correct figure (or a zero oval) has been blackened in that column of the item. If this is not done, the erased oval may be read as your entry.

THANK YOU!

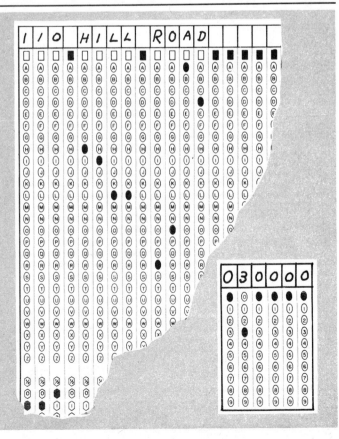

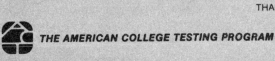
THE AMERICAN COLLEGE TESTING PROGRAM

STATE CODES

Alabama	01	Illinois	14	Nevada	29	Texas	44
Alaska	02	Indiana	15	New Hampshire	30	Utah	45
Arizona	03	Iowa	16	New Jersey	31	Vermont	46
Arkansas	04	Kansas	17	New Mexico	32	Virginia	47
California	05	Kentucky	18	New York	33	Washington	48
Colorado	06	Louisiana	19	North Carolina	34	West Virginia	49
Connecticut	07	Maine	20	North Dakota	35	Wisconsin	50
Delaware	08	Maryland	21	Ohio	36	Wyoming	51
District of		Massachusetts	22	Oklahoma	37	Canada	53
Columbia	09	Michigan	23	Oregon	38	Amer. Samoa	61
Florida	10	Minnesota	24	Pennsylvania	39	Canal Zone	62
Georgia	11	Mississippi	25	Rhode Island	40	Guam	63
Hawaii	12	Missouri	26	South Carolina	41	Puerto Rico	64
Idaho	13	Montana	27	South Dakota	42	Trust Territories	65
		Nebraska	28	Tennessee	43	Virgin Islands	66
						All Other	55

SECTION A. STUDENT'S INFORMATION

1. Enter your last name, first name, and middle initial.

2-5. Enter the address where you can be certain of receiving notification of the processing of this form.

6. Enter your Social Security number. Your Social Security number is required if you are applying for a Basic Educational Opportunity Grant (BEOG).

7. Enter your date of birth.

8. Indicate your sex.

9. Indicate whether you are a veteran of the U.S. Armed Forces.

10. Indicate your U.S. citizenship status. If you are not a U.S. citizen, see the BEOG eligibility criteria on page 1 of these instructions.

11. Indicate your present marital status.

12. Indicate your educational level for fall 1978. For example, if 1978-79 will be your first year of education beyond high school, blacken the "Undergraduate: 1st year" oval. If you indicate "5th year or more" of undergraduate education, see the BEOG eligibility criteria on page 1 of these instructions.

13. Indicate your academic classification for fall 1978.

SECTION B. STUDENT'S STATUS

The term "parent," for the purposes of this form, is generally defined to be the student's mother and/or father. The three questions in Section B should be completed in regard to your mother or father. If you answer "YES" for any question for any year, your parents' financial information must be reported on page 3 of the form.

If you are able to answer "NO" to every question for every year with regard to your mother and father, their financial information will not have to be provided. However, if some person other than a parent (or spouse) provided or will provide more than half your support during 1978, you would complete page 3 of the form with that person being considered to be your "parent." If you can still answer "NO" to every question for every year, you would complete Section C. If you answer "YES" to any question for any year with regard to your "parent," you would complete page 3 of this form using their financial information. In no case would a spouse be considered to be the student's "parent."

14-16. Answer these questions using the above definition of parent.

If you answer "YES" to **any** question for **any** year in Section B, skip Section C and complete all items on pages 3 and 4. Exception: If you are married, or have persons dependent upon you for more than half their support, complete Section C and pages 3 and 4.

If you answer "NO" to **every** question for **every** year in Section B, complete all items in Section C and on page 4. Skip page 3.

GENERAL INSTRUCTIONS FOR SECTIONS C, D, E, and F

For all dollar items that do not apply to you or your parents, enter a zero in the right-hand box and blacken the corresponding zero oval. Enter all figures in dollars; omit cents. For example:

Enter $9,345.15 as | 0 | 9 | 3 | 4 | 5 |

NOTE: Funds received by you or your parents as an award under the Distribution of Judgment Funds Act or the Alaska Native Claims Settlement Act should NOT be reported as income or assets on this form. Property should not be reported as an asset if: (a) it may not be sold or have loans placed against it without consent of the Secretary of the Interior, or (b) the property is held in trust for you or your family by the U.S. Government.

If you or your parents are residents of Puerto Rico, the Virgin Islands, Guam, American Samoa, or the Trust Territories and filed a 1977 Income Tax Return with that Government, enter information corresponding to that requested in the following items.

SECTION C. STUDENT'S (AND SPOUSE'S) FINANCIAL STATEMENT

Complete this section only if you answered NO to EVERY question in Section B (or if you answered "YES" to any question in Section B and are married or have persons dependent upon you for more than half their support). Items apply to **both** you and your spouse. If you are divorced or separated from your spouse, provide only the information which applies to you.

1977 Actual Income and Expenses

17. Enter the total nontaxable income received during 1977. Include Social Security benefits received, welfare benefits, child support, unemployment compensation, and earned income that will **not** be reported in item 20. Also include all veterans benefits except those educational benefits received by you or other members of your household, and any income (such as interest on tax-free bonds, untaxed portions of pensions and capital gains, military and other subsistence and quarters allowances, etc.) which was not subject to income tax. Do not include any amounts received from student aid programs (educational loans, work-study earnings, grants, or scholarships), veterans benefits for education (G.I. Bill or War Orphans' and Widows' Education Assistance), or any "adjustments to income" reported on your 1977 U.S. Income Tax Form 1040, line 28. **Do not** include any income reported in item 20.

In completing items 19 through 24, if you and your spouse are married and filed separate income tax returns, add the figures from both returns and report the total.

18. Indicate whether the 1977 U.S. Income Tax Return figures provided are from a completed return, or are estimated, or that you will not file a U.S. Income Tax Return for 1977. If you and your spouse did not and will not file a 1977 U.S. Income Tax Return, enter zeros for items 19 through 24.

19. Enter the number reported on line 7 of your 1977 U.S. Income Tax Form 1040, or line 6 of Form 1040A.

20. Enter the amount reported on line 31 of your 1977 Form 1040, or line 10 of your Form 1040A. Do not include any income received as the result of employment provided by student financial aid programs. If this amount was negative (i.e., due to a farm or business loss), blacken the θ oval above the item heading "1977 Adjusted Gross Income."

21-22. Enter the amount of wages, salaries, tips, and other compensation reported on line 8 of your 1977 Form 1040, or line 7 of Form 1040A, for: (21) yourself and (22) your spouse. Income reported in this item should also be included in item 20 above. Do not include any income received as the result of employment provided by student aid programs.

23. Enter your total U.S. Income Tax paid as reported on line 47 of your 1977 Form 1040, or line 13 of Form 1040A. Do not copy tax withheld from a W-2 Form.

24. If you itemize deductions on your 1977 U.S. Income Tax Return, enter the amount from line 39 of Schedule A, Form 1040. If you do not itemize deductions, enter a zero.

25. If you itemize deductions on your 1977 U.S. Income Tax Return, enter the total of lines 2 and 6 from Schedule A. If you take a standard deduction or will not file a 1977 return, enter the amount of your household's medical and dental expenses for 1977 which were not covered by insurance. Do not include the cost of medical/dental insurance premiums.

26. If you itemize deductions on your 1977 U.S. Income Tax Return, enter the amount reported on line 29 of Schedule A. If you take a standard deduction or will not file a 1977 return, determine the amount of each loss not covered by insurance, due to theft, or to damage by fire, storm, or accident. Subtract $100 from the amount of each loss, then add the net amount of each of these losses and enter the total.

27. Enter the amount of elementary, junior high or high school tuition and fees that you paid in 1977 for dependent children included in item 44. Do not report any amounts which were paid by scholarships or other forms of student aid.

Student's/Spouse's Assets and Debts

Enter the present market value of each of the assets listed. Do not use such valuations as Assessed Value, Insured Value, Taxed Value, etc. Do not report personal or consumer loans or any debts that are not related to the assets listed. Do not report any asset or debt more than once. Do not include any parents' assets or debts.

28. Enter the present amount of your cash, savings, and checking accounts. Do not include any amounts received through educational loans or grants.

29. Enter the amount you presently owe in consumer debts. Include credit cards, motor vehicle and appliance loans, educational loans, etc. Do not report these debts anywhere else on this form.

NOTE: Items 30-35 are six boxes long. Enter figures (dollars only) so they end in the right-hand box. (E.g., enter $1,000 as | 0 | 0 | 1 | 0 | 0 | 0 | .)

30. Enter the present market value of your home.

31. Enter the amount of present unpaid mortgage and related debts on your home.

2

32. Enter the total of the present market value of your investments (including stocks, bonds, and other securities) and present market value of other real estate. Report farm and business only in items 34 and 35.

33. Enter the total unpaid debts on the investments and other real estate listed in item 32.

34. Enter the present market value of your farm or business (including value of land, buildings, machinery, equipment, animals, inventories, etc.). Do not include value of home; report home value only in item 30. If you are not the sole owner, enter only the amount of your share of the total farm or business market value.

35. Enter the present mortgage or related debts for which the farm or business assets were used as collateral. If you are not the sole owner, enter only the amount of your share of total farm or business debt.

36. Indicate whether the assets reported in item 34 are primarily from a farm or from a business.

1978-79 Student's/Spouse's Information

37. Enter the amount you (and your spouse) expect to receive in nontaxable income between July 1, 1978 and June 30, 1979. Include only those types of nontaxable income outlined in the instructions for item 17, except your Social Security benefits. Do not include amounts you expect to receive from student aid programs, veterans benefits for education, or other amounts excluded in instruction 17.

38-39. Enter the amounts you expect to earn from wages, salaries, tips, etc., for the time periods shown. Do not include anticipated earnings from college work-study programs.

40-41. Enter the amounts your spouse expects to earn from wages, salaries, tips, etc., for the time periods shown. Do not include anticipated college work-study earnings.

42. Enter all taxable income not entered in items 38 through 41 that you and your spouse expect to receive between July 1, 1978 and June 30, 1979. Include interest income, dividends, alimony, estate or trust income, business or farm profits, and rental or property income.

43. Enter the total financial assistance (cash, gifts, etc.) to be received from your parents and your spouse's parents between July 1, 1978 and June 30, 1979.

44. Enter the total number of persons for whom you (and/or your spouse) will provide more than half support between July 1, 1978 and June 30, 1979. Include yourself, your spouse, your dependent children, and other persons who live with you and receive more than half their support from you.

45. Enter the appropriate number of persons (including yourself) reported in item 44 who will be enrolled in a college, university, vocational or technical school, or other education beyond high school, on at least a half-time basis, during the 1978-79 academic year.

Please check again to make sure you have completed every item and have entered zeros for those items that do not apply to you. Then go on to Section G.

SECTION D. STUDENT'S INFORMATION

46-47. Enter the amounts you expect to earn from wages, salaries, tips, etc., for the time periods shown. Do not include anticipated earnings from college work-study programs.

48. Enter the nontaxable income you will receive between July 1, 1978 and June 30, 1979. Include Vocational Rehabilitation benefits, welfare, child support, income tax refunds, etc. Do not include your Social Security and veterans benefits (to be reported in items 84 through 87). Do not include any amounts to be received by your parents.

49. Enter the total of your present cash, savings, and checking accounts and the present net value of your other assets, including investments, real estate, inheritances, and trust funds. Do not include your automobile, stamp or coin collection, or other personal property. Do not include any amounts received through educational loans or grants.

SPECIAL INSTRUCTIONS FOR SECTIONS E AND F

If your parents are divorced or separated, provide information for the parent who has or had custody of you. If no custody was awarded, or if parents have or had equal custody of you, provide the information for the parent with whom you resided for the greater portion of the 12-month period preceding the date of completing this form.

If your parents are divorced, or if your mother/father is widowed, and your parent has remarried, the financial information of your stepparent may need to be reported. Your stepparent's information should be reported (together with your parent's information) IF either (a) you did or will live with your stepparent (and parent) for six weeks or more during 1977, 1978, or 1979; OR (b) you did or will receive $600 or more in financial assistance from your stepparent in 1977, 1978, or 1979.

SECTION E. PARENTS' INFORMATION

50. Indicate parents' present marital status.

51. Enter parent's age.

52. Enter the occupational code of the main earner of parental income, using the codes below.

53. Enter the code for the parents' state of residence, using the code listing on page 2 of these instructions.

54. Enter the total number of persons, including student, for whom parents will provide more than half support between July 1, 1978 and June 30, 1979. Be sure to include student, parents, parents' other dependent children, and parents' other dependents.

55. Enter the appropriate number of persons (including student) reported in item 54 who will be enrolled in a college, university, vocational or technical school, or other education beyond high school, on at least a half-time basis, during the 1978-79 academic year.

56. Enter the amount reported on parents' 1976 U.S. Income Tax Return Form 1040 (line 15c) or Form 1040A (line 12). If this amount was negative (i.e., due to a farm or business loss), blacken the θ oval above the item heading "1976 Adjusted Gross Income."

57. Enter the total nontaxable income received by parents in 1976. Include only those types of income outlined in instruction 59 below.

58. Unusual debts: if parents owe debts **from 1976 or before** for funeral or medical expenses; legal fees; loans for parents' education; uninsured natural disaster losses; unreimbursed job-related moving expenses; remaining business indebtedness if business has been dissolved; or living expenses if business failure, prolonged illness, and unemployment have forced indebtedness; enter the total here. Do not include any other type of debt. Consumer debts, credit card balances, motor vehicle loans, etc., should be entered in item 71.

SECTION F. PARENTS' FINANCIAL STATEMENT

1977 Income and Expenses

59. Enter the total nontaxable income parents received during 1977. Include Social Security benefits received by or for all household members listed in item 54 above (including student), welfare benefits, child support, unemployment compensation, and earned income that will **not** be reported in item 62. Also include all veterans benefits except those educational benefits received by the student or other members of the household, and any other income (such as interest on tax-free bonds, untaxed portions of pensions and capital gains, military and other subsistence and quarters allowances, etc.) which was not subject to income tax. **Do not** include any amounts received from student aid programs (educational loans, work-study earnings, grants, or scholarships), veterans benefits for education (G.I. Bill or War Orphans' and Widows' Education Assistance), or any "adjustments to income" reported on the parents' 1977 U.S. Income Tax Form 1040, line 28. **Do not** include any income reported in item 62.

_____ OCCUPATIONAL CODE LISTING _____

Retired/Disabled
110 Permanently disabled
111 Retired with no taxable income
112 Retired with taxable income

Professional/Technical
113 Accountant
114 Architect
121 Author or editor
122 Clergy
123 College professor or administrator
124 Physician or dentist
131 Engineer
132 Lawyer
133 Musician or artist
134 Nurse
141 Scientist
142 Teacher (elementary or secondary)
143 Technician (health fields)
144 Technician (industrial)
145 Superintendent
146 Coach (athletics)
211 Other professional
212 Other technical

Farmers/Ranchers
213 Farm owner
214 Sharecropper
215 Ranch owner
216 Rancher (renting)
221 Tenant farmer
222 Farm laborer

Proprietors/Managers
223 Business owner
224 Business manager (salaried)
225 Self-employed
226 Inspector
231 Government official
232 Other salaried manager

Clerical Workers
233 Bookkeeper
234 Typist or secretary
241 Postal or bank worker
242 Other clerical worker

Sales Workers
243 Insurance or real estate sales
244 Retail sales
311 Wholesale sales
312 Other sales

Craftsman/Foremen
313 Craftsman
314 Foreman
315 Carpenter
321 Mechanic

Operatives
322 Assembler
323 Driver (taxi, truck, etc.)
324 Laundry/dry cleaning worker
331 Mine worker
332 Manufacturing worker
333 Other operative

Service Workers
334 Barber or cosmetologist
341 Cook or domestic
342 Fireman or policeman
343 Janitor
344 Waiter or bartender
345 Plumber
411 Other service worker

Labor (except mining)
412 Construction worker
413 Longshoreman
414 Lumberman
415 Railroad worker
421 Other labor (not elsewhere specified)

Other
430 Homemaker

If none of the occupational codes listed above describes occupation of main family earner, enter 444.

60. Indicate whether the 1977 U.S. Income Tax Return figures provided are from a completed return, or are estimated, or that parents will not file a U.S. Income Tax Return for 1977. If parents did not and will not file a U.S. Income Tax Return, enter zeros for items 61 through 66.

In completing items 61 through 66, if parents are married and file separate income tax returns, add the figures from both returns and report the total.

61. Enter the number reported on line 7 of parents' 1977 U.S. Income Tax Form 1040 or line 6 of Form 1040A.

62. Enter the amount reported on line 31 of parents' 1977 Form 1040, or line 10 of Form 1040A. If this amount was negative (i.e., due to a farm or business loss), blacken the θ oval above the item heading "1977 Adjusted Gross Income."

63-64. Enter the amount of wages, salaries, tips, and other compensation reported on line 8 of parents' 1977 Form 1040 or line 7 of Form 1040A for: (63) father (or male guardian) and (64) mother (or female guardian). Income reported in this item should also be included in item 62.

65. Enter parents' total U.S. Income Tax paid as reported on line 47 of 1977 Form 1040, or line 13 of Form 1040A. Do not copy tax withheld from a W-2 Form.

66. If parents itemize deductions on their 1977 U.S. Income Tax Return, enter the amount from line 39 of Schedule A. If parents do not itemize deductions, enter a zero.

67. If parents itemize deductions on their 1977 U.S. Income Tax Return, enter the total of lines 2 and 6 from Schedule A. If parents take a standard deduction or will not file a 1977 return, enter the amount of parents' household's medical and dental expenses for 1977 which were **not** covered by insurance. Do not include the cost of medical/dental insurance premiums.

68. If parents itemize deductions on their 1977 U.S. Income Tax Return, enter the amount reported on line 29 of Schedule A. If parents take a standard deduction or will not file a 1977 return, determine the amount of each loss not covered by insurance, due to theft, or damage by fire, storm, or accident. Subtract $100 from the amount of each loss, then add the net amount of each of these losses and enter the total.

69. Enter the amount of elementary, junior high and high school tuition and fees parents paid in 1977 for all dependent children (other than student) included in item 54. Do not report any amounts which were paid by scholarships or other forms of student aid.

Present Assets and Debts

Enter the present market value of each of the assets listed below. Do not use such valuations as Assessed Value, Insured Value, Taxed Value, etc. Report personal or consumer loans only in item 71. Do not report any asset or debt more than once.

70. Enter the present amount of parents' cash, savings, and checking accounts.

71. Enter the amount parents currently owe in consumer debts or personal loans. Include credit cards, motor vehicle and appliance loans, etc. Do not report these debts anywhere else on this form.

NOTE: Items 72-77 are six boxes long. Enter figures (dollars only) so they end in the right-hand box. (E.g., enter $30,000 as $\boxed{0}\boxed{3}\boxed{0}\boxed{0}\boxed{0}\boxed{0}$.)

72. Enter the present market value of parents' home.

73. Enter the amount of present unpaid mortgage and related debts on parents' home.

74. Enter the total of the present market value of parents' investments (including stocks, bonds, and other securities) **and** present market value of parents' other real estate. Report farm and business only in items 76 and 77.

75. Enter total unpaid debts on the investments and other real estate listed in 74.

76. Enter the present market value of parents' farm and business (including value of land, buildings, machinery, equipment, animals, inventories, etc.). Do not include value of home; report home value only in item 72. If parents are not the sole owners, enter only the amount of their share of the total farm or business market value.

77. Enter the present unpaid mortgage or related debts for which the farm or business assets were used as collateral. If parents are not the sole owners, enter only the amount of their share of total farm/business debt.

78. Indicate whether the assets reported in item 76 are primarily from a farm or from a business.

Parents' Estimated Income for 1978

79. Enter parents' estimated Adjusted Gross Income for 1978. This is the same type of income as reported in item 62.

80. Enter the amount parents expect to receive in nontaxable income during 1978. Include only those types of nontaxable income outlined in instruction 59.

Please check again to make sure you have completed every item and have entered zeros for those items that do not apply to you or your parents. Then go on to Section G.

_____PAGE 4 OF FFS_____

SECTION G. OTHER STUDENT INFORMATION

81. Enter the month and year you received or expect to receive a high school diploma or G.E.D.

82. Enter the beginning and ending dates of the term(s) for which you wish to receive assistance.

83. Enter the code for your state of legal residence. See the state code listing on page 2 of these instructions.

84. Enter the amount of Social Security educational benefits per month you expect to receive between July 1, 1978 and June 30, 1979. Include only amounts that you (not other members of your household) will receive if you are between 18 and 22 years of age and enrolled in an educational institution.

85. Enter the number of months you expect to receive Social Security benefits between July 1, 1978 and June 30, 1979.

86. Enter the amount of veterans benefits per month you expect to receive between July 1, 1978 and June 30, 1979. Include only amounts that you (not other members of your household) will receive from the G.I. Bill or War Orphans' and Widows' Education Assistance Program. If you are unsure of these amounts, contact your local Veterans' Administration office.

87. Enter the number of months you expect to receive these veterans benefits between July 1, 1978 and June 30, 1979.

88. Unusual Debts: if you owe debts **from 1976** or before for funeral or medical expenses, legal fees, or uninsured natural disaster losses, enter the amount here. Do not include consumer debts, credit cards, motor vehicle loans, educational loans, or any debt reported elsewhere on this form.

89. Enter your date of birth exactly as it was entered in item 7 on page 1 of the FFS. This item is repeated to allow matching of information on pages 1 and 2 with that on pages 3 and 4 if they should become separated.

90. Indicate whether you authorize ACT to release your record to recognized student aid programs not coded on this form.

SECTION H. Complete as indicated.

SECTION I. REPORT REQUEST, AUTHORIZATIONS, CERTIFICATION, AND SIGNATURES

91. Enter the ACT codes of the schools or programs to which you wish ACT need analysis reports sent. See the enclosed ACT Financial Aid Code Listing. Use only ACT codes. If you are applying for a BEOG (by answering "YES" to item 92), your eligibility results will be sent to the first two schools listed. If you want BEOG eligibility results sent to a school not listed, enclose with your FFS a note with the full name, city, and state of the school. Do not staple or tape the note to the FFS.

FEE: Enclose the appropriate fee for the number of codes listed. Checks must be written on U.S. banks. Do not send cash. Please write student's Social Security number on your check.

92. Indicate whether you wish to apply for a Basic Grant. There is no charge for doing so.

93. Indicate whether you authorize the BEOG Program to release your record to the agency administering student financial aid in your state of legal residence (entered in item 83).

94. If you are using this FFS to apply **only** for the BEOG Program and **do not** want ACT need analysis reports sent to the schools or programs coded in item 91, answer "YES" to this question. If you answer "YES", do not send money with this FFS.

95. This form must be signed by the student, the student's spouse (if married), and, if parental information is provided, at least one of the student's parents.

Print parent's name in the area provided.
Enter parent's Social Security number.
Print parent's address.

96. Enter the month, day, and year that this form is signed.

Please check again to make sure that all items have been completed and that zeros have been entered for items which do not apply to you or your parents (except in those sections you have been instructed to skip).

If other forms are included in this packet, complete and mail them as instructed on those forms.

 THE AMERICAN COLLEGE TESTING PROGRAM

SAVE THESE INSTRUCTIONS! They will help you to verify the information that is reported back to you as a result of processing this form.

4

NOTES ON FINANCIAL AID FORMS

FAF Form

1) This is a very important choice point. If you are able to answer "no" to *all three* of these questions (13–15), you probably will qualify for aid as an independent student, which will in most instances mean a far better chance of getting meaningful financial aid. But it must be all three; a "yes" to any of them means that you will be a dependent student for aid purposes. Note that some colleges will still require that the Parents' Confidential Statement be filled out.

2) This is basic information taken from income tax statements, and should be taken from 1976 and 1977 income tax returns. The 1978 estimates are likely to be similar to 1977 actual figures, unless major new expense factors are clearly visible at the time this form is filled out.

3) Items 30, 31, 33 and 34 ask for estimates of the present market values of homes, other real estate, businesses and farms. Note that estimates like these are at best educated guesses, and that many factors come into play that may raise or sharply lower the value of such properties when they are actually sold. As the value of these properties is taken into account in determining how much financial aid will be granted, it is wise to estimate their market values reasonably conservatively. Note that owners of businesses and farms must file supplementary forms. We suggest that these be done with the help of an accountant.

4) Items 68–71 call for the same kinds of market value estimates from students and should be treated with the same kind of conservatism.

FFS Form

5) Items 14–16 raise the same very important question discussed in (1) above. If you are able to answer "no" to all three, you probably will qualify for aid as an independent student.

6) Items 30–41 raise a series of questions involving estimates of market values and future earnings. Again, while it would be wrong to seriously underestimate, it would be equally wrong and potentially quite costly to overestimate in these areas.   •

7) Items 72–80 raise similar estimate questions, and should be treated equally conservatively.

ACT Student Data Form

8) Note that the Student's Estimated Resources section calls for more estimates.

5

DEVELOPING YOUR STRATEGY FOR COLLEGE AND FINANCIAL AID APPLICATIONS

YOU now know how to derive very important information with which to proceed in getting money for college. This basic number is how much money you will be expected to spend toward college costs—in official determinations (by colleges and government agencies). As you've seen, we call this your "total expected." (The internal official phrases for this dollar sum are downright misleading—"total family contribution" in the College Scholarship Service's pioneering system and the deliberately opaque "student eligibility index" used in the federal Basic Opportunity Grant Program.) Of course, it's the key number for you that's used officially to prove whether you have "financial need"—and how much in the case of each college.

With your "total expected" figure, you can now set up your general strategy for applying to colleges and for applying for financial aid. Your strategies here will naturally also take into account your decisions across the range of college-cost options open to you.

Let's see how you could plan your strategies through three examples —one somewhere in the middle ground and two at high and low extremes in terms of total expected.

THE WILSONS: HIGH-EXTREME EXAMPLE—NO FINANCIAL NEED (OFFICIALLY)

Sue and Jim Wilson of the affluent St. Louis suburb Webster Groves were shocked to see from the last chapter that their total expected came out to about $7,700 a year. They felt appalled to think that financial aid people would expect them to be able to pay some $30,800 to put Deborah through four years of college—and with all their really pressing money obligations!

But then they felt better when they thought about their range of cost options (explained in Chapter 2) and the availability of quite a lot of "no-need" financial aid in which financial need is not a factor (explained in Chapter 6). They decided first to look at the full range of their college-cost options, at least for Debbie's first two years of college. They jotted down these figures, with Debbie herself doing most of the work:

Debbie Wilson's College-Cost Options—Full Range (Approx. Figures, '77-'78) *

Most expensive college	$7,650	(Harvard and Radcliffe Colleges)
Mid-expense private college	4,800	(average for all private four-year colleges, dorm student)
State university, four-year	2,900	(average, dorm student)
Community college (commuting)	1,450	(omitting home room and board budget costs of $864)

This looked more encouraging to them. Compared to what official sources expected they could spend on college, they save $2,900 a year if Debbie were to go to a mid-expense private college. Or they could save as much as some $6,250 a year were Debbie to live at home and commute to Meramec Community College over in Kirkwood (one of three community colleges in their county).

That listing at least mapped out the extreme ends of the spread in which their strategy on what cost levels of colleges to apply to would work.

They then turned to consider their possible aid strategy. They realized clearly that they would be limited only to "no-need" types of aid. Debbie jotted down these possibilities (based on Chapters 6, 8, 9, 10):

Debbie Wilson's Financial Aid Possibilities

Colleges—maybe a no-need scholarship like $500 a year from a good but not great private college (I've got pretty good marks), or one from the University of Missouri at Columbia or Southeast Missouri State College (if they have any)

* These figures come from the annual booklet mentioned before as about the only general source of the crucial "student expense budget" costs at almost all colleges. This is the booklet of the CSS (College Scholarship Service of the College Entrance Examination Board) called *Student Expenses at Postsecondary Institutions, 1977–78* (or subsequent year for which the expense budget figures are effective; the figures used in this book are those for the 1977–78 academic year). Some colleges give their own student expense budget figures in their literature.

Federal and state governments—maybe I'll try ROTC (but I doubt it); sure bet is a 7-percent Guaranteed Student Loan (if we really need it)

Private-agency aid programs—I could give one of the few no-need programs here like the Betty Crocker Search of General Mills a try; we might keep our eyes open for a few hundred dollars in prize money from a no-need scholarship contest, especially one open just to students in this area.

Sue and Jim Wilson then set about figuring what they might want to do (or have to do) beyond financial aid, including guaranteed loans.

They all faced many further inquiries and decisions on specific colleges, programs, and details (like summer and school-year work for Debbie, or a co-op college work-study program for her). But this first overall review set the framework for their college-choice and aid strategies.

THE SMITHS: MID-GROUND EXAMPLE—FINANCIAL NEED AT SOME COLLEGES BUT NOT OTHERS

Jane and Don Smith in Rochester, N.Y., were also shocked to see from the last chapter that financial aid officials would expect them to provide $3,000 a year toward college for young Tim ($3,000 was their total expected).

Tim blocked out their full range of cost options much as Debbie Wilson had done. To it, though, he added second and third columns that would show their "financial need" (as officially defined) for each option. The result looked like this:

Tim Smith's College-Cost Options and Financial Need (Approx., '77–'78)

College type and cost		Our total expected	Our financial need there
Most expens.	$7,650	$3,000	$4,650
Mid-exp. pvt.	4,800	3,000	1,800
State U, four-yr.	2,900	3,000	none
CC (commute)	1,450	3,000	none (save $1,450/yr. vs. State U)

This lineup showed them a number of points that could involve thousands of dollars they'd save or spend.

It showed them, for instance, that they could prove financial need of some $1,800 at typical four-year private colleges. They hence might qualify for aid on that order in the many need-based financial aid programs (insofar as only need is concerned). They also saw that they would have to get that much aid if they decided Tim should go to such a college. (And similar conclusions but with higher amounts held for any more expensive colleges Tim might try for.)

It showed them also that they would be likely to have no need at their state university campuses (for New York's four state university centers, total student expense budgets for dorm students in '77–'78 are Albany, $3,050; Binghamton, $3,205; Buffalo, $3,600; Stony Brook, $3,250).

And it showed them that they could save some $1,450 a year were Tim to commute to Monroe Community College in town rather than be a dorm student at a state university campus.

Tim next hustled into their financial aid questions. He put down a first listing that looked like this (based on Chapters 6, 8, 9, 10):

Tim Smith's Financial Aid Possibilities (Lots)

Colleges

1. Apply for aid as well as admission at all colleges I'll try for—except maybe State U and Monroe Community. Look for private colleges with those low, 3-percent-interest National Direct loans in case we need one. Admissions chances a long shot for me at a most-expensive private college, but aid chances good *if* I get admitted. I might get a fat scholarship offer from a faraway private college that's good enough but not known much beyond its region.

Federal government

2. Basic Grant—Try for anyway, especially since I don't have to fill out any extra application forms for it.

3. Guaranteed Student Loan—That's our backup in case we might need it; we'd probably get the federal subsidy covering all interest (at 8 percent now in New York State) while I'm in college.

4. ROTC, Social Security, Veterans Administration? They're all out in my case.

State government

5. Regents Scholarship—I'm not bad on tests and I might get one around the average of $280 a year if I go to college in the state.

6. Grant aid, TAP (Tuition Assistance Program) in our state—Try for it by all means if I go to college in the state. Need for TAP is figured only on the basis of state income tax returns and does not take family assets into account. Maybe I could qualify for half the average amount in a TAP grant, or $250 a year. We'll be sure to apply for it anyway.

Private-agency aid programs

7. Sure, we'll look hard for any and all possibilities. Dad works for Eastman Kodak, and they may very well offer scholarships for employees' kids. And there seem to be lots of lodges, clubs, and civic groups offering scholarships around town.

My guidance counselor at school is pretty good, and I'll be sure to ask her about private aid programs for me. I've seen lots of notices about them over in the guidance office. I'll see about any national programs, and we'll all ask at the church and all the different clubs we belong to.

THE SLOANS: LOW-EXTREME EXAMPLE—TOTAL FINANCIAL NEED (OFFICIALLY)

Marv and June Sloan in the Watts section of Los Angeles weren't too surprised to see from the last chapter that their total expected equaled zero —minus $123 a year, in fact.

Marv's irregular work as a piano-player in local nightspots supplemented by occasional half-days as a parking-lot attendant had brought in only some $6,000 through the previous year, and they were struggling to pay off heavy medical bills run up for five children. Danny, the eldest, had always been strong on books, and now he thought he might go off to college.

It was Danny and an interested counselor in his high school who took the lead in noting down their college-cost options. With Marv's and June's help, they set up a listing that showed their heavy financial need for each option:

Danny Sloan's College-Cost Options and Need (Approx., '77–'78)

College type and Cost		Our total expected	Our financial need there
Most expens.	$7,650	–$123	$7,773
Mid-exp. pvt.	4,800	–$123	4,923
State U, four-yr.	2,900	–$123	3,023
CC (commute)	1,450	–$123	1,573

Marv and June were staggered by the cost of even their least expensive option—a community college like Los Angeles City College. But Danny worked at a possible solution for their most expensive possibility as if it were an especially fascinating puzzle. To do it, he drew on information in Chapter 7 of this book as well as in Chapters 6, 8, 9 and 10.

Then he showed his parents how it might work, with his possible strategy for meeting needs of theirs even as high as $7,773 a year. Here are his rough figures:

Danny Sloan's Financial Aid Strategy (All Out—the Works!) Top of the Heap ($7,773/year)

Federal aid

Basic Grant	$1,400	(that's the maximum amount; may be $1,600 in '78–'79)
Supplementary Grant	1,000	(must be matched by college or state)
College work-study job	400	(not too heavy a work load while studying)

State aid

State scholarship	1,500	(higher than average; I'll really try! college must be in California)
Coll. Oppty. Grant	1,200	(a little higher than average amount; California college)

College aid

Scholarship	1,000	(with luck; needed to match Supp. Grant)

Private-agency aid programs

National Ach. (Merit)	1,000	(maybe! one-year only)
National Scholarship Service and Fund for Negro Students	273	(just the kind of fill-in aid they give)
	$7,773	(wow! I could *make it!*)

Reserve aid (if needed)

Community Schol. Prog.	500 (??)	(we'll all look hard; Dad's a veteran)
National Direct Loan	2,500	(maximum, only if needed; 3 percent interest)
Guaranteed Loan	2,500	(maximum, only if needed; 7 percent)
ROTC Scholarship	big	(consider; all costs except room and board but you get paid $100/month)

The rest was fairly simple to map out for Danny's less-expensive cost options. The whole family was elated at his chances.

YOU MIGHT SIMILARLY FIGURE YOUR OWN ROUGH COST OPTIONS AND NEED HERE

Setting up a table showing your own college-cost options, total expected, and financial need for each option at this point should be helpful to you. You can do it in much the same form illustrated by the last two young people. Feel free to use either their typical cost figures for 1977–78 or total "student expense budget" figures (current ones) for colleges you're actually considering.

Figuring what your financial need would be for different college-cost options can help you by providing a focus for going through the next four chapters on all the financial aid offered today, and how to find and get it. What you'll need to find out from those chapters differs according to whether or not you'd have financial need at one or more colleges and how much your financial need would be.

You won't yet be able to figure out your financial aid possibilities as shown in this chapter; the necessary background hasn't been covered yet. But you should be able to do it as readily as the three young people of the examples here once you have gone through the next chapters.

YOUR SEARCH STRATEGY TO CHECK ALL SOURCES OF THE BILLIONS OFFERED IN AID FOR COLLEGE

AT this point you have learned how to make (and have possibly made) strategic plans for going ahead on a spread of basic college-cost options. These probably involve inquiries and applications with perhaps five or more colleges.

Some of those options and possible colleges may require financial aid beyond all that you can reasonably mobilize from your own resources. If so, you may already have figured about how much financial aid each college possibility would call for as explained in the previous chapter. Even if you don't have financial need at any of your college options, you might still apply for some billions in financial aid awarded regardless of need—as we explain later in this chapter.

Your chances of getting what aid you need will be increased if you use an effective search strategy in seeking it out. Two large facts about financial aid for college make it advisable for you to have a good strategy. These are:

1. More than $10 billion a year is available in financial aid for college and you might as well get your fair share of it for either saving your own money or obtaining a better (or at least more-expensive) college education.

2. Financial aid is offered in extremely fragmented and complex ways in the United States and not through any one overall system; making sure that no major financial aid opportunities are overlooked thus takes a well-framed, strategic approach.

In order to apply your search strategy with some insight, though, you first need to know basically what financial aid for college is available.

THAT CHAOTIC, $10-BILLION-A-YEAR BONANZA OFFERED YOU IN FINANCIAL AID FOR COLLEGES

Students who have not only grappled with but conducted research on college financial aid wax eloquent about the field's complexity and lack of information. In 1976 the CEEB commissioned eight students to serve as a student advisory committee of the College Scholarship Service (CSS). Their mission was to analyze and recommend improvements in financial aid. The committee remarked in its report on "the maze of application forms, deadlines, eligibility criteria, and other program requirements." It also found that "students cannot get adequate information about what programs are available, how to apply, and their rights and responsibilities under aid programs."

You face literally thousands of sources of financial aid, each varying in what it provides and requires, and all wrapped up in red tape that's usually more complicated than your federal income tax return. But let's trace the major outlines here to help you thread your way through the maze to aid worth possibly thousands of dollars.

 Three major types of sources provide financial aid today. You should keep these in mind as the big blocks across your range of aid possibilities and as the kinds of sources to be sure to investigate and possibly apply to. These major sources are:

1. *Colleges.* Getting aid must of course begin with applying for admission to a college; applying to it also for financial aid is highly advisable. Colleges are the source of not only the sizable aid they themselves provide but often of very large programs of federal aid. But college financial aid offices are unevenly skilled, and some might not tell you about federal aid programs for which you can apply through them.

2. *Government, federal and state.* Government agencies on the federal and state levels are by far the largest sources of college financial aid today.

3. *Private agencies of all kinds.* Scholarship programs (and a few loan programs) are sponsored by hundreds of corporations, labor unions, foundations, church bodies, civic and fraternal organizations, veterans associations, and still other private (noncollege and nongovernmental) groups. Such programs usually have quite special eligibility requirements.

You can tell from the following table how much aid is available from each of these three major sources. The table also gives you an idea of the staggering sums available in aid programs—the sums it cites are in *millions* of dollars. It should also give you some idea of the jumbled character of the field. The figures shown are estimates for the 1977 federal fiscal year and were made by Alexander G. Sidar, CSS executive director.

The $10-Billion-Plus Offered Per Year in Financial Aid for College Students

(figures given are in millions of dollars)

Colleges	
Scholarship (grants)	$ 600
Loans	60
Jobs	320
Government—Federal	
Veterans Administration (GI Bill)	3,600
Social Security benefits	1,183
Basic Educ. Oppty. Grants (BEOG)	1,315
Supplementary Educ. Oppty. Grants (SEOG)	240
College Work-Study Program (CWSP)	455
Natl. Direct Student Loans (NDSL)	496
Special programs	
LEEP (Law Enforcement Educ. Program)	40
Nursing loans	15
Bureau of Indian Affairs	33
TRIO (special low-income student services)	70
Government—State programs	500
Government—Federal and state programs	
Guaranteed Student Loan Program (GSLP)	1,300
Nursing scholarships	6
State Student Incentive Grants (SSIG)	44
Private Agencies	
Scholarships	50
Loans	10
	$10,337

You might note two things in connection with the table. First, you would not need to have unusually high academic (or athletic) ability in order to qualify for aid from most of the sources. Ability as judged in competitive selection is a factor in winning only the scholarships shown (scholarships from colleges, nursing scholarships, and scholarships from private agencies) and scholarships offered in some of the state programs.

Second, you would be required to have either demonstrated financial need or income lower than specified levels in order to qualify for most of the aid shown, with three major exceptions: Veterans Administration benefits for ex-servicepersons (often called GI Bill benefits), Social Security benefits (paid to college-attending children of retired, disabled, or deceased family breadwinners), and Guaranteed Student Loans.

Incidentally, the table does not include some additional millions of dollars in federal defense funds for college studies that are also awarded without regard to need. Among these are the funds for ROTC (Reserve Officer Training Corps) scholarships and the funds for free education plus monthly cash payments to students at the U.S. service academies. Complete information about these funds is given in Chapter 9.

YOUR SEARCH STRATEGY FOR FINANCIAL AID—WHAT IT CAN DO FOR YOU

Faced by this welter of financial aid possibilities, where do you begin? How do you hunt to be sure of not missing either your widest possibilities or obscure good bets? The answer is to follow the search strategy outlined for you here.

This strategy consists essentially of a sensible sequence of steps. These help you proceed systematically, without annoyance, doubts, or pressure. They lead you through checking all sources likely to be open to you. They should protect you from missing any prime possibilities.

Only brief information about specific financial aid programs is given in this chapter—only the information you need to understand and begin applying the strategy. More detailed information about individual programs is given in the next three chapters. Those chapters treat applying the strategy and basic actions to take when you actually go about getting aid. The next chapters also present mailing addresses to which you may write for full and current program information, while those chapters and the Appendix on "Additional Information Sources" list books you may consult for extensively detailed information on programs.

Several principles underlie the search strategy suggested for you:

1. Try first from the widest and likeliest sources of the most desirable form of aid—grants or scholarships.

2. Avoid loans (and later debt) if possible; if not, try for lowest-interest loans first. Try for job aid instead of even lowest-interest loans to avoid later debt, but don't impossibly overload study time with job hours.

3. Try for maximum amounts of grant aid and minimum amounts of job aid.

TIMING FOR USE OF YOUR SEARCH STRATEGY

If possible, start applying this strategy in the spring of the junior year in high school for your college-bound offspring or yourself—generally, that is, about a year and a half before expected college entrance. Starting in the fall of the high school senior year (a year before entrance) should still prove workable though tight for all the digging and work you'll probably have to do.

Application deadlines for aid programs commonly begin coming up in November and December of the high school senior year. Deadlines for registering to take tests required by some scholarship programs may occur as early as late September of the senior year. (The National Merit Scholarship Program test must be taken in October of the junior year.)

You can apply for aid in a few programs, like the federal and state guaranteed student loan programs, as late as several weeks before entering college and still receive aid money in time to help pay fall college bills. However, a great many colleges today demand payment of bills for September entrants as early as mid-August.

But set out on your aid search early if you can. Doing so will improve your chances for getting the most in aid, for not missing any possible sources, and for spreading the sheer work involved.

YOUR SEARCH STRATEGY OUTLINED—BIG BLOCKS

 Here is the search strategy suggested for you. It is sketched in very broad outline, so that you may fix its major features clearly in mind. Its four principal parts are:

1. A basic question—whether or not you have *demonstrable* financial need (and how to proceed if you do not); the other parts depend on your having such need.

2. Acting on your widest possibilities for grant aid.

3. Acting on scholarship possibilities—all your chances for them.

4. Setting work, loan, and other alternatives to hold in reserve.

Basic Question: Do You Have Demonstrable Financial Need? How You Can Still Apply for Billions in Aid Even If You Don't Have Need

Just about everyone feels he or she has financial need when it's time to pay soaring college costs these days. But colleges and other financial aid sources define financial need very specifically, through the systems explained earlier in Chapter 6 on proving your financial need. By using what was said in that chapter, you should be able to tell approximately how much need you have that is demonstrable to sources of aid, according to major systems of financial need analysis.

In recalling or figuring whether you probably have demonstrable financial need, you should remember that your financial need varies from college to college. It is the difference between what the need-analysis systems estimate you can reasonably afford toward college costs and the annual cost budget for the student at each college you're considering. You can thus have substantial financial need at more expensive colleges and no need at less expensive colleges.

Your answer to this basic question of having need would therefore be "yes" if you would have need for any one or more college possibilities you've chosen.

Large aid sources for you if you do not have demonstrable financial need. You still might get financial aid for college from some sources even if your answer to the questions of having demonstrable need is "no." These sources include the ones briefly mentioned earlier as major programs that do not consider need in awarding aid. Again, these are:

U.S. Veterans Administration benefits (for veterans holding any but dishonorable discharges and who had at least ten months' active duty between 1956 and 1976, these can pay $270 a month or more during full-time college study; altogether they represent the largest single college aid source, totaling $3.6 billion a year, as you saw).

U.S. Social Security benefits (to children whose parent qualified for Social Security and is retired, disabled, or deceased, these can pay some $70 to $130 a month during the child's full-time college studies; also a large aid source, totaling some $1.2 billion a year).

Guaranteed Student Loan Program (of federal and state governments; if you must borrow, you can get a GSLP loan of up to some $2,500 a year regardless of financial need and take advantage of its subsidized 7-percent interest to save hundreds of dollars in interest costs compared to loans at commercial rates; another large aid source, this one totals $1.3 billion a year).

ROTC scholarships and U.S. service academies (Reserve Officers Training Corps scholarships should cover all but some $300 to $1,800 a year of college costs depending on the college, while the service academies represent the option that pays you to go to college; in both program types students aided are picked regardless of need).

Two other no-need possibilities besides those mentioned before might be noted. Some scholarships awarded by colleges are also exempt from the usual practice of colleges to adjust the amount of aid awarded according to need. Scattered private colleges that are anxious to attract more students with rather good academic capability offer a number of those no-need awards. Athletic scholarships offered by the collegiate sports powers of the country (outside the Ivy League) are also often no-need awards and cover just about all college costs. Any good high school athlete can find out about these from his or her coach.

Basic details for actually sizing up and applying to these sources (and many others) are given in Chapters 8, 9 and 10. But these sources just highlighted represent the major checkpoints for your search strategy if you don't have financial need.

Now, what if you do have demonstrable financial need for college, as most American families have today? Your search strategy in that event is outlined in this chapter's remaining sections.

Acting on Your Widest Possibilities for Grant Aid

Over the last decade or two, scholarship aid has usually been viewed by students as the most desirable type to get. It's "free money"—cash payments to your college account with no obligations to earn or repay the funds. Two common requirements for scholarships, though, are (and have been) to demonstrate financial need and to qualify for it by evidence of unusually good ability—usually judged in a competitive selection with the best candidates winning.

But in only the last years, massively increased college aid funds have been made available in what are often called "grant" programs. The federal and state governments provide these programs—as in the federal BEOG program (awarding some $1.3 billion a year to more than a million students) and the Illinois Monetary Award Program (granting some $70 million a year to more than 90,000 students). Such offerings are widely called "grant programs," and we accordingly also call them programs of grant aid in this book.

Grant aid of this type is even more desirable for you than scholarship aid. For grant aid programs, while also requiring you to demonstrate financial need, can also bring you "free money"—cash payments to your college account with no earning or repayment obligations. But for grant aid, however, you are not required to have unusually good ability. And even if you do have such ability, you're not required in grant programs to go to what is often in scholarship programs the extra trouble of giving evidence of high ability (by special tests, transcripts, forms, recommendations, interviews, and the like).

Your only academic requirement in grant programs is that you get into college, which you're doing anyway.

From this you can see why your first step should accordingly be to look into grant aid programs and apply to any that seem possibly open to you. These should certainly include:

1. BEOG (Basic Educational Opportunity Grant Program, which provides grants today to about one in every ten college students. Grants have averaged about $800 a year and can range up to $1,400 a year through 1977–78, with a higher top under discussion for future years. Families with annual incomes of $15,000 to $20,000 or more might qualify for BEOG awards, depending on family circumstances and costs at the college attended.)

2. Your state's grant aid program, if your state has one. (Many states do, including California, Georgia, Illinois, New York, Ohio, Oregon, Pennsylvania, and Washington. Grants in these programs run from a few hundred dollars to about $1,500 a year; they often may be used only at colleges in the state.)

A second main step will open your way to still more grant aid programs. This step is to apply for financial aid as well as admission to the colleges you choose. Your colleges will then consider you for three other large federal aid programs, one of which provides grants. It is SEOG, the Supplementary Educational Opportunity Grants program for students of exceptional financial need. (The other two are NDSL, National Direct Student Loan program, which provides college loans at a very low interest rate of 3 percent, and CWSP, College Work-Study Program, which provides federal funds for part-time campus jobs awarded by the college as financial aid.)

The U.S. Office of Education terms these "campus-based programs." In them, federal funds are allocated among colleges. Colleges in turn award those funds to their financial aid applicants.

Should you be interested in law enforcement studies in college, your colleges could also consider you for a special federal aid program of grants and loans, LEEP (Law Enforcement Education Program, supplying some $40 million a year to more than 90,000 students).

It has probably occurred to you already that you should consider in addition two other large federal sources of aid as convenient as grant aid if you're eligible—Veterans Administration and Social Security benefits.

Acting on Scholarship Possibilities—All Your Chances for Them

Your third major move in applying a good search strategy if you have financial need is, manifestly, to cover all your chances for getting scholarships. Winning a scholarship takes unusually good ability—academic and often extracurricular ability or athletic ability in the case of athletic scholarships.

If you think your child or you might have abilities in the scholarship range (on the basis of what's explained in the next chapter), you should consider the four main sources of scholarships that encompass all your possibilities:

1. Colleges. The basic step toward competing for college scholarships is to apply not only for admission to all the colleges you've chosen, but to apply to each one for financial aid as well. You might increase your chances of getting a scholarship by doing some special hunting and choosing among colleges to find ones with larger scholarship programs. Generally (and ironically), colleges that are more expensive in student charges award more funds in scholarships than less expensive colleges. Colleges strong in intercollegiate sports represent just about the only source of athletic scholarships, which are often no-need, full-cost awards.

2. Your state's scholarship program, if your state has one. Many states do have scholarship programs, often a large one open to any college students and smaller programs only for such special types of students as those studying to become nurses, those who are children of deceased or disabled veterans, or those who are poverty-level members of minority groups.

3. What are essentially the federal scholarship programs—ROTC scholarships and the U.S. service academies. There are also some federal scholarship programs (and other college aid programs) for minority-group members like American Indians.

4. Scholarship programs sponsored by private agencies of all kinds. Efficient ways to hunt out your possibilities among the hundreds of such programs are explained in Chapter 10.

Setting Work, Loan, and Other Alternatives to Hold in Reserve

Your fourth and last search-strategy move is to prepare for alternatives that consist mainly of job aid or loan aid. These come last because they're less desirable to you than grant or scholarship aid. You also might want to hold them in reserve rather than committing yourself early to them in case you should get enough grant or scholarship aid to meet your need. You should nevertheless explore and take standby steps on these alternatives, however, so that you'll have them ready should you not get enough (or any) grant or scholarship aid.

Broad types of alternatives for you to check out and get set on in this move are:

1. Work aid. Part-time campus jobs awarded by colleges you apply to represent a major kind of possibility for such aid; these would include federally funded CWSP jobs. You might also consider cooperative work-study programs of colleges or the few special colleges where all students work.

2. National Direct Student Loans (NDSL) at 3-percent interest. Applying to colleges for aid as well as admission puts you in a position to be offered one of these federal loans as noted earlier. Colleges tend to reserve these desirably low-interest loans for high-need students from low-income families. NDSL loans are in short supply compared to the interest in having them.

There are also a few loan programs of colleges themselves and of private agencies that offer loans at attractive interest under 7 percent.

3. Guaranteed Student Loan Programs of federal and state governments, providing loans at 7-percent interest. Applying to college for admission with aid also often puts you in line for a GSLP loan, which has the advantage of carrying a lower interest rate than commercial loans you might get. Many students applying to colleges for financial aid today find that their "aid package" offered by the college is made up in large part by GSLP loans. (Small-amount scholarship, small-amount campus job, and large-amount GSLP loan make up the typical "aid package" of a college today.)

Some colleges make GSLP loans directly, from their own funds. But most GSLP loans are made by banks (as well as by savings and loan associations and credit unions), and students getting these obtain application forms and make application at the bank itself.

4. Should all these preceding possibilities fail to produce enough money to meet your financial need at a college, you could either take more from your income or assets (including the step of getting a loan at high rates of commercial credit) or you could shift to a lower-cost college option.

But even if you have no financial need, you may be able to get some of the $10 billion a year provided to aid college students. How to go about getting that aid in detail is explained in the next chapters.

7

SPECIAL HELP FOR STUDENTS HANDICAPPED BY POVERTY AND DISCRIMINATION

A four-year college education today can cost as much as three or four Coup de Villes—brand-new, loaded, power everything.

And there are these people who can juggle their stocks and their bank accounts and their insurance and taxes to save a few thousand on what college would otherwise run them.

But you have barely enough money to live on. And you're Black, or Latino, or Oriental, or Native American Indian.

Where does that leave you on college?

Better than people in your shoes ever had it before.

No joke.

It's a kind of revolution, a big one. Maybe not quite the kind of revolution this country really needs. But there's been an enormous change in the chances that people like you have for college, if you've already made it pretty big through probably rotten schools but are still game for more.

You see, the more unbelievably expensive it's gotten to pay for college, the better the chances have become for people like you to get money for college.

And today, lots of times, you can get all the money. All the money you need to live on while in college. Plus all the money to pay for everything else about college. This is often true even at top-cost colleges.

How come? First, there are quite a few programs providing special help for college-bound students from minority-group families who have very low incomes. Their help consists of financial aid for college, and also special teaching and guidance in some programs. We'll describe such programs shortly, especially the financial aid ones. These programs can and do help a great deal.

But the tremendous new advantage for you results very largely from huge new programs of financial aid developed by Uncle Sam and many state governments in recent years. And it's particularly a basic ground rule in these programs (and other large aid programs) which gives you that advantage.

That ground rule calls for setting the amount of aid granted according to the student's financial need. In some programs, need alone (plus, of course, admission to a college) determines not only how much aid but whether or not the student gets any aid at all.

So, while you're short on everything else that's worth money, you're very long on financial need. And hard as it may be to believe, your need can prove to be worth all the money it will take to put you through college.

You see, many people better off than you run out of need pretty fast in trying for college aid. But you're in a position to go on and on and on before you run out of financial need.

And the number and size and ground rules of aid programs today all make it possible for you to do just that—to go on and on and on, from program to program to program, until your need for college money is met. Need's the big thing in aid for college these days. You've got lots and lots. Make the most of it.

It's funny, sure. And for once, the joke isn't on you.

THE MAJOR PROGRAMS IN WHICH YOU CAN PILE UP AWARD AFTER AWARD

Here's the real muscle to put into getting money for college if you're coming from this kind of place in the United States to go on to college. It's largely the muscle of the country's big, mainline financial aid programs we mentioned. We show you here how to pile up award after award in them. First, though, a few general pointers.

• **Pour it on in your studies, because you have good reason for hope.** You have easily some $3,000 to $5,000 a year for college open to you in these programs—*if* you can rack up grades of A or B in academic courses like college-prep math, English, and science, with the pretty good scores on college-entrance and scholarship tests that usually go along with A and B grades in the last couple of years of high school. Feel free to put lots of serious work into these courses, then, if you've so far kind of liked them but hadn't bothered much because it wouldn't do you any good anyway. Now you know it can do you some good—some $12,000 to $20,000 worth, for starters.

• **Latch onto a good counselor if you can.** You'll face seemingly endless facts and details and questions about colleges and financial aid programs. A capable, interested, with-it guidance counselor can help you tremendously with them. Try to find one—in your school, if you can; if not, through one of the special programs described shortly.

• **Get to know the colleges and the aid programs.** Even with a counselor, there's a great deal about colleges and aid programs that you'll have to find out on your own. Haunt the school guidance office and the school or community library to bone up heavily about colleges—especially all the different ones, near and far away, to which you might go. Read up on the kinds of careers that colleges lead to, particularly on the money they pay and what chances for starting jobs they offer today.

Much information about financial aid programs can be gotten by writing to them at the addresses given in this book. Get it and read it till you can see clearly what it might do for you, and how you should apply and meet requirements.

• **Line up at least minimum cooperation from your parent or other guardian.** Maybe your parent or other legal guardian would be enthused and helpful about your going to college. If so, fine. But if not, try to get at least grudging cooperation from your parent or guardian. If you apply for aid in the most common way—as a "dependent student" (financially dependent on your parent/guardian)—that person will have to supply some personal and financial information and sign some applications and other forms (or could even fill them all out, if willing).

You can apply as a "self-supporting" student, though, if you have broken off or lost touch with your parent/guardian. The person then wouldn't have to sign any form except one stating that for the last year, present year, and next year, he or she hasn't-doesn't-won't house you, provide more than $600 a year toward your financial support, nor claim you as a dependent on income tax (for not one but the two preceding years). This parent-signing requirement makes it tough for some self-supporting students who have broken away from a parent/guardian with really hard feelings on both sides. But it's still there, anyway.

• **Don't blow up at all the incredible paperwork, red tape, and possible brush-offs.** Getting financial aid on top of applying to college is the absolutely worst tangle of forms, mixed-up instructions, checkboxes, rules, cut-off dates, and general nit-picking you can ever imagine. The only reason you have for putting up with it all is the thousands of dollars it can bring you. So don't blow up over it. Start months and months early. Expect it to be annoying in the extreme.

Some people who work in financial aid offices at colleges with whom you'll have to deal may also be rude enough to give you brush-offs, long waits, and even wrong information. Things like this have been reported by students across the country. But don't blow up over them, either—at least not to the extent of quitting altogether. Hang in there, and you'll succeed in spite of them. (But don't be surprised if the financial aid people you meet are interested and tremendously helpful. Most of them are good-hearted, hard-working people.)

• **Get waivers for the fees you'll keep running into.** Don't let your way be blocked by the fees you'll keep running into, either. These will be like the application fees at each college you apply to ($10 to $25), the fees for required admissions and scholarship tests (from some $7 to $18 or so), and the fees for having copies of your financial need forms sent to colleges and aid programs (some $4.50 and up). Colleges will waive their application fees if you write to them asking them to and explaining your financial situation. So will the testing agencies and the need-form agencies. It's their policy to waive fees this way for poverty-level students, and one of the first forms of special help provided—comparatively small, but it can mean a lot.)

Now, Go for These Programs for Sure—for $3,600 a Year as Openers

Let's start with five aid programs or kinds of programs for you to go after. The first four of these are certainly open to you, and your state probably has the fifth kind of program—a program of state grants to college students who have financial need that would certainly also be open to you. Your chances of getting aid in all five are just about 100 percent if you're the sort of student we've been talking about—and aid that's worth thousands of dollars, as you'll see.

 Important information about each of these aid sources is given in the later chapters on getting financial aid (Chapters 8–10). Here we only highlight these sources in giving you the big picture.

The first five sources for you to be certain to go after are these, along with the amount of aid each year you could probably get from each one:

Basic Educational Opportunity Grant program (federal)	$1,400
Supplementary Educational Opportunity Grant program (federal)	$ 500
College work-study program (federal; job aid)	$ 400
Scholarship from the college you go to	$ 500
State grant program (which your state probably has)	$ 800
TOTAL	$3,600

So there's $3,600 a year in aid that you're very likely to get if you just apply for it and follow through on requirements. That's enough to cover all your costs for a four-year college education living on campus at your state university (in just about any state).

And you have still more very good possibilities—lots more as long as you don't run out of financial need.

Want More? Go on to These Programs for Another $1,000 or More a Year

Three more kinds of programs and what they might be worth a year are these:

State scholarship program (if your state has one)	$500
A community, private-agency scholarship program	$500
ROTC scholarship	jackpot all by itself

For any of these three kinds of scholarships, you'd be competing on the basis largely of test scores, marks, and character with other young men and women who have had more advantages than you. Your character could give you an edge here. You should certainly try in such competitions, anyway; many young people with backgrounds like yours win in them every year. On an ROTC scholarship, incidentally, you'd get all your college expenses paid except some part of room-and-board costs (which could be covered by a surefire aid form like a Basic Educational Opportunity Grant, mentioned before). And on graduating you'd become an officer in the army, navy, marines, or air force to go on active duty for a few years and 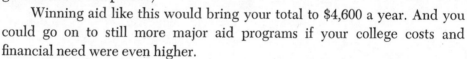 inactive reserve duty for several years more—all at pretty good pay. (More details on ROTC scholarships—as with all the other aid programs—are given later in Chapter 9.)

Winning aid like this would bring your total to $4,600 a year. And you could go on to still more major aid programs if your college costs and financial need were even higher.

Still Further Aid—Absolutely Sure up to $2,500 a Year More

Two more large financial aid programs in which you'd be completely certain to get still further aid you might need (in the hefty amounts shown) are these:

National Direct Student Loan Program	up to $2,500 a year
Guaranteed Student Loan Program	up to $2,500 a year

You'd probably take out aid totaling no more than $2,500 a year between the two programs or from one or the other (rather than the $2,500 maximum a year from both for a $5,000 total). The programs provide loan aid that has to be paid back in installments (over a period as long as ten years after college), and it's wise for a college student not to take on debts of more than about that $2,500 a year for the four college years. (It's also wise for a student who does run up $10,000 in college debts to train for a good-paying field in college.)

Between the two programs, by the way, the National Direct Student Loans are better for you because interest on them is only 3 percent (compared to 7 percent on the guaranteed loans).

Getting $2,500 a year like this would bring your total aid up to $7,100 a year—an amount well within range of the few top-cost colleges in the country. If you got admitted to one—and these and most other colleges work hard to interest students like you in applying—the college would almost surely make up the several hundred dollars beyond $7,100 you'd need for its costs (probably in additional scholarship funds).

That's how you really could make it into any college today—right on up through the top-cost ones—by using one after another of the big major programs of financial aid. You can do it, given the ability and the need.

Beyond all this major financial aid, you also have programs of special help that could prove very important to you. We tell you about these and give you their addresses below.

HELP THAT'S YOURS FOR THE ASKING FROM SPECIAL PROGRAMS FOR POVERTY-LEVEL, MINORITY-GROUP STUDENTS

Most programs designed specifically to help poverty-level, minority-group students go to college provide special counseling and/or special help with studies. Some are entirely or partly financial aid programs, though. Almost all are only for U.S. citizens. This section includes only a few of the better-known special programs for poverty/minority students. You might locate smaller ones in your own area—ones run by school systems, community service organizations, or individual colleges—by asking in your school, library, or other community center. We give the financial aid programs first, then the others.

✓ Special Programs Providing Financial Aid

For any minority-group student, any study field. Supplementary scholarship program of the National Scholarship Service and Fund for Negro Students (NSSFNS). The main work of the service is counseling students of any minority group to help them get college admission and financial aid. It also awards supplementary scholarships of up to some $600 a year, each designed to fill the need gap of students it has helped to get far more aid from other sources. (Some fifty students a year have received such awards in past years.)

Addresses of the National Scholarship Service and Fund for Negro Students are 1776 Broadway, New York, N.Y. 10019 and Southeastern Regional Office, 931-1/2 Hunter St., Atlanta, Ga. 31314.

For any minority-group student, accounting studies. Education fund of the American Institute of Certified Public Accountants. The small fund provides grants for minority-group students who plan full-time studies with accounting majors (assisting some thirty-five students in amounts from $250 to $1,000 each in past years). The institute also provides minority-student aid funds through many colleges.

Address of the institute is 1211 Avenue of the Americas, New York, N.Y. 10036.

For any Black student. National Achievement Scholarship Program for Outstanding Negro Students of the National Merit Scholarship Corporation. For details on this substantial program, see page 135.

For any Native American Indian student. Bureau of Indian Affairs Higher Education Assistance Program. For details on this substantial program, see page 115.

States providing special college aid funds for Native American students include Alaska, Arizona, Florida, Minnesota, Montana, Nebraska, New York, North Dakota, South Dakota, and Wisconsin. Information about each of these state funds may be requested from the addresses listed under the state names on pages 118–30.

Special Programs Providing Counseling and Help with Studies

For any poverty-level student, federally backed "TRIO" programs. TRIO is the official name for three types of widespread federal programs of special services for poverty-level students, with the services funded by federal support totaling $70 million annually in past years. Each program type and the services in it are as follows:

Talent Search programs. Talent Search programs are for students currently enrolled in high school. They provide counseling and other help with getting admission and aid for college on an individual basis. Talent search agencies are located in many major cities and on many college campuses throughout the country.

Upward Bound programs. Students are usually admitted to Upward Bound programs after they finish their second or third year of high school. Students in the programs generally live on a college campus during the summer and continue Upward Bound activities (tutoring sessions, meetings, field trips, home visits, special counseling with special tutors, counselors and teachers) throughout the school year. Parents often join in the programs. Help is given in the programs with applying to college and getting financial aid.

Special Services programs. These programs are for students who have already been admitted to college or are already attending college. The programs help students through tutoring during the college year or in summer and with reading and English-language capabilities. The programs also assist students with finding and applying for financial aid, and with planning careers and finding jobs.

You may ask if one or more of these three types of TRIO programs are available to you by writing:

> Division of Student Services and Veterans Programs, Bureau of Postsecondary Education, Office of Education, U.S. Department of Health, Education and Welfare, Washington, D.C. 20202.

For any minority-group student, engineering studies. Minority Engineering Education Effort (ME³) is a program backed by several professional engineering societies. It provides free information on college programs and financial aid for students with interest and aptitude for studies in engineering, and refers students to other sources of help.

> Address of the Minority Engineering Education Effort is 345 E. 47th St., New York, N.Y. 10017.

For any Black student. Black students may obtain counseling and information about colleges and financial aid from chapters of each of two organizations across the country. Locations of chapters offering these services are available on request to each organization, as follows:

> *National Association for the Advancement of Colored People* (NAACP), 1790 Broadway, New York, N.Y. 10019.
>
> *National Urban League,* 477 Madison Ave., New York, N.Y. 10022.

For any Latin-American student. Financial aid information is available to Latin-American students from:

> League of United Latin American Citizens, National Education Service Centers, 400 First St., N.W., Washington, D.C. 20001.

For any Mexican-American student. Counseling and assistance with applying for college admission and financial aid may be gotten by Mexican-American students from either of two organizations:

> *El Congreso Nacional De Asuntos Colegiales,* 6601 Dyer St., El Paso, Tex. 79904.
>
> *Director of Office of Spanish Speaking Fomento,* American Association of Community and Junior Colleges, One Dupont Circle, N.W., Washington, D.C. 20036.

For any Puerto Rican student. ASPIRA of New York, Inc., is an organization that serves Spanish-speaking students, primarily Puerto Ricans. Its services include free counseling on college and financial aid and counseling after students enter college.

> ASPIRA of New York's address is 245 Fifth Ave., New York, N.Y. 10016.

PUBLICATIONS FOR COLLEGE-BOUND, MINORITY-GROUP STUDENTS

It might be helpful for you to write for a copy of these publications giving information and advice for minority-group students interested in college and financial aid:

> *Going Right On.* Available free from College Board Publication Orders, Box 2815, Princeton, N.J. 08540.
>
> *How to Pay for Your Health Career Education; A Guide for Minority Students.* Available from Bureau of Health Resources Development, Health Resources Administration, U.S. Department of Health, Education and Welfare, 9000 Rockville Pike, Bethesda, Md. 20014.
>
> *Scholarships for American Indian Youth.* Available from Bureau of Indian Affairs Higher Education Program, 5301 Central Ave., N.E., Albuquerque, N. Mex. 87108.
>
> You might also want to consult in a library the latest edition of *Directory of Special Programs for Minority Group Members* (published by Garrett Park Press, Garrett Park, Md. 20766).

GETTING AID
FROM COLLEGES

APPLY. Apply, that is, not only as an applicant for admission but most certainly also as an applicant for financial aid at the colleges you're considering.

That's your first essential rule for getting aid from colleges. Does it sound too simple to you? Well, a New Jersey commission found in 1974 that, of all college students in the state, only 44 percent had applied to their colleges for aid—and that some seven out of every ten students who had failed to apply came from families having annual incomes of $10,000 or less!

Much the same findings have been made by other states across the country. California's State Scholarship and Loan Commission learned that in 1972, for instance, some two-thirds of its college students from low-income families had failed to apply for aid. A 1975 Pennsylvania study discovered that nearly one in five college students whose families had incomes of less than $9,000 a year had also failed to apply.

Apply *early*.

That's rule two. Many colleges set their application deadlines for scholarships *earlier* by several months than their application deadlines for admission. By delaying, you might miss chances at many college-awarded scholarships.

Applying early can help even at colleges with comparatively late application deadlines for financial aid—ones in May or June. For at colleges like these, the more desirable grant funds and scholarship funds tend to be awarded first, to the early birds. Latecomers tend to be offered mostly or only job or loan aid.

What's early? Before January 1, if you're planning to enter college the following fall, more than nine months later. January 1 is about the earliest deadline date for financial aid applications you'll run into as a fall entrant. It's been the actual deadline date for Harvard, Yale, and Stanford in recent years, for example. (But watch out for up-to-date deadline details in current college bulletins you get: The University of Colorado has wanted applications in from out-of-state students as early as December 1.) Of course, making it before January 1 or still earlier means that you've got to get rolling months ahead of that, picking out possible colleges and writing to them for their information and forms.

By the way, try to avoid being a midyear college entrant and applicant for financial aid if you can. Some colleges (possibly including ones you may want to attend) admit no midyear entrants. And at most colleges financial aid tends to be completely committed to the large majority of students who enter each fall. Only awards that become available by chance may be on hand for midyear entrants.

MANY REASONS FOR APPLYING TO COLLEGES FOR AID— AND ALMOST NONE AGAINST

Whatever your situation, you have all kinds of reasons to apply for aid as well as admission from colleges.

• It's the only way to be considered for the college's aid if you would have financial need at the college.

• Even if you absolutely would not have need, it could put you in line for no-need scholarships offered by the college that you may not know of.

• It's the only avenue to several large federal programs of financial aid.

• It almost never detracts from your chances of admission at a college where you'd especially like to go. A college most often decides first on admission among its applicants, and then goes back and decides on its offers of financial aid. After all, when it's deciding, the college has no way of knowing whether you'll get aid from some of the many other sources providing aid today. The college can easily admit you yet deny your application for financial aid (making you one of those "admit-deny" applicants we talked about earlier).

About the only reason against applying for college aid is the extra trouble and expense to which it would put you. This expense could be as low as $4 or $5 for having a copy of your family financial statement form sent to a college (plus $2 or $3 per college for each additional college to which you want a copy sent). It might also include some $12 to $15 in fees for tests a college requires for financial aid applicants in addition to those it requires for admissions applicants.

STEPS TO TAKE FOR GETTING AID FROM COLLEGES—
AND FOR INCREASING YOUR CHANCES OF GETTING IT

Now that you realize how it could benefit you to apply and apply *early* to colleges for aid, you'll want to know how you might best go about it. The rest of this chapter gives you helpful pointers in outlining a series of major steps to take. These are:

1. *Selecting colleges to increase your financial aid chances.* (There's quite a lot to this step, as you'll see, because your opportunities for aid from colleges are many and complex.)

2. *Applying for admission with financial aid.* (This steers you through the involved process of actually applying.)

3. *Pressured decisions you may face after applying.* (This gives you background information on a painful step that may be forced on you under present systems used by colleges for offering you admission and aid.)

Selecting Colleges for Your Best Financial Aid Possibilities

Virtually all colleges today award financial aid. But which colleges you choose can make a difference of perhaps a thousand dollars a year or more in the financial aid you might get—and also in whether you get more desirable scholarship or grant aid instead of loans. We tell you here how you might adapt your selections of colleges to increase your chances of getting aid—aid of the more desirable, no-strings types.

You probably realize already that students with higher academic qualifications have better chances of getting college-awarded aid, scholarship aid in particular. Trying for scholarships will result in more likelihood of success if you're an above-average student and test-taker. That's especially true for no-need scholarships, which a college offers in order to attract high-ability students. But students who can get admitted to a college at which they have financial need are today often awarded enough loan aid and job aid (with perhaps small amounts of grant aid) to meet their need. Don't worry too much about your academic qualifications for aid, then, except for scholarship possibilities. Generally speaking, if you can get into a college where you have need today, then the college will offer you at least loan and job aid.

Start with Your "Natural" Choices of Colleges

Begin with those college possibilities that come naturally to you. These are the colleges your family, friends, teachers, or neighbors talk about as ones you might go to, or that they think are good ones. They're colleges you've read about, ones you've heard about in your part of the country, or ones where older brothers and sisters of your friends are going or have gone.

To improve your financial aid chances, start looking into colleges if possible not later than about a year and a half before you'll enter—in the winter of your third high school year (if you'll start college the fall after finishing high school). This is a little earlier than guidance counselors in your school probably schedule formal sessions with college-bound students and their parents for college guidance. But you might go out of your way then to press for an early preliminary conference on good colleges for you with your counselor. Doing this can help give you lead time to hunt for more or better financial aid than you'd otherwise get.

Expand Your "Natural" College Choices to Cover the Range of Your College-Cost Options

Once you've reached decisions on your "natural" college choices, you'll perhaps have something like your state university and two or three private four-year colleges. Or you may have your local community college plus a state four-year college.

At this point, consider what we said earlier in Chapter 2 about your full range of possible college-cost options. If you didn't do it then, this is the time to do some thinking and figuring to set up the particular range of college-cost options that seems most advisable in your own case. The range you work out should span from the least-expensive possibility that could feasibly realize the kind of college education you want to the most-expensive you might be able to manage (using full fair shares of assets and income plus all the financial aid for which you could conceivably qualify).

For example, here's a set of cost options like those across which you should spread your college-financing alternatives:

1. Community college (a low-cost option of about $400 per year for tuition and fees)

2. State university or state four-year college (a moderately low-cost option of about $620 per year for tuition and fees)

3. Private college of moderately high cost (with tuition-and-fees charges running from about $2,700 to $4,000 a year)

4. Private college of high cost (tuition and fees per year from about $4,000 and up)

(Your own options could of course run to still less-expensive possibilities and include refinements like alternatives of commuting to college rather than paying room and board as a dorm student or special options like co-op work-study programs, service academies, or credit-by-examination that were identified in Chapter 2.)

Now, take your own set of cost options like these and compare your initial "natural" college choices against them. (You'll obviously be able to get costs at different colleges that you'll need in doing this from current college directories and catalogs in your high school or community library.)

Do you then see any options for which you have no college names? Maybe you've skipped the community-college possibility. Or perhaps you have no high-cost private colleges.

For any blanks like these, go back to what you've heard about colleges and to your directories and catalogs to find other appropriate colleges for you that fill in those open options.

Don't shrink from extending your least-expensive options for fear of being completely out of place at a college for just very low-income people if certain low-cost colleges offer academic work of the kind you want with adequate academic quality. Remember that "subcultures" exist within any college's student body. While students at some low-cost college may be mainly from low-income families, you're apt to find that small groups of students (subcultures) from affluent families also go there.

In addition, don't shrink from extending your most-expensive options, either, for fear of crushing college expense. A college with very high charges might not prove expensive at all in your case. The somewhat involved reasons for this are explained in the following sections.

Your "High-Cost" Options Might Be Made "Low-Cost" Ones to You through Financial Aid

Through financial aid, it might be no more costly in your case to go to an expensive college than to a low-cost college.

Many students for whom this generally holds true don't realize it. In one recent study, costs were judged by college-bound students to be the most important kind of information about colleges they needed in order to decide on which ones to try to attend.

Having more information about costs and financial aid at different types of colleges would lead many college-bound students to change their minds about the kind of college they would attend, it was found in another recent study. This was a survey of some 5,000 young people in seven states (California, Massachusetts, Virginia, Illinois, Oregon, Michigan, and Ohio; the survey was made in the "Better Information for Student Choice" project of the College Scholarship Service, College Entrance Examination Board).

Large proportions of these students at all family income levels planned to attend lower-cost public colleges (low-income, 92 percent; middle-income, 89 percent; high-income, 75 percent).

But more than half of these students reported that more information about costs and financial aid at different types of colleges would change their minds about the kinds of colleges they'd attend. Proportions of those who said that better aid information would change their minds varied by income level (low-income, 71 percent; middle-income, 57 percent; high-income, 38 percent).

Surprising Fact:
For Many Students Today, Colleges Charge on a Sliding Scale

Clearly, students in the survey had begun to understand a surprising fact that could be vital for you to realize in selecting possible colleges:

A college's financial aid awards mean that, in effect, the college charges some students not at its stated, fixed rates (for items like tuition and fees, room and board), but on a sliding scale.

Let's take a typical example illustrating this. Suppose that you (or your child) had been a student at a well-known liberal arts college in Ohio, Oberlin College, in 1975–76. Oberlin at that time figured on total student expense budgets of some $5,600 a year (a figure that had risen to about $6,400 in 1977–78, incidentally).

But in a special, new kind of report on its financial aid program for 1975–76, Oberlin showed these "net costs" to families for the student's 1975–76 year, according to family income levels:

Dependent Students from Families with Incomes

Average net cost to the family for 1975–76	under $9,000	$9,000– $15,000	$15,000– $21,000	$21,000– $27,000	$27,000 and above
	$1,138	$1,927	$2,527	$3,069	$3,407

The difference between each of these "net costs" for the year and Oberlin's student-expense-budget total of $5,600 was made up by financial aid.

Rather clearly, then, this looks very much like a sliding scale of charges, with amount based on family ability to pay.

First Proviso: The picture isn't quite as rosy as only this suggests, however. Those "net costs" above held true only for the 43 percent of Oberlin undergraduates getting aid that year. A majority of the students— the other 57 percent—paid the full $5,600 expenses.

Second Proviso: Oberlin also points out that the first $1,500 in aid it awarded 1975–76 students at any family income levels was what it admirably calls "self-help," i.e., job and loan aid. That left the most desirable, no-strings grant aid received by the students (and from all sources, not just Oberlin) ranging in averages from $3,043 (for the under-$9,000 students) to only $791 (for the $27,000-and-above students). It seems fair to say that what is in effect Oberlin's "sliding scale" of charges slid that year only as far as these grant amounts, not to the lower "net cost" amounts shown above.

Main Point:
Financial Aid Frees You Somewhat to Consider High-Cost Private Colleges
What all this comes down to is that you should not arbitrarily rule out considering high-cost private colleges because you can't afford them. If you've got the academic and other qualifications to get you admitted to these expensive colleges, go ahead. Ironically, today more than ever, the lower your family income, the better chance you have of getting enough

aid to go to an expensive college—with especially high proportions of non-returnable (grant or scholarship) aid.

Your prospect at an expensive college isn't quite as enticing if you're in a middle-income or high-income family, however. Expensive colleges that admit you will probably see that your need is met. But in doing so they are likely to award you some job aid that ties up your time and substantial amounts of loan aid that you must repay.

By contrast, at a low-cost public college of good academic quality, you could probably get through with less or perhaps nothing to repay in loans.

You'll have to decide in your specific situation if probably heavier loan obligations after graduating from a more-expensive college would be worth it. Many thousands of people today think they are. However, many thousands of other people think they're not.

Special Case:
For Athletic Scholarships, Talk to Your Coach
You have very special opportunities for financial aid from colleges, incidentally, if you're a very outstanding athlete in a popular intercollegiate sport and want to spend much of your time in college on athletics. A whole system of athletic grants-in-aid or scholarships awaits you. These grants pay tuition and fees, room and board plus some $15 a month, and are awarded regardless of need. They are offered by several hundred colleges that are powers in sports.

Your high school coach is probably your best source of information on these colleges and grants, and on which coaches at these colleges might be interested in you. Talk to your present school coach about these special opportunities for financial aid. However, for academic guidance concerning these colleges, talk also to a guidance counselor at your school.

There's one possible drawback to these grants-in-aid that could pose serious problems for your college education. Under present regulations of the NCAA (National Collegiate Athletic Association) on the grants, they are renewable from year to year only if you continue to make the team in your sport. Should you be injured, otherwise off your game, or have a major disagreement with your college coach, your grant could accordingly end. That could finish your college education if you had to have the grant in order to attend.

As noted before, the Ivy League colleges do not award such athletic scholarships. Athletes at these colleges are awarded need-based, renewable scholarships on the same terms as all other scholarship recipients. (These colleges are Brown, Columbia, Cornell, Dartmouth, Harvard, Pennsylvania, Princeton, and Yale.)

Look into your chances for an athletic grant in aid, then, if you're interested and are also among the comparatively few students who might qualify for one. But keep your other options open at the same time in case you wouldn't get one, or might later decide against the regimentation often imposed on star college athletes.

Check Your Expanded College Choices To See What Financial Aid They Offer

Next on your agenda for selecting colleges to increase your overall aid chances comes the step of checking up on the possible colleges you've chosen across your own range of cost options.

1. Take each college you've picked and see what financial aid it offers. Look first in the directories and catalogs in which you've already found out about such other features of these colleges as their costs and academic programs.

2. Put a big question mark next to any college at which you'd have financial need that does not appear to offer at least some scholarships, federal or state guaranteed loans, and job aid. Put a plus mark after any college that reports especially extensive or large scholarship offerings (as far as you can tell), or offerings of the 3-percent interest National Defense Student Loans.

3. Then go after financial aid information in earnest for each of the colleges remaining that don't have a big question mark or do have a plus. Write to each one requesting complete, up-to-date information and forms sent to applicants for admission with financial aid, along the lines of the sample letter shown here.

Sample Letter for Requesting Financial Aid Information and Forms

(Type if possible; otherwise handwrite very legibly and neatly)

> Your street address
> Your town, state, postal zipcode
> Date

Director of Admissions
Name of college
Street address of college (may not be needed)
Town, state, postal zipcode

Dear Sir or Madame:

Please send me the complete, current information and application forms that you provide for applicants for admission with financial aid.

I am a student at (full name of your present high school) in (its town, state), and will graduate in (month, year).

I am interested in entering (name of college) as a freshman in (month, year).

Thank you.

Sincerely yours,

(Your signature)

Your name (printed or typed)

What To Look for—and Look Out for— in Financial Aid Information from a College

In the folders or booklets you'll get from each college, look for incisive and specific facts from which you can estimate your chances of qualifying for each kind of aid it offers and how much of each kind of aid you might get. Look especially for data like this about scholarships and grants—the most desirable forms of aid. Look for such facts on no-need scholarships if that's what you're hunting for.

Look out, on the other hand, for high-flown general statements and long lists of named scholarships that, though broadly encouraging, leave you in the dark on what specific aid might be realistic to expect in your own case.

It's likely that you'll see little of the first kind of information and lots of the second kind. Colleges thus far are often lofty but evasive in leveling with the public about the financial aid they offer. Public as well as private colleges often compete strenuously for students (and consequent income) in this era of declining college enrollments. Most colleges are thus under pressure to make their financial aid offerings sound much better than they really are. They're similarly pressed to obscure their full (and rising) costs.

What would reasonably detailed and factual information look like? You can tell from several samples given on pages 100–102. These are reports worked out as a public service by a few pioneering colleges, in cooperative efforts between the U.S. Office of Education and associations of colleges to provide better consumer information on colleges.

The sample reports give fairly incisive data on costs and financial aid programs in the 1975–76 academic years for three colleges representative of types you may be choosing:

University of California at Irvine—a state university

Oberlin College—a rather high-cost, private four-year liberal arts college (in Oberlin, Ohio)

Mount Empire Community College—a typically low-cost, public two-year community college (in Big Stone Gap, Virginia)

The form of these reports and the information given in them by these colleges were developed in the "Better Information for Student Choice Project" of the College Scholarship Service, College Entrance Examination Board. (This work in the project was carried out under a grant from the Fund for the Improvement of Postsecondary Education, U.S. Office of Education, as part of the National Task Force on Better Information for Student Choice. These three college reports are reprinted by permission from the College Entrance Examination Board publication *Making It Count; A Report on a Project to Provide Better Financial Aid Information to Students*, issued by the board in 1977.)

With luck, you'll get financial aid information in this detailed form from increasing numbers of colleges in years ahead.

Let's look at a few of the important things you could tell about your own case from these reports, as examples of actually using information like this.

All three reports start with a full listing of what your costs would be at the college (the top half of the page headed "I. STUDENT EXPENSE BUDGETS"). The listings also represent the kind of student expense budget that the financial aid office at each college would use in figuring your financial need.

But that second half of the reports—the bottom half of the page headed "II. AID RECEIVED BY STUDENTS"—can give you answers to all kinds of important questions about possible aid. Here are some examples, using these three college reports.

Where might you get the most in scholarship aid? Look across the line labeled "Average grant." Oberlin's figures there range from $3,043 for the lowest-income bracket to $791 for the highest income bracket. Irvine's similarly range from $1,857 to $237. Clearly, Oberlin is the better bet for larger amounts in scholarship aid.

But where would you be saddled with less cost in loans? Look at the "Average loan" line. Oberlin's figures are about $1,000 in loan aid a year across all income brackets. Irvine's, by contrast, range from some $500 to $300 a year in loan aid across income brackets (for students dependent on their families). From a lower-loan standpoint, Irvine appears the better bet. It might be even better than the community college, Mount Empire, if you're in the $9,000–$15,000 income bracket where Mount Empire shows an "average loan" figure of $1,366.

Would you find any fellow students from upper-income families at Mount Empire? Yes—5 percent of its students are from families with $21,000-and-up income; 2 percent are in the $27,000-and-up bracket. At Irvine? Yes—some 8 percent of the students receiving aid there are in the $21,000-and-up brackets (with lots more from such affluent families not receiving aid). You might also note that more than half of Oberlin's students are from $21,000-and-up families—and also that more than half receive no form of aid (but that one in every ten students in the $27,000-and-up bracket receives total aid averaging $2,193).

Does financial aid at Oberlin tend to equalize what families pay out of pocket (their "average net cost") compared to a state university? In one sense, yes. The report's bottom line tells this story. In Oberlin's report, that "average net cost" line ranges from $1,138 to $3,407 across income brackets (as we saw before), and these figures are all lower than Irvine's "student expense budget" total of $3,720 for students living on campus. But in another sense, no. When you take into account the effect of financial aid at Irvine as reflected in its bottom line, its "average net cost" figures for aid recipients across income brackets are consistently lower than Oberlin's by several hundred dollars.

You can similarly cross-check reports in this form for many other questions you have. Take job aid or "work aid," for instance. You'd be almost certain to get some aid through a campus job as an aid recipient at Irvine, where percentages of those awarded work aid range across income brackets from 95 to 100 percent. But your chances of being awarded work aid would be less at Oberlin if you're in a $15,000-and-up income bracket (where those percentages range from 77 percent to 42 percent with increasing income).

What about no-need scholarships? A second page of these reports (which isn't reprinted here) states that for each of these three colleges the institution's policy concerning no-need scholarships (gift assistance to students who do not have any financial need) is the following:

> *Oberlin*—"Oberlin does not grant no-need awards."

> *Irvine*—"The University of California, Irvine, has few no-need scholarships. The university does award no-need scholarships when monies are available for them."

> *Mount Empire*—"Restricted funds predetermine recipients. Non-restricted scholarships are based on need." (What this probably means is that Mount Empire has a few no-need scholarships, probably small in amount, for which the scholarship fund donor has restricted the field of study or other requirement for the scholarships.)

One big question you still can't answer from reports of this type is, "What qualifications do I need in order to have good chances of winning a scholarship at this college?"

How you can get answers to this basic question is explained in the next section, which focuses on hunting down colleges with your best possibilities for scholarships and other aid.

Look for Colleges that Increase Your Chances for Aid, Scholarship Aid in Particular

In your hands at this stage are your range of college-cost options, names of colleges corresponding to each option, and current financial aid and admissions information from each college. Your main step now is to see if you can add to or substitute among those colleges in order to increase your chances of getting college-awarded aid.

Among colleges fitting your options and study plans, it's not like adding or substituting for community colleges or state universitie. colleges would have much effect on your aid prospects. Aid at commu colleges is offered mainly for very low-income students and drawn ma. from state and federal sources. Aid programs are likely to be much t same for all community colleges in your state.

Aid programs at state universities and colleges in any one state similarly tend to be about the same, as they depend on current funding by the state legislature for all state institutions as a whole. There's one possible exception to this that you might look into, though. The largest or oldest state university in a number of states may have more aid funds than newer state universities or state colleges—places like the University of Michigan, the University of Mississippi, or the University of Oregon. You might write to the institution like this in your state for financial aid information and forms if it would be feasible in your plans and you haven't yet included it on your list.

It's among private colleges, though, that your choices might make the most difference in the financial aid you get. Look for several private colleges feasible in your plans that seem to have larger or better financial aid programs than the private colleges you've already chosen. In general, colleges with more-expensive tuition charges offer larger financial aid programs and scholarships.

You have several places to look. Ask your guidance counselor and your friends. Search further in those by now well-thumbed directories and catalogs. One directory widely available in high schools and libraries that's especially good for such financial aid searching is *The College Handbook*, issued in revised editions every other fall by the College Entrance Examination Board.

The College Handbook is put out by:
  College Entrance Examination Board
  Publication Orders
  Box 2815
  Princeton, N.J. 08540

Another college directory that pioneers in reporting on "no-need" scholarships provided by colleges—as well as giving unique facts on the size and extent of their need-based scholarships and athletic grants-in-aid —is written by a co-author of this book. It is:

Guide to Colleges, by Gene R. Hawes
New American Library, Inc.
1301 Avenue of the Americas
New York, N.Y. 10019

Watch the local news media for information, especially of new scholarship programs offered by colleges in your area. When you find clues to more or better aid at a college, write to it for information and compare its offerings with those of colleges you already know about.

Be alert to possibilities wherever they may crop up. For instance, had you been reading the May 16, 1977, issue of *Newsweek* you would have seen a full-page ad on the University of Delaware's Freshman Honors Program for 150 students. The ad noted, among other features, that "special scholarships" are awarded to all students in the program and that "additional aid based on need" is also available to them. Obviously, here is an offering of 150 no-need scholarships for students with unusually high academic qualifications. (But note that these are scholarships for one year only. Sound practice on college scholarships calls for the donor to provide them on an annually renewable basis until the recipient earns the degree sought—usually in two or four years of full-time study.)

You'll probably have a chance to look into many college possibilities all at once on certain occasions you can watch for. These are the "college days," "college nights," or "college fairs" that your high school may run (or join in sponsoring with other high schools). Admissions representatives from dozens of different colleges typically attend these affairs in order to talk with the college-bound students for whom they are given. At such a meeting you can talk firsthand with the representatives of a number of colleges about financial aid, getting answers to key questions relevant to your specific situation and interests. Doing this could save you much literature searching and letter writing.

If you want, you can even open up avenues for possibly getting offers of financial aid from colleges at their initiative. Two means for doing this follow. If you'll be taking the Scholastic Aptitude Test (SAT) of the College Board to meet college admissions requirements, you can open one avenue by indicating on your SAT registration form that you want to be included in the board's Student Search Service. Also, give the answers requested in the "student descriptive questionnaire" part of the form.

Colleges interested in attracting groups of students with characteristics like yours may then obtain your name and address from the board and write to you about their academic and aid offerings. Naturally, the characteristics of yours most likely to attract such mailings are high SAT scores and academic record in school, or possibly minority-group status on your part. (Incidentally, private agencies offering scholarships may also approach you through the service.)

You would have to pay a fee of some $35 to open the other avenue for possibly getting offers of admission and financial aid from colleges that first contact you rather than the other way round. You would take this approach through the College Admissions Center of the National Association of College Admissions Counselors. Registration at this center (for which the fee is charged) would put records you file there before hundreds of colleges across the country that use its services. The records you file would be much like those you complete in applying to a college for admission and aid. Registering should bring letters from at least several colleges—or from dozens, if your qualifications are unusually good. If you're interested, request information by writing:

> College Admissions Center,
> National Association of College Admissions Counselors,
> 801 Davis St., Evanston, Ill. 60201.

One Key Tactic for Maximizing Your Scholarship Chances: Apply to Colleges Where You'd Be a Very Desirable Student

Colleges use scholarships to attract students of the kinds they particularly want. Acting on this with some insight is one of the most effective ways of increasing your chances at scholarships, especially of large scholarship proportions in college-awarded aid.

Remember in your college searching that you can be rejected for admission by some colleges yet still be admitted with scholarship aid by other colleges. This actually happens to many thousands of students every year. It does because high-prestige colleges attract large pileups of applicants with qualifications ranging from good to excellent among whom the colleges pick and choose. But hundreds of other colleges are straining to attract, admit, and aid students with high qualification—students like those whom prestige colleges are often rejecting.

You need at least quite good qualifications for college in order to take advantage of these facts—qualifications like entrance test scores above the seventy-fifth or eightieth percentile among college-bound students, high school course grades averaging about B-plus (3.5 on an A = 4.0 scale) or, better, high school class rank in the top quarter or top tenth, and preferably a record of extracurricular activity in high school with some distinction.

If you have qualifications of this order, look for perhaps two or three colleges in other parts of the country at which these qualities would put you in the top quarter or top tenth of the college's student body. It isn't at all easy to identify such colleges. Most colleges today try to hide the ability levels of their students from the public in order to protect their reputations. (Ability levels of students at most private colleges today are relatively low.) But you should be able to find colleges like this by talking with your guidance counselor, digging in directories like *The College Handbook* and perhaps in college catalogs, and talking with college representatives at "college night" meetings.

These would be quite good private colleges, well known in their locales but not nationally, and probably ones that get stiff competition from large, strong, low-cost state university systems (as in the Midwest and West). Picking such colleges in other parts of the country adds luster to your application, for these colleges give preference to faraway applicants in admission. Attracting students from many distant states and some foreign countries is part of a private college's reputation for which it is willing to pay in scholarship aid. Another prized part of its reputation is its attraction for students with high qualifications. (Even good state universities feel the need to go to some lengths to draw high-caliber students, as evidenced in the special University of Delaware ad mentioned earlier.)

Short of turning yourself into a genius-level, minority-group, school-activities-celebrity applicant, a step like this should give you your largest chances for getting college-awarded scholarship aid, and aid with the largest scholarship proportions in financial aid "packages" you'll be offered.

One last word of caution. Some colleges will award a rather large proportion of scholarship aid in a student's financial aid package for the freshman year but then, for later years, reduce the student's scholarship substantially while raising the loan amount. Private colleges especially may feel unavoidably forced to this expedient by today's fiscal pressures. Nevertheless, this could deeply change your long-term college costs if it happened to you. You'd find it very hard to ascertain if this has typically occurred at a college you're considering. One way might be to ask various students there who hold scholarships if this did happen to them while you were on a visit to the campus to judge it generally firsthand. Or, if your scholarship were thus cut while you were already in college, you might plan to transfer to a lower-cost college.

Set Your Final College Choices for Applying

After all your exploring and talking along the lines outlined above, you'll have a well-chosen selection of colleges to which you plan to apply for admission with aid. Take one last look through your possible colleges to weed out ones that may be least attractive to you or least promising for aid. Also, be ready to add another good bet or two if you should learn of them while you're in the process of applying to colleges that we describe next.

Applying to Colleges for Admission with Financial Aid

Get used to the idea that it's real work and often exasperating to apply to colleges for admission with financial aid. Expect the process to involve bureaucratic red tape at its most annoying, for it can combine all the worst features of government-agency dealings, job applications, and income tax returns. Applying for aid seems so confusing, frustrating, and laborious to some students and families that they simply throw up their hands and say to hell with it. But they forget the stakes they may have in going through with it—stakes that can amount to $10,000 or more over a four-year college education.

Your attitude right from the outset can therefore be crucial. Start early. Relax. Take your time. Remember all the money this should bring you. Be very systematic, going ahead in an alert, step-by-step way after you've first organized carefully just how you'll complete each application. Answer any questions or requests that seem confusing in the most reasonable and simple way that occurs to you after reflection. Don't get upset. If you feel yourself about to blow up at some point, leave it. Then go back to it when you've calmed down.

Assume that everything asked for is needed, whether or not it seems to make any sense at all. Everything will be needed to keep you in the running for money. It's standard operating procedure for colleges to consider only applications that are complete and that contain all required supporting documents. Leaving out one piece or answer might make all your other work on an application go for naught.

Applying itself will cost you an aggravating amount of money as well as an aggravating amount of time. Application fees that you send with your completed application form to a college run some $15 to $25 and up these days. Applying to five colleges can hence cost $75 or more in college application fees. There's no additional college fee charged applicants who apply for financial aid, presumably because they're needy.

There are fees beyond those for college applications, though. Fees for tests that colleges require for admissions applicants can run from some $8 to $20 and are also payable in advance when sending in your registration for the tests. Fees due when sending in your filled-out family financial statement form run some $4 or $5 plus $1.50 to $3 for each college (or private scholarship program) beyond one to which you want copies of the form sent (as required by the college).

All in all, figure on up to $100 or more in your direct, out-of-pocket costs in applying. But if you're really impoverished and can't afford these fees, you or your guidance counselor can write to the colleges and testing/scholarship-service agencies to request that the fees be waived in your case and briefly explain why. The testing/scholarship-service agencies will waive fees at such requests, and most colleges will also.

Here are important general rules to follow through the application process:

1. Make sure to be consistently respectful of any college and serious in characterizing your interest in going there—in all your application answers, interview statements, letters, and even preliminary contacts and conversations with a college's representatives. Each college takes itself and all that it does very seriously. Whatever you may think privately, never deprecate anything about a college from which you're trying to get admission with aid. Be genuinely wise in pursuing your interests instead of an antagonizing "wise guy" who shows off all that he or she knows about colleges. The more you actually know, the more careful you'll be to avoid prejudicing the people associated with an individual college against you.

What if you're asked point-blank, "Is Siwash your first-choice college?" This is a very rude question for a college to ask an applicant, and most colleges don't raise it. But if one should in a conversation or interview, your best answer might be to say that you're extremely interested in Siwash but haven't made your final decision yet (unless, of course, it is your first choice).

2. Set up and follow without fail a schedule of yours for each college. Get current information very early (twelve months before your planned college entrance) from each college on its deadlines for not only the completed application forms themselves but for all the other requirements, like test scores, family financial statement, high school transcript, interviews, school recommendations, possible teachers' recommendations, recommendation letters from former employers, and the like. Set up a checklist of required items and deadline dates, and schedule your efforts to get all of them in to the college on time.

3. Be scrupulously careful in all your paperwork. In filling out any form or writing any letter or other statement that may go into your application file folder at the college, typewrite the document if at all possible. If this is absolutely not possible, fill out all forms in the neatest, most legible careful printing you can do, and handwrite with extreme neatness any letter. First make on scratch paper a working draft of your answers to any application or other form, reviewing and correcting it thoroughly to make sure your answers are exactly right. Follow all instructions to the letter, and check draft answers to see that you have done just as instructed. Then copy your answers, very clearly and error-free, on the form itself. Do the same with any written statements required—such as the short essays on topics like your main reasons for wanting a college education or recent reading you've done that are often called for on admissions applications.

Why go to such trouble? Because everything you send to a college reflects what kind of person you are, and every scrap of it will be gone over by college officers who decide whether or not to award you money. Consider your trouble an investment.

Pressured Decisions You May Face after Applying

Most colleges in the country use schedules for offering you admission and financial aid that can put you through a meat grinder of suspense, as explained below. You can get off the hook by a possible dead-loss cash outlay of $200 or more. In doing this they are being entirely selfish, looking out for their interests and trampling all over yours. But that's the way it is and no one's doing anything that seems at all likely to change it.

We forewarn you here about this obscure, complex, college-application shakedown so you'll know what's happening if you get caught in its grip. We also suggest countermeasures that may be of some help if you do. And you probably will if you follow the advice we've given in the preceding pages.

A few hundred colleges out of the 2,500 or more in the country are the "good guys" in this situation. These few hundred colleges sign the "Candidates Reply Date Agreement" sponsored by the College Entrance Examination Board. Any college signing the agreement pledges that it will not require applicants (whom the College Board has called "candidates" for years) to reply to their offers of admission and aid until May 1.

May 1 is the magic date by which any applicant (for the fall college term) will have received similar offers from all other colleges to which he or she has applied. Usually, the latest offers sent in the spring by sought-after colleges are those of the Ivy League colleges and their self-selected peer colleges, offers that all go out together on April 15 and not before by policy. Another background fact is that almost all the other hundreds of colleges operate on what are called "rolling admissions" schedules in which they notify each applicant of admission and aid offers something like four weeks after all required documents are received.

Now, here's how all this could hit you in the nerves and pocketbook. You've gone ahead and pitched in applications to four or five colleges, including some in that select, Ivy League category. You've gotten all your application credentials in early to better your aid chances.

So it's January 20 of your senior year in high school. In that day's mail comes a letter from a state university or a private college that you like quite well but less than your prestige-college possibilities: "We admit you and offer you a $1,200 renewable scholarship, $600 loan, and $400 campus job," says the letter. It adds that you must accept the offer within two weeks or it will be withdrawn. Your acceptance, it also advises, must be accompanied by a $300 deposit toward your fall-term college bill. It notes too that the $300 is nonreturnable if you don't happen to show up on campus that fall.

That's the shakedown. The generous college has deliberately put you under as much pressure to accept as it dares, out of fear of losing you to a competitor who might do more for you. It exacts a $300 consolation settlement if it loses. There are palliative explanations that can be made (the college of course assumes it's your first-choice institution, it's letting you know early to relieve your suspense, it needs the early reply for orderly planning, and so on). But these seem simply not true.

What do you do then besides rave or sweat? One choice is of course to pay the $300 and stand ready to take it as a complete loss (nondeductible on taxes, at that). About your only other option is to write or phone one or more of the prestige colleges (from which you may not otherwise have a decision until just after April 15) to tell them of the other offer and ask for informal but firm assurances now, or possibly even an official full offer. In some cases they'll help. In others they can't or won't.

It's a tough situation that obviously exploits a substantial sector of the college-going public. Making a reply date like May 1 mandatory for all colleges is the manifest remedy. But there are no signs that anything is under way along these lines to help you out of such a predicament.

Fortunately, pressures like these do not arise in the course of your getting aid from the very large government sources we tell you about in the next chapter.

STUDENT FINANCIAL AID
Statement of Cost and Policy
1975-76 Academic Year

(Insert the Name of the Institution)

OBERLIN COLLEGE

I. STUDENT EXPENSE BUDGETS: The following budgets are those typically used to calculate the financial need of students with the characteristics indicated below. Other
typical budgets can be obtained from the office listed at the bottom of this statement.
Adjustments to these typical budgets are made to reflect special needs of different individual students.

	SINGLE STUDENTS LIVING			MARRIED STUDENTS	
	AT Home	ON Campus	OFF Campus	No Children	Additional Each Child
Number of months covered by budget	9	9	9	Enrollment of married students is too low to establish budgets. Each case is treated indi- vidually.	
Tuition and fees	$ 3588	$ 3588	$ 3588		
Books and supplies	$ 150	$ 150	$ 150		
Room and board	$ 1470	$ 1470	$ 1470		
Transportation –Depends on state of residence.	$_____	$_____	$_____	$_____	$_____
Personal and miscellaneous expenses	$ 300	$ 300	$ 300	$_____	$_____
TOTAL ESTIMATED BUDGET	$ 5508	$ 5508	$ 5508	$_____	$_____

II. AID RECEIVED BY STUDENTS: The following information describes the way in which
financial aid (from all sources) was awarded to undergraduate students last year. It
is provided as an indication of institutional practices with the understanding that individual awards vary according to need and that changes in funding levels may influence
awards in subsequent years.

The number of full-time undergraduates in 1975-76 was   2549

The number and percent of that group receiving some form of aid was   1105   43 %

	DEPENDENT STUDENTS FROM FAMILIES WITH INCOMES					INDEPENDENT STUDENTS	
	Under $9,000	$9,000- $15,000	$15,000- $21,000	$21,000- $27,000	$27,000 and Above	Single	Married
Estimated % of full-time undergraduate students	10.6%	16.6%	16.3%	18.0%	35.5%	2.0%	1.0%
% of aid recipients	26%	40%	20%	9%	3%	1.5%	.5%
Average expense budget	$ 5600	$ 5600	$ 5600	$ 5600	$ 5600	$ 5600	$_____
% receiving any grant	98%	93%	75%	60%	40 %	50%	50%
Average grant	$ 3043	$ 2300	$ 1650	$ 1120	$ 791	$ 2190	$-----
% receiving any loan	97%	95%	94%	96%	97 %	95%	-----%
Average loan	$ 1032	$ 986	$ 1035	$ 1026	$ 1015	$ 916	$_____
% receiving work aid	97 %	96 %	77%	71%	42 %	50%	-----%
Average work income	$ 387	$ 387	$ 387	$ 387	$ 387	$ 387	$----
AVERAGE TOTAL AID	$ 4462	$ 3673	$ 3073	$ 2531	$ 2193	$ 3493	$_____
AVERAGE NET COST TO STUDENT AND PARENT	$ 1138	$ 1927	$ 2527	$ 3069	$ 3407	$ 2107	$_____

Additional information about student expense budgets
and aid received by students can be obtained from
the financial aid office at the address or telephone
number shown here.

Oberlin College, Oberlin, Ohio
(specific location of aid office)
(216) 775-8142
(area code, telephone number, ext.)

STUDENT FINANCIAL AID
Statement of Cost and Policy
1975-76 Academic Year

(Insert the Name of the Institution)
UNIVERSITY OF CALIFORNIA, IRVINE

I. STUDENT EXPENSE BUDGETS: The following budgets are those typically used to calculate the financial need of students with the characteristics indicated below. Other
typical budgets can be obtained from the office listed at the bottom of this statement.
Adjustments to these typical budgets are made to reflect special needs of different individual students.

| | SINGLE STUDENTS LIVING | | | MARRIED STUDENTS | |
	AT Home	ON Campus	OFF Campus	No Children	Additional Each Child
Number of months covered by budget	9	9	9	9	9
Tuition and fees	$ 627	$ 627	$ 627	$ 627	
Books and supplies	$ 243	$ 243	$ 243	$ 243	
Room and board	$ 1600	$ 1900	$ 1900	$ 3000	$
Transportation	$ 400	$ 400	$ 400	$ 650	$
Personal and miscellaneous expenses	$ 200	$ 550	$ 550	$ 850	$
TOTAL ESTIMATED BUDGET	$ 3070	$ 3720	$ 3720	$ 5370	$

600

II. AID RECEIVED BY STUDENTS: The following information describes the way in which
financial aid (from all sources) was awarded to undergraduate students last year. It
is provided as an indication of institutional practices with the understanding that individual awards vary according to need and that changes in funding levels may influence
awards in subsequent years.

The number of full-time undergraduates in 1975-76 was _____ 6484 _____

The number and percent of that group receiving some form of aid was _____ 1912 _____ 24.49 %

| | DEPENDENT STUDENTS FROM FAMILIES WITH INCOMES | | | | | INDEPENDENT STUDENTS | |
	Under $9,000	$9,000-$15,000	$15,000-$21,000	$21,000-$27,000	$27,000 and Above	Single	Married
Estimated % of full-time undergraduate students	N/A%	N/A%	N/A %	N/A %	N/A %	N/A %	N/A %
% of aid recipients	19.56%	21.44%	14.91%	6.17%	1.05%	29.71%	7.16%
Average expense budget	$ 3750	$ 3605	$ 3616	$ 3599	$ 3736	$ 4032	$ 6490
% receiving any grant	99 %	99 %	98 %	87 %	90 %	92 %	100 %
Average grant	$ 1857	$ 1464	$ 895	$ 476	$ 237	$ 931	$ 1032
% receiving any loan	68%	70 %	72 %	72 %	100 %	93 %	100 %
Average loan	$ 514	$ 450	$ 473	$ 361	$ 303	$ 960	$ 1530
% receiving work aid	97%	99 %	97 %	95 %	100 %	92 %	100 %
Average work income	$ 722	$ 699	$ 544	$ 426	$ 455	$ 1019	$ 1262
AVERAGE TOTAL AID	$ 3093	$ 2613	$ 1912	$ 1263	$ 995	$ 2910	$ 3824
AVERAGE NET COST TO STUDENT AND PARENT	$ 657	$ 992	$ 1707	$ 2336	$ 2741	$ 1122	$ 2666

Additional information about student expense budgets
and aid received by students can be obtained from
the financial aid office at the address or telephone
number shown here.

204 Administration Building
Irvine, California 92717
(specific location of aid office)
(714) 833-5337
(area code, telephone number, ext.)

STUDENT FINANCIAL AID
Statement of Cost and Policy
1975-76 Academic Year

(Insert the Name of the Institution)

MOUNT EMPIRE COMMUNITY COLLEGE

I. STUDENT EXPENSE BUDGETS: The following budgets are those typically used to calculate the financial need of students with the characteristics indicated below. Other
typical budgets can be obtained from the office listed at the bottom of this statement.
Adjustments to these typical budgets are made to reflect special needs of different individual students.

| | SINGLE STUDENTS LIVING | | | MARRIED STUDENTS | |
	AT Home	ON Campus	OFF Campus	No Children	Additional Each Child
Number of months covered by budget	9	N/A	N/A	9	9
Tuition and fees	$ 225	$ N/A	$ N/A	$ 450	
Books and supplies	$ 150	$ N/A	$ N/A	$ 150	$
Room and board	$ 900	$ N/A	$ N/A	$ 1900	$ 700
Transportation	$ 300	$ N/A	$ N/A	$ 1050	$ 0
Personal and miscellaneous expenses	$ 150	$ N/A	$ N/A	$ 400	$ 300
TOTAL ESTIMATED BUDGET	$ 1725	$ N/A	$ N/A	$ 3950	$

II. AID RECEIVED BY STUDENTS: The following information describes the way in which
financial aid (from all sources) was awarded to undergraduate students last year. It
is provided as an indication of institutional practices with the understanding that individual awards vary according to need and that changes in funding levels may influence
awards in subsequent years.

The number of full-time undergraduates in 1975-76 was   422

The number and percent of that group receiving some form of aid was   166   39 %

| | DEPENDENT STUDENTS FROM FAMILIES WITH INCOMES | | | | | INDEPENDENT STUDENTS | |
	Under $9,000	$9,000- $15,000	$15,000- $21,000	$21,000- $27,000	$27,000 and Above	Single	Married
Estimated % of full-time undergraduate students	70 %	18 %	7 %	3 %	2 %	62 %	38 %
% of aid recipients	68.57 %	8.57 %	N/A %	N/A %	N/A %	9.52 %	13.33 %
Average expense budget	$ 1725	$ 1725	$ 1725	$ 1725	$ 1725	$ 2550	$ 3950
% receiving any grant	86.14 %	19.27 %	N/A %	N/A %	N/A %	7.83 %	14.45 %
Average grant	$ 729	$ 523	$ N/A	$ N/A	$ N/A	$ 749	$ 678
% receiving any loan	0 %	3.8 %	N/A %	N/A %	N/A %	0 %	0 %
Average loan	$ N/A	$ 1366	$ N/A	$ N/A	$ N/A	$ N/A	$ N/A
% receiving work aid	41 %	7.22 %	N/A %	N/A %	N/A %	8.1 %	6.62 %
Average work income	$ 668	$ 489	$ N/A	$ N/A	$ N/A	$ 613	$ 857
AVERAGE TOTAL AID	$ 1397	$ 1009	$ N/A	$ N/A	$ N/A	$ 1362	$ 1535
AVERAGE NET COST TO STUDENT AND PARENT	$ 388	$ 716	$ N/A	$ N/A	$ N/A	$ 1188	$ 2415

Additional information about student expense budgets
and aid received by students can be obtained from
the financial aid office at the address or telephone
number shown here.

Drawer 700
Big Stone Gap, Virginia 24219
(specific location of aid office)

(703) 523-2400
(area code, telephone number, ext.)

GETTING AID FROM
FEDERAL AND STATE GOVERNMENTS

THERE'S a lot of that aid provided by colleges which you saw how to get in the last chapter nationwide, a total of more than $900 million a year. But there's some ten times as much aid provided by the federal and state government programs identified and explained for you in this chapter—more than $9 *billion* dollars a year.

Open to you is a whole confusing welter of these federal and state programs, as briefly indicated in an earlier chapter. Some of these programs award aid regardless of your financial need. This chapter describes all the major federal programs from which you might get aid and gives you the mailing addresses or other sources of current information and applications for each program. It also summarizes the aid programs of each state providing aid, and lists addresses and even phone numbers in each state for getting full information.

Federal aid programs are presented here in order of desirability outlined in the chapter on your search strategy: grant programs first, then scholarship programs, job aid programs, and finally loan programs. But grant, scholarship, and loan programs open to you regardless of need are given in the first section, while programs open only to those with need follow in a second section.

For the various programs, we tell you when and how to apply, how much aid you might get, when you should be notified about your aid award, and any other facts useful for getting aid. We also give the abbreviation by which the program or type of aid is commonly identified in college and government bulletins.

Unless we specifically note otherwise, these programs have one basic feature in common: Your aid under the program is paid not to you but to the college where you will be (or are) enrolled.

You may find it helpful to read this checklist for quickly setting your strategy on all the multibillion-dollar federal and state aid programs described in this chapter (with aid programs given in the list in the order they're described in the chapter):

1. If you do *not* have (or *do* have) financial need, look into:

    • U.S. Veterans Administration—benefits for veterans (if you did or will have active duty in the U.S. armed forces)

    • U.S. Social Security—student benefits (if you have a parent covered by Social Security who is retired, disabled, or deceased)

    • ROTC scholarships (if you're interested in—or don't mind—some military studies and drill while in college and four years or so as an officer in the armed forces after you graduate)

    • U.S. service academies (if you have fairly high qualifications and are interested in heavy military training in college and at least five years or so as an officer in the armed forces, Coast Guard, or merchant marine after you graduate)

    • Guaranteed Student Loan Program (if you may want or need loan funds at 7 or 8 percent interest—lower than commercial rates—and long repayment terms)

2. If you *do* have financial need, look into:

    • Basic Educational Opportunity Grant Program (be sure to apply)

    • Special federal grant and loan programs (if you're in or plan to enter law enforcement work or nursing, or if you're a Native American Indian)

    • College Work-Study Program (if you want a college aid job instead of or with loan aid)

    • National Direct Student Loan Program (if you'd like loan aid with *very* low 3 percent interest)

    • Your state's financial aid programs (check the introduction and then the summary under your state; be sure to apply in your state's grant programs)

FEDERAL AID PROGRAMS OPEN TO YOU EVEN IF YOU DON'T HAVE FINANCIAL NEED (AND IF YOU DO HAVE NEED)

Here are the major federal aid programs open both to students without any financial need and to those with need. They provide desirable gift aid that doesn't have to be either repaid or earned except for the last one, which is the country's biggest loan-aid program for college.

U.S. Veterans Administration—Benefits for Veterans

Veterans benefits providing financial aid for college differ substantially, depending on whether you were on active duty in the U.S. armed forces before 1977 or after 1976. These two veterans benefits programs are described accordingly under the separate headings below.

For Veterans with Active Duty 1956–1976

Abbreviation by Which Commonly Known: VA (or GI Bill) aid.

Who Is Eligible: Veterans holding any but dishonorable discharges and who had at least eighteen months' active duty at any time from 1956 through 1976 qualify for the maximum period of thirty-six months of benefit payments. This is designed to cover the four academic years of nine months each in which bachelor's degrees are normally earned. (Any veteran with at least 180 consecutive days of active duty 1956–1976 is eligible, but those with less than eighteen months' service receive benefit payments only for 1½ months for each month of active duty.) Eligibility ends ten years after your last discharge or release from service whether or not you've used all your entitlement months (so be careful to begin a four-year program, for instance, within six years after your discharge).

Award Amounts Paid: Monthly benefit payments are made. In recent years these have been $270 a month for a full-time student with no dependents (or $321 with one dependent; $366, two dependents). Payments to three-quarter-time students have similarly been $203 (one dependent, $240; two dependents, $275). Payments to half-time students have been $135 (one dependent, $160; two dependents, $182).

Payments are made directly to the veteran.

In all, some $3.6 billion a year is provided by this program in aid for study in colleges or other postsecondary institutions, making it the largest single aid program in the country.

How You Apply: Get a Veterans Administration "Certificate of Eligibility" application form (from a local or the national VA office, your school, or American Legion or Red Cross offices) and fill it out. If you're not yet in college, send it with a copy of your "DD214" service-separation document to the nearest regional office of the VA. If you're in college, turn in these documents to the financial aid office.

Schedule by Which You Apply and Get the Aid: If you're starting college, it's a good idea to get your application in at least two months before you'll need your first monthly check. You can have an advance payment check sent to the college to be given to you when you register by checking items requesting this on the application. After that, you should receive checks around the tenth of every month to go toward your expenses of the month before.

You need to reapply each academic year by getting and filling out in advance a "request for enrollment certification" form.

Address for Information: Request information and forms concerning this and still other (though much smaller) aid programs of the VA from Veterans Administration, Washington, D.C. 20420.

Information about this and many other types of scholarship, loan, and job aid programs for veterans is given in the annually revised booklet of the American Legion, *Need A Lift?* Look for it in your local library or get it by writing (and paying a small sum like 50¢ or 75¢ a copy, as you'll be advised) to:

American Legion,
Dept. S, Box 1055,
Indianapolis, Ind., 46206.

For Veterans with Active Duty in or after 1977

Abbreviation by Which Commonly Known: VEA (for Veterans Education Assistance Act, passed in 1977).

Who Is Eligible: Any person who starts active duty in the armed forces in or after 1977 and arranges to join in the program while in service.

Award Amounts Paid: Veterans who join in this savings/double-matching program while in service receive aid benefits of $2 contributed by the government for every $1 the veteran contributed out of military pay from $50 to a limit of $75 a month for the veteran's contributions. Thus, for each month of participation, the veteran accumulates up to $75 in his or her savings plus up to $150 double-matched by the government, for maximum totals of $225 a month, $2,700 a year, and $8,100 for a three-year enlistment.

How You Apply: You apply for this program after starting active duty through your commanding officer. Within your first days in service, you will have an appointment with an educational counselor who should offer you the chance to sign up for VEA benefits. You can also apply later while in service.

Schedule by Which You Apply and Get the Aid: You apply just after entering or any other time you are in service, as noted above. You cannot apply after active duty ends. Benefit payments are made from your accumulated fund total on a monthly basis, in amounts and schedule like those for the pre-1977 veterans benefits.

Address for Information: You may obtain information on this program from your local recruiting office, through your commanding officer after you go on active duty, or by writing:

REACT Center,
P.O. Box 1000,
Mt. Vernon, N.Y. 10550.

U.S. Social Security—Student Benefits

Abbreviation by Which Commonly Known: SS

Who Is Eligible: Full-time students in college (or even high school) who are unmarried, between the ages of eighteen and twenty-two, and have a retired, disabled, or deceased parent who qualified (by payments while working) for Social Security benefits.

Aid Amounts Awarded: Monthly benefits payments are made directly to the student or to a parent or guardian. They vary according to current Social Security policies, but in recent years have averaged about $110 a month overall. Specific averages have been $70 a month to a student with a disabled parent, $80 to a student with a retired parent, and $127 to a student with a deceased parent. Monthly payments continue through vacations of not more than four months if the student is in full-time study both before and after the vacation. Students can earn up to $3,000 a year without reducing their Social Security benefits, but the monthly check is reduced by $1 for every $2 the student earns beyond $3,000 a year.

This is a "Cinderella" program in which your benefits end when you reach age twenty-two, marry, or stop full-time studies.

More than $1 billion a year has been paid in student benefits under this program, making it one of the country's largest programs of financial aid for college. However, as this book went to press, the Carter administration had mounted efforts to persuade Congress to limit benefits in it to the maximum payable under the Basic Educational Opportunity Grant program (described below).

How You Apply: At your local Social Security office, which will give you information and forms.

Schedule on Which You Apply and Get Aid: Apply several months before age eighteen if you think you're eligible. Should you learn of it after you're already eighteen or older, you can apply for back payments. But these will be paid only for up to twelve months' full-time attendance from the time you file your application. Monthly benefits checks are sent, as noted before.

Address for Information: You can get information and forms from the local Social Security office identified in the "U.S. Government" listings of your local telephone book.

ROTC (Reserve Officer Training Corps) Scholarships

Abbreviation by Which Commonly Known: ROTC (Army ROTC, Navy-Marine Corps ROTC or NROTC, Air Force ROTC or AFROTC).

Who Is Eligible: Men or women who are U.S. citizens (or shortly will be), who will be at least age seventeen when the scholarship takes effect and less than age twenty-five when graduated from college, who can meet demanding physical requirements, and who can qualify for admission to one of the several hundred colleges or universities having army, navy, or air force ROTC units. You must also be willing to enlist in your armed forces branch both during your four college years and for some years after—currently, four years' active duty followed by two years in the reserves.

Aid Amounts Awarded: ROTC scholarships pay tuition and fees, laboratory fees, textbooks expense plus a tax-free subsistence allowance of $100 a month for up to ten months an academic year in 1977 program provisions. An army ROTC scholar also earns some $500 during a six-week summer camp session while in college. (Navy ROTC scholars have three summer training sessions.)

The three separate ROTC programs (army, navy, air force) are not large ones compared to other government aid programs; altogether they provide perhaps some $75 million a year in scholarships. But the numbers of ROTC scholarships offered are not inconsiderable: The army ROTC program offered 1,000 new four-year scholarships in 1977, for instance, and then had 6,500 four-year, three-year, and two-year scholarships in effect.

Scholarship Program Requirements and Other Key Details: Acceptance of an ROTC scholarship requires enlistment in the army, navy, or air force through college, and agreement to accept an officer's commission on graduation and also enlist for some six years in the reserves with several years' active duty immediately after graduation (in 1977, a minimum of four years' active duty with the remaining years in inactive reserve duty). Scholars who don't make it through college and the program according to reasonably high standards of performance and conduct (for reasons judged within their control) go on active duty in noncommissioned ranks for a few years (in 1977, four years for army ROTC; two years for navy ROTC).

While in college you would have to take one or two military courses a year and drill weekly in uniform.

You would qualify for an ROTC scholarship in fairly stiff competition based on the usual college-admission-and-scholarships criteria. For instance, among new army ROTC scholarship winners for 1975–76, 35 percent were class presidents or other student-body officers, 59 percent were varsity-letter winners, 100 percent had top-half rank in their high school graduating class (with 13 percent ranking first), and the mean verbal plus math score on the Scholastic Aptitude Test was 1216 (though 8 percent of the winners had verbal plus math scores in the 600–999 range; the American College Test composite-score mean was 27). The picture was similar for new navy ROTC scholarship winners in 1975: Average SAT scores of 570 verbal and 650 math or average ACT composite score of 28; 89 percent had top-fifth class rank, 33 percent had held school office, and 62 percent had been in varsity sports.

How You Apply: By getting and filling out an application blank for your choice among the three programs—army, navy, or air force. Information you're sent on request also lists colleges with ROTC units for the service branch you want. You can use this list to choose the colleges you would like to be admitted to, but the admission process is one you must complete on your own.

Schedule on Which You Apply and Get Aid: Start a year and a half before fall college entrance on applying for a four-year ROTC scholarship. Applications become available and are accepted starting in the spring of your third high school year—on March 1 in the navy ROTC program and on April 1 in the army's (in their competitions for ROTC scholars entering college in September, 1977). Application deadlines are the following November 15 (in the fall of your fourth high school year). The first 300 army ROTC scholarship winners (among those who got completed applications in by September 1) are notified by letters sent on October 15; the remaining 700 winners are announced the following April 1. Navy ROTC winners are notified by letters sent March 1.

Schedules differ for three-year and two-year ROTC scholarships, with full details given in current ROTC scholarship bulletins. You can be awarded these after you've finished one or two years of college.

Addresses for Information: You can request full information and application forms from:

Army ROTC Scholarships, P.O. Box 12703. Philadelphia, Pa. 19134

Commander, Navy Recruiting Command (Code 314), 4015 Wilson Blvd., Arlington, Va. 22203

Air Force ROTC, Maxwell Air Force Base, Ala. 36112

U.S. Service Academies

So remarkable is the opportunity for you to be paid for going to college expense-free at one of the five U.S. service academies (military, naval, air force, Coast Guard, or merchant marine) that eligibility, benefits, and addresses for information were covered in Chapter 2 "What You Face— Your Range of College Cost Options."

The only advice that might be added here is to get information and start planning early in your third high school year if you're interested.

Guaranteed Student Loan Program (of Federal and State Governments)

Abbreviation by Which Commonly Known: GSL or GSLP

Who Is Eligible: Any student enrolled in (or accepted for) half-time to full-time study in college is eligible. Applicants must also be U.S. citizens or permanent residents (or must intend to become such residents).

Your financial need would not be a factor either in eligibility for a guaranteed loan nor in setting the amount you could borrow.

Loans are either guaranteed by a state agency or private nonprofit agency or insured by the federal government on a state-by-state basis. Many state agencies guaranteeing the loans set state residency requirements like six to twelve months for recipients, with only attendance in a college not counting as residency. (New York State, for instance, requires twelve months' residence.) You hence might not be eligible for a loan as yet if your family recently moved into your present state of residence.

Aid Amounts Awarded: You may borrow up to a maximum of $2,500 a year for undergraduate study or up to $5,000 a year for graduate study (but less than $5,000 is authorized in some states). Your total guaranteed loan indebtedness may not be more than $7,500 through undergraduate study or $15,000 through undergraduate and graduate study combined. Lending agencies will usually not approve loans for an amount more than your actual college expenses for the year (and often that amount less the other financial aid you are getting). Loans are applied for and promissory notes are signed by the student alone on a year-by-year basis. No cosigner for the loan is required.

Guaranteed loans comprise one of the country's largest aid programs, now totaling some $1.3 billion a year.

Interest Charged and Repayment Requirements: Your basic interest rate on a guaranteed loan would be 7 percent, charged as simple annual interest on the loan amount outstanding. The basic interest rate is 8 percent as of 1977 in New York State (and possibly other states). You are also charged a borrowing fee of one-half of 1 percent in most states (one-quarter of 1 percent in others). This fee is deducted from your loan proceeds at the time each loan is issued.

You pay no interest on your loans while in college if your "adjusted family income" is less than $25,000 a year. (In the special definition used for "adjusted family income," it is, essentially, the family's "adjusted gross income" from the federal income tax return, less 10 percent of adjusted gross income, less the number of dependents claimed on the federal return times $350. The actual formula is of course more complex and subject to change.) This freedom from interest payments while in college is made possible by federal interest benefits that pay the interest. If your adjusted family income is more than $25,000 and you still have officially defined financial need, you may possibly obtain the federal interest subsidy by submitting a "recommendation" form from your college (which incorporates a financial need analysis of your case) to the lender from which you got your loan.

The student must normally begin repaying the loan some nine to twelve months after graduation (or leaving college); the number of months varies by state. Up to ten years is allowed for repayment, except that most states require you to repay a minimum of $360 a year (unless your lender agrees to less due to hardship). You would earlier sign a repayment agreement converting your total indebtedness into a schedule of monthly installments. Typical schedules at 7 percent interest might look like this (note that required payments can be *heavy* and *long*):

Total borrowed	Monthly payment	Number of monthly payments	Total amount repaid (interest amount)
$ 1,000	$ 36.43	30	$ 1,092.90 ($92.90)
$ 6,000	$ 69.66	120	$ 8,359.20 ($2,359.20)
$10,000	$116.11	120	$13,933.20 ($3,933.20)

Repayment obligations are suspended for up to three years while the student serves in the armed forces, Peace Corps, or in a full-time volunteer program conducted by ACTION (a federal agency).

How You Apply: Your family bank or credit union may be one of the 20,000 authorized lenders in the guaranteed loan program. If so, you might find it simplest to pick up an application form from your bank. If not, ask the financial aid officer at your college to suggest a lender—perhaps the college itself (some colleges act as lenders), or one of the banks enlisted or located as sources by the college. You apply simply by filling out the application blank (which contains a section in which you try for the federal interest benefits while in college). Return your completed application to the lender, who in turn passes it along to your college to certify enrollment.

Schedule by Which You Apply and Get Aid: Apply for a guaranteed loan after you've gotten and accepted admission, and about two or three months or more before you'll need the money to pay college bills at registration time (which will allow time for processing). It shouldn't take too many weeks for you to get the promissory note (which you sign) and the check that is made payable to the student (and to the college, in some states).

Address for Information: Ask first for information about a Guaranteed Student Loan from your family bank, the financial aid officer at your college, or your high school guidance counselor. One of these should have what you need. If not, request a current state-by-state list of the regional branches of the U.S. Office of Education or state agencies that provide information for each state by writing:

> Guaranteed Student Loan Program, Office of Education, U.S. Department of Health, Education and Welfare, Washington, D.C. 20202.

FEDERAL AID PROGRAMS OPEN TO YOU ONLY IF YOU HAVE FINANCIAL NEED

Even though this section lists the major federal aid programs in which students with no financial need either may not receive awards or are not eligible to apply, you should probably apply in the first program listed anyway—the Basic Educational Opportunity Grant Program.

This is advisable for various reasons. First, it is difficult to set some income ceiling above which a family absolutely would not qualify for a

Basic Grant. A few families with annual incomes well over $20,000 receive them (because varying family circumstances as well as expense at the college chosen influence Basic Grant amounts). Second, many colleges today require any financial aid applicants to apply also for a Basic Grant—even applicants for no-need scholarships the college may offer. Third, starting in 1978, applying for a Basic Grant may involve no more paperwork on your part than applying for financial aid at colleges or in aid programs of states or private agencies (as explained shortly).

Basic Educational Opportunity Grant Program

Abbreviation by Which Commonly Known: BEOG

Who Is Eligible: Students admitted for (or enrolled in) half-time to full-time study in college (or other postsecondary institution approved for the grants) may apply. Applicants must be U.S. citizens or permanent residents (or must intend to become such residents), and must not have previously received a bachelor's degree. Whether or not you get an award depends on your officially determined financial need at the college you attend.

Aid Amounts Awarded: Overall Basic Grants funding in any one year depends on appropriation by Congress and hence varies. Individual grants for 1977–78 are estimated to range from $200 to $1,400, with the actual amount set according to financial need at the college you attend. (The intended maximum for 1978–79 is $1,600.)

Basic Grants are designed to serve as the foundation of a financial aid package. Their amounts are accordingly figured (with tables issued annually and used by the financial aid office at your college) to meet only part of your need (the difference between your total expense budget at the college and the sum you can reasonably afford toward expenses as determined by need analysis). Your Basic Grant therefore may not be more than half of your total expense.

How You Apply: Starting in 1978, you may apply for a Basic Grant by filling out either the Financial Aid Form (FAF) of the College Scholarship Service or the similar Family Financial Statement (FFS) of the American College Testing Program. Since these financial statement forms are widely required by colleges and scholarship programs of states and private agencies, you're likely to be filling them out anyway. Allowing them to be used for Basic Grant application saves an estimated 2.5 million families a year the trouble of filling out separate Basic Grant application forms (and makes possible saving you that extra paperwork).

In case you're not otherwise filling out a FAF or FFS form, you may also apply by getting and completing a Basic Grants application for the academic year in which you'll use the grant while enrolled in college.

Schedule on Which You Apply and Get Aid: If you're entering college in the fall, you would get and complete a FAF, FFS, or Basic Grants application form and send it in *no earlier than January 1*. You are urged to provide family financial data on the form after you finish your latest federal income tax return. Doing so should make it easier for you anyway, since many items called for on the financial aid blanks are drawn directly from the federal return. Schedule dates in later years should be much like these for 1978–79.

Within six weeks after you file your application, you should get a "student eligibility report." Check it over as requested and have any errors fixed. The "student eligibility index" number that it shows for you is, by the way, the dollar amount that the Basic Grants formula figures you can reasonably afford toward college expenses. If it's higher than your student expense budget at your college, you can't get a Basic Grant; if it's lower, a Basic Grant awarded you would cover no more than part of the difference—perhaps a fourth or a third. Naturally, Basic Grants for half-time study are smaller than for full-time study.

You then give your student eligibility report to the financial aid officer of the college you will be (or are) attending. He or she figures the amount of your grant on the basis of your eligibility index number, official tables, and your student expense budget. The officer can also tell you how much it is.

You are urged to apply for a Basic Grant at least five or six months before you'll need the funds. Doing so would allow the financial aid office time to build your financial aid package around it. However, application deadlines in past years have permitted students to apply as late as March 15 of the academic year in which they actually use the grant.

Basic Grants are awarded and must be applied for annually.

Should your family financial situation suddenly change much for the worse, by the way, you can use a current supplemental form to report the disaster and hopefully get your Basic Grant increased. Details on this are given in the Basic Grants application.

Addresses for Information: You may obtain a "Student Guide" booklet explaining the program and financial aid generally, a "Basic Grant Eligibility" booklet giving information on the method used to determine your eligibility index, and/or an application form from BEOG, P.O. Box 84, Washington, D.C. 20044.

Application blanks are also widely available in high schools, libraries, and colleges.

Supplemental Educational Opportunity Grant Program

Abbreviation by Which Commonly Known: SEOG

Who Is Eligible: Undergraduate students "of exceptional financial need who without the grant would be unable to continue their education," according to the U.S. Office of Education. Half-time to full-time attendance is required.

Aid Amounts Awarded: Between $200 and $1,500 a year, with the actual amount based on financial need. Grants are renewable annually up to a total of $4,000 for a four-year undergraduate program (or $5,000 for undergraduate degree programs extending over five years of required study). If you are selected for a Supplementary Grant, your college or your state must award you additional aid at least equal to the amount of the grant. Grants in the program nationwide total some $240 million a year.

How You Apply: Only through the financial aid officer at a college in the course of applying to the college for financial aid.

Address for Information: Information and application forms may be obtained from financial aid officers at colleges.

State Student Incentive Grant Program (of the Federal Government)

You would not even be aware of this federal financial aid program in applying for financial aid. It supplies funds to states (funds which the state must match) for their state grant programs to college students. SSIG is a fairly large program, providing more than $44 million a year to the states.

SPECIAL FEDERAL GRANT AND LOAN PROGRAMS

Law Enforcement Education Program

Abbreviation by Which Commonly Known: LEEP

Who Is Eligible: U.S. citizens already employed in a public law enforcement agency or agreeing to obtain employment in one on graduation.

Aid Amounts Awarded: Grants of up to $600 a year and loans of up to $1,800 a year. Loans are canceled at the rate of 25 percent per year of full-time employment in a public law enforcement agency. A total of some $40 million a year is awarded in the program.

How You Apply: In the course of applying for financial aid to a college.

Schedule on Which You Apply and Get Aid: According to each college's schedule for applications and aid awards.

Address for Information: Information and applications may be obtained from financial aid officers at colleges participating in the program.

Nursing Student Loans

Who Is Eligible: Students at nonprofit schools of nursing (including collegiate schools) who have financial need in half-time to full-time study for associate's, bachelor's, or graduate degrees.

Aid Amounts Awarded: A uniform $800. Some $15 million a year is awarded in this federal aid program.

How You Apply and Schedule: In applying to a nursing school for financial aid, according to its schedule for financial aid applications and awards.

Address for Information: Information is available from financial aid administrators at or for nursing schools.

Bureau of Indian Affairs Grants

Abbreviation by Which Commonly Known: BIA grants

Who Is Eligible: Students with financial need and proof of descent from at least one parent or grandparent who is or was a Native American (American Indian) or Native Alaskan belonging to a tribe recognized by the U.S. Bureau of Indian Affairs. Students must also be admitted to or attending accredited colleges (or other postsecondary institutions).

Aid Amounts Awarded: Awards range from $100 to $2,300, and are adjusted in amount according to finanical need. In all, they assist more than 15,000 students and total some $33 million a year.

How to Apply and Schedule: Applications are sent to the Bureau of Indian Affairs area office responsible for the applicant's tribal group. Addresses of these offices may be obtained from the central bureau office given below. May 1 is the application deadline.

Addresses for Information: Information and application forms may be requested from U.S. Bureau of Indian Affairs, Room 201, 5301 Central Avenue., N.E., Albuquerque, New Mexico 87108.

College Work-Study Program

Abbreviation by Which Commonly Known: CWSP

Who Is Eligible: Students in half-time to full-time study on undergraduate or graduate levels who have financial need.

Aid Amounts Awarded: In this job aid program, you earn at an hourly rate, ranging generally from the minimum wage or higher depending on the type of job you are awarded by your college financial aid office. Jobs are on campus or off campus at public agencies or private nonprofit organizations like hospitals. The work is usually part-time, though it can range up to twenty hours a week during studies; pay comes from the college from funds allocated among colleges by the federal government. Federal funding of the program totals some $400 million a year.

How You Apply: Application for aid in this program is made in the course of applying to a college for financial aid. Extent of financial need is a major factor considered by college financial aid officers in making awards.

Schedule on Which You Apply and Get Aid: You apply according to the college's schedule for financial aid applicants. Payment is made directly to you after you start working, as with any regular wage or salary.

Address for Information: Information about the program may be obtained from financial aid officers at colleges.

National Direct Student Loan Program

Abbreviation by Which Commonly Known: NDSL

Who Is Eligible: Half-time to full-time students at colleges participating in the program who have financial need are eligible for these comparatively very desirable loans, which are made at only 3 percent interest that is charged only during the repayment period. Quite a few colleges don't participate, since federal funding of the loans is relatively small (some $300 million a year in provision of new loan funds) and colleges must themselves provide $1 of every $10 loaned.

Aid Amounts Awarded and Repayment: Loan amounts are adjusted according to financial need. They may total no more than $2,500 through the first two years of bachelor's-degree study, $5,000 through the normal four years of bachelor's-degree study, and $10,000 through graduate study. Colleges offering these loans tend to award them first to students with highest financial need. Repayment begins nine months after you graduate or leave college and may extend over ten years. Repayment is suspended for up to three years during service in the armed forces, Peace Corps, or VISTA. Part of the loan total is canceled if you enter designated teaching fields or types of military duty.

How You Apply and Schedule: In the course of applying for financial aid from a college participating in the program and in accordance with each college's general schedule for financial aid applicants.

Address for Information: Information about the program may be obtained from financial aid officers at participating colleges.

YOUR STATE'S FINANCIAL AID PROGRAMS OF GRANTS, SCHOLARSHIPS, JOBS, AND LOANS

State financial aid programs represent a large and growing source of help with college—providing more than $645 million a year in grants and scholarships alone nationwide (and not including large state shares of the $1.3 billion a year in guaranteed loans).

What's your possible stake in a state aid program? Individual awards in these grant/scholarship programs averaged $440 to students at public colleges and $833 to students at private colleges in 1976–77 across the country as a whole. These figures may give you an idea of the sums for which you might qualify in your state's programs.

This section presents information on college financial aid programs in each state in alphabetical order of the states, with programs of Guam, Puerto Rico, and the U.S. territories given last.

Look under your state's heading below for identification of its major financial aid programs and also figures indicating the number of awards and dollar values of those awards in 1976–77. Also given is the address to which you may write (and phone number if you prefer to call) for full, current information on all your state's financial aid programs, including ones of job aid and loan aid. Write early if you're interested—around the middle of your third year of high school—to give yourself time to examine possibilities and meet deadlines.

Data on state programs given here is based on the eighth annual survey of the National Association of State Scholarship and Grant Programs, covering the 1976–77 academic year. The survey was compiled and published by Joseph D. Boyd, executive director of the Illinois State Scholarship Commission.

You might find some general information on these state programs helpful before looking into specific information on your state's programs below.

In almost all these programs, financial aid awards are based on financial need. You therefore are not likely to qualify (except possibly in some small, special program of your state) unless you'd have financial need at one of your college choices.

You may have to apply for a Basic Grant in the federal program as a condition for a state award. Basic Grant application is required by eighteen states (in 1976–77): Alabama, Arkansas, California, District of Columbia, Hawaii, Kentucky, Louisiana, New Jersey, New York, North Carolina, Oregon, Pennsylvania, South Carolina, South Dakota, Tennessee, Vermont, Washington, and Wisconsin (and also by American Samoa and the Trust Territory of Micronesia in the Pacific).

Awards in state grant programs are made to you simply if you meet the specified requirements—most often, financial need, with grant amount almost always adjusted according to need. You can also usually use a state grant (or scholarship) only at colleges in your state. Only eight states allowed grants or scholarships to be used at out-of-state institutions in 1976–77: Connecticut (state scholarships, higher education grants), Delaware, District of Columbia, Massachusetts, New Jersey (state competitive scholarships, county college graduate scholarships, educational opportunity grants), Pennsylvania, Rhode Island (state scholarships, nursing scholarships), and Vermont (plus American Samoa, Guam, Virgin Islands, and the Trust Territory). You may also come upon certain other grant requirements, such as use only at public or private colleges.

Awards in state scholarship programs are made (as you might expect) on a competitive basis to applicants judged to have the highest qualifications. It's fairly common for a state to have several small state scholarship programs, such as programs for veterans or veterans' children or for nursing or other health-care studies.

Most state grant or scholarship aid based on financial need is for undergraduate study. Only seven states provided such need-based aid for graduate study in 1976–77—Connecticut, Delaware, Michigan, New Jersey, New York, Texas, and Vermont (plus Guam and Virgin Islands).

Now, here's the state-by-state information and addresses and phone numbers on major aid programs.

Alabama

Programs: Student Assistance Program—awards to 2,350 students averaging $180 each and totaling $423,000.

Address: Alabama Student Assistance Program, Room 812, State Office Building, Montgomery, Ala. 36130, Phone 205-832-3946.

Alaska

Programs: State Scholarship Loan Program, State Memorial Scholarship Loan Program. (No 1976–77 data available.)

Address: Alaska Department of Education, Pouch F (118 Seward), Juneau, Alaska 99811, phone 907-465-2962.

Arizona

Programs: Seeking Authorization and funds in 1976–77.

Address: Arizona Commission for Postsecondary Education, 4350 Camelback Rd., Suite 140-F, Phoenix, Ariz. 85018, phone 602-271-3109.

Arkansas

Programs: State Scholarship Program—awards to 1,095 students averaging $177 each and totaling $487,000.

Address: Student Aid Office, Department of Higher Education, 122 National Old Line Building, Little Rock, Ark. 72201, phone 501-371-1441.

California

Programs: State Scholarship Program—awards to 45,998 students averaging $1,026 each and totaling $47,228,000.

College Opportunity grants—awards to 12,783 students averaging $1,098 each and totaling $14,036,000.

Occupational Education/Training grants—awards to 1,374 students averaging $1,096 each and totaling $1,506,000.

Other aid programs—Graduate Fellowship Program, Medical Student Contract Program, Special Clinical Internship Program, Law Enforcement Personnel Dependents Scholarship Program, Real Estate Scholarship Program, Statewide Student Financial Aid Information Program.

Address: California Student Aid Commission, 1410 Fifth St., Sacramento, Calif. 95814, phone 916-445-0880.

Colorado

Programs: Student grants—awards to 12,200 students averaging $617 each and totaling $9,019,000.

Other programs—Colorado student scholarships, athletic grants, Colorado graduate grants, Colorado graduate fellowships, Colorado Work-Study Program, Matching Funds for Health Professions, federal nursing and NDSL loans, Colorado Tuition Assistance.

Address: Student Services Office, Colorado Commission on Higher Education, 1550 Lincoln St., Denver, Colo. 80203, phone 303-892-2723.

Connecticut

Programs: State Scholarship Program—awards to 2,684 students averaging $732 each and totaling $1,964,000.

Higher Education grants—awards to 1,329 students averaging $321 each and totaling $427,000.

College Continuation grants—awards to 590 students averaging $500 each and totaling $295,000.

Restricted Education Achievement grants—awards to 533 students averaging $488 each and totaling $260,000.

Contracted Students/Independent Colleges Program—awards to 3,357 students averaging $850 each and totaling $2,853,000.

Other programs—State Work-Study Program, awards to children of deceased/disabled veterans.

Address: The Commission for Higher Education and the State Scholarship Commission, P.O. Box 1320, Hartford, Conn. 06101, phone 203-566-3910.

Delaware

Programs: Higher education scholarships—awards to 300 students averaging $1,167 each and totaling $350,000.

Address: Department of Public Instruction, John G. Townsend Building, Dover, Del. 19901, phone 302-678-4620.

District of Columbia

Programs: State scholarships—awards to 650 students averaging $1,058 each and totaling $688,000.

Other programs—Guaranteed Loan Program.

Address: Scholarship Program Office, Higher Education Council, Government of the District of Columbia, 1329 E St., N.W., Room 1050, Washington, D.C. 20004, phone 202-737-5334.

Florida

Programs: Student Assistance grants—awards to 6,141 students averaging $1,048 each and totaling $7,308,000.

Other programs—Florida insured student loans, Florida student loans, scholarships for children of deceased and disabled veterans.

Address: Student Financial Aid Office, Department of Education, 563 Knott Building, Tallahassee, Fla. 32304, phone 904-487-1800.

Georgia

Programs: Incentive scholarships—awards to 6,153 students averaging $316 each and totaling $1,943,000.

Other programs—Independent College Tuition Equalization Grant Program (for undergraduates only), Law Enforcement Personnel Dependents Scholarship Program (parent death or disability required; for undergraduates only), State Direct Student Loan Program.

Address: Georgia Higher Education Assistance Authority, Suite 110, 9 Lavista Perimeter Park, 2187 Northlake Parkway, Tucker, Ga. 30084, phone 404-939-5004.

Hawaii

Programs: Student Incentive grants—awards to 800 students averaging $453 each and totaling $362,000.

Other programs—State Scholarship Program, Hawaii Merit Scholarship Program, Tuition Waiver Program, State Higher Education Loan Fund.

Address: Board of Regents, University of Hawaii, 2444 Dole St., Honolulu, Hawaii 96822, phone 808-948-7487.

Idaho

Programs: Scholarship Program—awards to 69 students averaging $1,493 each and totaling $103,000.

Incentive grants—awards to 1,500 students averaging $194 each and totaling $291,000.

Address: Office of the State Board of Education, Room 307, Len B. Jordan Building, Capitol Mall, Boise, Idaho 83720, phone 208-384-2270.

Illinois

Programs: Monetary Award Program—awards to 90,978 students averaging $762 each and totaling $69,370,000.

Other programs—Illinois Guaranteed Loan Program, bilingual scholarships, National Guard/Naval Militia awards, POW-MIA dependents' awards, firemen/policemen/correctional officers dependent awards, Student-to-Student Grant Program.

Address: Illinois State Scholarship Commission, 102 Wilmot Rd., Deerfield, Ill. 60015, phone 312-945-1500.

Indiana

Programs: State scholarships—awards to 15,879 students averaging $894 each and totaling $14,200,000.

Educational grants—awards to 4,495 students averaging $569 each and totaling $2,559,000.

Freedom of Choice grants—awards to 5,164 students averaging $465 each and totaling $2,400,000.

Other programs—Top Twenty Hoosier Scholar awards.

Address: State Scholarship Commission of Indiana, 2d Floor, EDP Building, 219 N. Senate Ave., Indianapolis, Ind. 46202, phone 317-633-5445.

Iowa

Programs: Tuition grants—awards to 7,791 students averaging $1,236 each and totaling $9,633,000.

Scholarship Program—awards to 965 students averaging $563 each and totaling $543,000.

Vocational/Technical grants—awards to 860 students averaging $349 each and totaling $300,000.

Address: Student Aid Program Office, Iowa Higher Education Facilities Commission, 201 Jewett Building, 9th & Grand, Des Moines, Iowa 50309, phone 515-281-3501.

Kansas

Programs: Tuition grants—awards to 3,575 students averaging $951 each and totaling $3,400,000.

State scholarships—awards to 1,340 students averaging $470 each and totaling $630,000.

Other programs—loans and scholarships to medical and osteopathic students.

Address: Student Assistance Section, State Board of Regents, Merchants National Bank Tower, Suite 1316, Topeka, Kans. 66612, phone 913-296-3516.

Kentucky

Programs: State grants—awards to 8,104 students averaging $324 each and totaling $2,622,000.

Other programs—KHEAA Student Loan Program, Commonwealth Work-Study Program.

Address: Kentucky Higher Education Assistance Authority, 691 Teton Trail, Frankfort, Ky. 40601, phone 502-564-7990.

Louisiana

Programs: Student Incentive grants—awards to 1,500 students averaging $373 each and totaling $559,000.

Other programs—State Guaranteed Student Loan Program, State High School Rally Scholarship Program.

Address: Louisiana Higher Education Assistance Commission, P.O. Box 44127, Capitol Station, Baton Rouge, La. 70804, phone 504-389-5491.

Maine

Programs: Tuition Equalization Program—awards to 800 students averaging $719 each and totaling $575,000.

Vocational/Technical Program—awards to 125 students averaging $400 each and totaling $50,000.

Address: Division of Higher Education Services, State Department of Educational and Cultural Services, State Education Building, Augusta, Me. 04333, phone 207-289-2541.

Maryland

Programs: General state scholarships—awards to 2,500 students averaging $720 each and totaling $1,801,000.

Other programs—Delegate, war orphans, veteran (POW) grants; reimbursement of firemen; Residing-Family Practica.

Address: State Scholarship Board, Room 206, 2100 Guilford Ave., Baltimore, Md. 21218, phone 301-383-4095.

Massachusetts

Programs: General scholarships—awards to 22,000 students averaging $592 each and totaling $13,015,000.

Nursing scholarships—awards to 500 students averaging $300 each and totaling $150,000.

Special education scholarships—awards to forty-two students averaging $357 each and totaling $15,000.

Other programs—Honor Scholarship Program, Medical Scholarship Program, Dental Scholarship Program, Fire/Police, POW-MIA Scholarship Program, Consortium Scholarship Program.

Address: Student Affairs Office, Massachusetts Board of Higher Education, 182 Tremont St., Boston, Mass. 02111, phone 617-727-5366.

Michigan

Programs: Competitive scholarships—awards to 16,949 students averaging $778 each and totaling $13,189,000.

Tuition grants—awards to 11,136 students averaging $1,096 each and totaling $12,200,000.

Other programs—Guaranteed Student Loan Program, State Direct Loan Program, degree reimbursement programs (4), listing of schools for NDSL loan cancellation, Legislative Merit awards.

Address: Student Financial Assistance Services, Michigan Department of Education, P.O. Box 30008, Lansing, Mich. 48909, phone 517-373-3394.

Minnesota

Programs: State Scholarship Program—awards to 7,039 students averaging $867 each and totaling $6,100,000.

Grant-in-Aid Program—awards to 14,065 students averaging $874 each and totaling $12,300,000.

Other programs—State Student Loan Program, Medical and Osteopathy Loan Program, Minnesota-Wisconsin Tuition Reciprocity Program, Minnesota-North Dakota Tuition Reciprocity Program, State Work-Study Program, Veterans' Dependents Assistance Program, Foreign Student Assistance Program.

Address: Minnesota Higher Education Coordinating Board, Suite 901, Capitol Square, 550 Cedar St., St. Paul, Minn. 55101, phone 612-296-5715.

Mississippi

Programs: Student Incentive grants—awards to 1,422 students averaging $500 each and totaling $711,000.

Address: Governor's Office of Education and Training, Suite 182, Universities Center, 3825 Ridgewood Rd., Jackson, Miss. 39211, phone 601-982-6606.

Missouri

Programs: Student Grant Program—awards to 9,300 students averaging $456 each and totaling $4,197,000.

Address: Student Aid Programs, Department of Higher Education, 600 Clark Ave., Jefferson City, Mo. 65101, phone 314-751-3940.

Montana

Programs: Student Incentive grants—awards to 400 students averaging $288 each and totaling $115,000.

Address: Office of Commissioner of Higher Education, 33 S. Last Chance Gulch, Helena, Mont. 59601, phone 406-449-3024.

Nebraska

Programs: Incentive Grant Program—awards to 1,500 students averaging $400 each and totaling $600,000.

Address: Nebraska Coordinating Commission for Postsecondary Education, 1315 State Capitol Building, Lincoln, Neb. 68509, phone 402-471-2331.

Nevada

Programs: None in 1976–77.

Address: Office of the Chancellor, University of Nevada System, 405 Marsh Ave., Reno, Nev. 89502, phone 702-784-4901.

New Hampshire

Programs: Incentive grants—awards to 550 students averaging $545 each and totaling $300,000.
Address: Postsecondary Education Commission, 66 South St., Concord, N.H. 03301.

New Jersey

Programs: Competitive scholarships—awards to 13,404 students averaging $503 each and totaling $6,741,000.

Education Incentive grants—awards to 8,300 students averaging $295 each and totaling $2,450,000.

Tuition Aid grants—awards to 5,200 students averaging $923 each and totaling $4,800,000.

County College Graduate scholarships—awards to 400 students averaging $625 each and totaling $250,000.

Educational Opportunity Fund grants—awards to 12,361 students averaging $857 each and totaling $10,591,000.

Public Tuition Aid grants—awards to 12,656 students averaging $243 each and totaling $3,074,000.

Other programs—Higher Education Assistance Authority, State College Work-Study

Address: Office of Student Assistance, New Jersey Department of Higher Education, P.O. Box 1417, Trenton, N.J. 08625, phone 609-292-4646.

New Mexico

Programs: Incentive grants—awards to 500 students averaging $400 each and totaling $200,000.

Address: Office of the Academic Coordinator, Board of Educational Finance, Room 201, Legislative-Executive Building, Sante Fe, N. Mex. 87503, phone 505-827-2115.

New York

Programs: Tuition Assistance Program (TAP)—awards to 350,000 students averaging $504 each and totaling $176,500,000.

Regents scholarships—awards to 74,000 students averaging $281 each and totaling $20,800,000.

Other programs—Guaranteed Student Loan Program; Medical/Dental Loan Program; Regents Nursing Scholarship Program; Regents scholarships for medicine, dentistry, and osteopathy; Regents Physician Shortage scholarships; Herbert H. Lehman graduate fellowships.

Address: New York Higher Education Services Corporation, Tower Building, Empire State Plaza, Albany, N.Y. 12255, phone 518-474-5592.

North Carolina

Programs: Student Incentive grants—awards to 2,475 students averaging $649 each and totaling $1,606,000.

Other programs—Insured Student Loan Program, legislative tuition grants for residents enrolled in North Carolina private colleges, Board of Governor's Medical Scholarship Program, Turrentine Foundation scholarships, Brooks Foundation scholarships.

Address: North Carolina Education Assistance Authority, Box 2688, University Square West, Chapel Hill, N.C. 27514, phone 919-929-2136.

North Dakota

Programs: Student Financial Assistance Program—awards to 900 students averaging $330 each and totaling $297,000.

Address: North Dakota Student Financial Assistance Agency, Board of Higher Education, Tenth Floor, State Capitol, Bismarck, N.D. 58505, phone 701-224-2960.

Ohio

Programs: Instructional grants—awards to 54,000 students averaging $488 each and totaling $26,342,000.

Other programs—War Orphans' scholarship programs.

Address: Student Assistance Office, Ohio Board of Regents, Thirty-Sixth Floor, 30 E. Broad St., Columbus, Ohio 43215, phone 614-466-7420.

Oklahoma

Programs: Tuition Aid grants—awards to 5,000 students averaging $239 each and totaling $1,196,000.

Other programs—Oklahoma Student Loan Program, Guaranteed Student Loan Program.

Address: Oklahoma State Regents for Higher Education, 500 Education Building, State Capitol Complex, Oklahoma City, Okla. 73105, phone 405-521-2444.

Oregon

Programs: Need grants—awards to 5,422 students averaging $479 each and totaling $2,596,000.

Cash awards—awards to 702 students averaging $450 each and totaling $316,000.

Other programs—Foreign Student Fee Remission Program, State 2½ Percent Fee Remission Program at Eastern Oregon College, Oregon Guaranteed Student Loan Program, private awards.

Address: Oregon State Scholarship Commission, Suite 9, 1445 Willamette St., Eugene, Ore. 97401, phone 503-686-4166.

Pennsylvania

Programs: Higher Education grants—awards to 115,900 students averaging $607 each and totaling $70,360,000.

Other programs—Student Loan Guaranty Program, Statewide College Work-Study Program.

Address: Pennsylvania Higher Education Assistance Agency, Towne House, Harrisburg, Pa. 17102, phone 717-787-1937.

Rhode Island

Programs: State scholarships—awards to 2,740 students averaging $839 each and totaling $2,300,000.

Nursing Education scholarships—awards to 121 students averaging $578 each and totaling $70,000.

Business Education Teachers scholarships—awards to thirty students averaging $500 each and totaling $15,000.

War Orphans scholarships—awards to twenty-four students averaging $125 each and totaling $3,000.

Address: Office of Student Assistance, Rhode Island Department of Education, Roger Williams Building, Hayes St., Providence, R.I. 02908, phone 401-277-2676.

South Carolina

Programs: Tuition grants—awards to 7,800 students averaging $987 each and totaling $7,699,000.

Address: Tuition Grants Agency, 411 Palmetto State Life Building, Columbia, S.C. 29201, phone 803-758-7070.

South Dakota

Programs: Student Incentive grants—awards to 1,214 students averaging $200 each and totaling $243,000.

Address: Office of the Secretary, SSIG Program, Department of Education and Cultural Affairs, New Office Building, Pierre, S.D. 57501, phone 605-224-3119.

Tennessee

Programs: Student Assistance awards—awards to 1,750 students averaging $857 each and totaling $1,500,000.

Other programs—Medical Loan Scholarship Program, Graduate Nursing Loan Scholarship Program, Guaranteed Student Loan Program.

Address: Tennessee Student Assistance Corporation, 707 Main St., Nashville, Tenn. 37206, phone 615-741-1346.

Texas

Programs: Tuition Equalization grants—awards to 17,760 students averaging $507 each and totaling $9,000,000.

Student Incentive grants—awards to 2,168 students averaging $376 each and totaling $815,000.

Public Education Incentive grants—awards to 8,000 students averaging $374 each and totaling $2,988,000.

Other programs—Hinson-Hazelwood College Student Loan Program.

Address: Division of Student Services, Coordinating Board, Texas College and University System, Box 12788, Capitol Station, Austin, Tex. 78711, phone 512-475-4147.

Utah

Programs: Student Incentive grants—awards to 1,094 students averaging $612 each and totaling $670,000.

Address: Office of the Assistant Director for Finance, Utah System of Higher Education, Room 1201, University Club Building, 136 E. South Temple, Salt Lake City, Utah 84111, phone 801-533-5619.

Vermont

Programs: Incentive grants—awards to 5,420 students averaging $498 each and totaling $2,700,000.

Other programs—Honor scholarships, nursing scholarships, Vermont Guaranteed Student Loan Program, Talent Search, National Guard scholarships.

Address: Vermont Student Assistance Corporation, 156 College St., Burlington, Vt. 05401, phone 802-658-4530.

Virginia

Programs: College Scholarship Assistance Program—awards to 8,000 students averaging $237 each and totaling $1,897,000.

Other programs—Tuition Assistance Grant and Loan Program.

Address: State Council of Higher Education, 700 Fidelity Building, Ninth & Main Street, Richmond, Va. 23219, phone 804-786-2143.

Washington

Programs: Need grants—awards to 7,500 students averaging $401 each and totaling $3,010,000.

Other programs—Tuition Waiver Program for children of deceased or incapacitated veterans, Aid to Blind Students Program.

Address: Division of Student Financial Aid, Council for Postsecondary Education, 908 E. Fifth St., Olympia, Wash. 98504, phone 206-753-3571.

West Virginia

Programs: Higher Education grants—awards to 3,730 students averaging $523 each and totaling $1,951,000.

Other programs—West Virginia Undergraduate Tuition and Fee Waiver Program.

Address: West Virginia Higher Education Grant Program, West Virginia Board of Regents, General Delivery, Institute, W. Va. 25112, phone 304-768-7310.

Wisconsin

Programs: Higher Education grants—awards to 25,000 students averaging $464 each and totaling $11,611,000.

Tuition grants—awards to 7,890 students averaging $836 each and totaling $6,600,000.

Indian (Native American) Student grants—awards to 1,300 students averaging $762 each and totaling $991,000.

Other programs—Wisconsin state student loans, Wisconsin guaranteed student loans, medical student loans, Minnesota-Wisconsin reciprocity programs.

Address: Division of Student Support, State of Wisconsin Higher Educational Aid Board, 123 W. Washington Ave., Madison, Wisc. 53702, phone 608-266-2897.

Wyoming

Programs: Student Incentive grants—awards to eighty students averaging $800 each and totaling $64,000.

Address: Higher Education Council, State Office Building-West, 1720 Carey Ave., Cheyenne, Wyo. 82002, phone 307-777-7763.

American Samoa

Programs: Scholarship Program—awards to 105 students averaging $2,410 each and totaling $253,000.

Address: Department of Education, Pago Pago, American Samoa 96799, phone (overseas operator) 633-5237.

Guam

Programs: Professional/Technical awards—awards to fifteen students averaging $3,800 each and totaling $57,000.

Other programs—RCA scholarships, GOVCO scholarships.

Address: Board of Regents, University of Guam, P.O. Box EK, Agana, Guam 96910, phone (overseas operator) 734-9061.

Puerto Rico

Programs: Incentive grants—awards to 2,200 students averaging $327 each and totaling $720,000.

Address: Council on Higher Education, Box F, UPR Station, Rio Piedras, Puerto Rico 00931, phone 809-765-6590.

Trust Territory

Programs: Scholarships and grants—awards to 1,000 students averaging $591 each and totaling $591,000.

Other programs—Congress of Micronesia Student Revolving Loan Fund.

Address: Student Assistance Office, Department of Education, Office of the High Commissioner, Trust Territory of the Pacific Islands, Saipan, Mariana Islands 96950, phone (Saipan local) 9334 or 9468.

Virgin Islands

Programs: Territorial scholarships—awards to 381 students averaging $1,152 each and totaling $439,000.

Address: Virgin Islands Department of Education, P.O. Box 630, Charlotte Amalie, St. Thomas, U.S. Virgin Islands 00801, phone 809-774-0100.

10

GETTING AID FROM THE PRIVATE AGENCIES OF ALL KINDS

IN your overall search strategy for financial aid, you still have a third broad sector to scout (in addition to the first and second—college and government aid programs). This is the sprawling sector that takes in thousands of scholarship programs (and a few loan programs) sponsored by private agencies of all kinds. Among these agencies are companies, labor unions, churches, fraternal organizations, PTAs, foundations, civic groups, professional societies, and still others. Their programs come in all shapes and sizes, but most often are comparatively small and have very narrow eligibility rules.

You should nevertheless probably look into this sector. Hundreds of thousands of students find financial aid in it. It provides aid for college that has been estimated to amount in all to $50 million a year in scholarships and $10 million a year in loans.

Only two considerations might prompt you not to bother with it. First, little of this aid is offered on a no-need basis (though some is). You might possibly skip it if you have no financial need whatever. Second, academic ability is a factor to some or a large extent in the selection of winners in most of these programs. You might also let it pass, then, if your school record and test scores are very low—unless their low levels stem from some serious handicap like poverty or physical disability (or unless you are looking for one of the few loan programs in this private sector).

But do look into this sector even if you're only fairly good academically yet still very much want to go to college and have financial need. These programs often award scholarships to students whom colleges that are more academically demanding cannot aid with scholarships or even admit.

Don't be at all alarmed because aid of this type comes from so many programs of so many kinds that it would seem to take forever to explore. As in earlier chapters, we give you a strategy here that can cut your time to a minimum while also helping organize your efforts. Carry out this strategy over about the same period in which you make all your other financial aid efforts. That is, start if possible in about the middle of your third year in high school and wind up your applications in the early part of your fourth year.

Here's a checklist outlining a recommended strategy for getting aid from private agencies. Its most important phase is the extensive first one—search. Its later phase of applying and qualifying for aid differs little in the great majority of these programs from the similar phase in college or government scholarship programs.

This checklist is only a bare skeleton. You may well not understand it fully until reading the explanation of it that is given with frequent examples of actual programs in the rest of the chapter.

YOUR CHECKLIST FOR FINDING AND GETTING AID FROM PRIVATE AGENCIES

The key tactic in the search phase of this strategy hinges on a basic fact about almost all of this aid offered by private agencies: The aid is provided by donors who have some connection with the kind of students they want to help. Most donors of this aid try regularly to tell your school and parents and organizations that it's offered for you—if you're one of the students eligible. Your tactic consequently amounts to watching for their announcements and also tracing the connections of you and your family back to typical likely sources to see if they provide aid programs. Doing this is much simpler than it sounds.

Search Phase Checklist

1. Ask in your high school (at the guidance office or principal's office) for information about private-agency aid programs of these kinds that might be open to you:

   • *Community* programs—ones open to college-bound students in your community or school (pp. 134–35)

   • *National* programs—ones open widely to students coast to coast and often especially well known to schools, like the National Merit Scholarship Program and the National Honor Society Scholarship Program (pp. 135–36)

2. Have your parents ask for information about possible financial aid programs for children of employees or for children of members (putting the question to informed executives or officers, rather than just fellow employees or members) at:

- *Companies* where they may work
- Any *labor unions* to which they belong
- Any *fraternal organizations* or *lodges* (such as the Elks Club, Lions, Rotary) to which they belong
- Any other *community service organizations* to which they belong (like the PTA, Chamber of Commerce, or League of Women Voters)
- Any local chapters of *veterans organization* to which they belong

3. Ask at your *church* (or write to its national office after getting the address at your church)

4. Ask adult leaders of any *youth organizations* to which you belong (like the 4-H clubs, Scouts, or Catholic Youth Organization)

5. Ask the boss at any *company where you work* part-time or summers

6. Watch closely for word of still other possibilities through the spring and summer in:

- Local newspapers, including your school's newspaper
- Local radio news
- Bulletins or other news periodicals of your parents' (or your) company, labor union, fraternal order, other community service organizations, church, or clubs

7. Make special inquiries (as later explained on p. 139) about *aid programs in your chosen college-study field*, if you have reached a fairly final decision on such a field and related career (such as nursing, pharmacy, architecture, or the like)

8. Possibly look in a *directory of financial aid* for college (though these tend unavoidably to be laborious to use, incomplete, and outdated)

9. Possibly use a *computer service* for helping locate financial aid that is open to you (though these charge a fee and also tend to be unavoidably incomplete and outdated)

Applying and Qualifying Phase Checklist

1. For each aid program of a private agency for which you find you're eligible, write for complete information and application forms (or get them in your school), carefully fill out the application, and send it in.

2. For each one of these private aid programs, set up a checklist-schedule of all the other steps you're required to take and carry them out scrupulously. (In most private-agency programs, the steps are essentially the same ones you're taking at about the same time in trying for college and government aid.)

In a nutshell, that's how you might do it. Here are some helpful details, specific examples, background explanations, and certain names and addresses you might want to use.

PRIVATE-AGENCY AID YOU MAY LOCATE BY ASKING IN YOUR HIGH SCHOOL

Your high school guidance office is most likely to have information about two types of scholarship programs (or loan programs) of private agencies for which you might be eligible.

Community scholarship programs. There are large varieties and numbers of what might be called "community" aid programs. These are programs open to all college-bound seniors in a specified community (or communities). Across the land they're sponsored by all kinds of local companies, foundations, and civic, fraternal, and service organizations.

As examples, the Paramus, N.J., Chamber of Commerce awards scholarships annually to local high school seniors. The Northwest Paper Foundation has offered scholarships for high school seniors in Cloquet, Minn., and Brainerd, Minn. Pennsylvania Power and Light Co. has offered scholarships to customers' children both living and heading for colleges in the Allentown area.

Some $500,000 a year for scholarships are raised from local businesses, foundations, and individuals by the Cleveland Scholarship Programs, Inc. It awards these scholarship funds to students in fourteen high schools in Cleveland and seven more schools in Cleveland suburbs. (You can ask about the programs in your school or by writing it at 1380 E. 6th St., Cleveland, Ohio 44114.) Hundreds of local scholarship offerings for students in the Oakland, Calif., schools are listed in an eighty-page handbook issued by the Oakland Public Schools (1025 2nd St., Oakland, Calif. 94619). Many local scholarship offerings in Rhode Island are identified in a sixty-page directory prepared by the financial aid counselor at Cranston High School East (Cranston, R.I. 02910). Remember, these are only a few examples of the thousands of local scholarships available.

Your high school very probably has information on such programs in your community because the aid donor wants to make sure all eligible students apply and the school wants to help its students get aid.

Some aid programs of this type are for students in many communities. The Citizens Scholarship Foundation of America has more than 200 chapters throughout the country that each support and award scholarships in their communities. You can find out if there's a chapter in your community by writing:

The Citizens Scholarship Foundation of America, One South St., Concord, N.H. 03301.

The Union Pacific Railroad has a scholarship program open to students who live in counties through which it runs in a dozen midwestern and western states. Applicants must also be members of the 4-H farm youth club. To see if you're in a county that makes you eligible, ask in your school or write:

> The Union Pacific Railroad, 1416 Dodge St., Omaha, Nebr. 68102.

National scholarship programs. Several large private scholarship programs offering numerous awards and open widely to high school students nationwide are well known to most high schools. Competition is typically keen in these programs, but they're worth a try on your part if you have rather high qualifications.

One of these is the National Merit Scholarship Program. You'd have to start very early in trying for a Merit award—before most students even begin thinking much about college and aid. The first step in trying for a Merit award is to take a test in October of your junior year in high school. That test is the PSAT (Preliminary Scholastic Aptitude Test of the College Board, which is also called and used as the NMSQT—National Merit Scholarship Qualifying Test). You don't have to worry too much about missing this test, though, for schools commonly give it to all college-bound juniors for guidance purposes.

National Merit makes awards from its own funds to some 3,000 students a year—awards that are one-time grants averaging about $1,000. But Merit is far more important as the framework through which many scores of companies, foundations, and unions provide scholarships, often to the children of company employees or union members. These "sponsored" Merit scholarships range from some $100 to $1,500 a year (based on need) and are most often renewable for four years.

After taking the test, you don't have to do anything next to compete in the annual selection. You'll be notified by Merit if you scored high enough on the test to qualify as a semifinalist, and of what further steps to take if you want to try to qualify as a Merit finalist and winner.

Special opportunities are also open to you through Merit if you're a Black American. Through the test, it also makes available scholarships in its National Achievement Scholarship Program for Outstanding Negro Students (as mentioned in this book's earlier chapter "Special Help for Students Handicapped by Poverty or Discrimination"). Merit's National Achievement Program provides awards to some 400 students a year, averaging $1,000 each in one-time awards and giving additional four-year scholarships funded ("sponsored") through Merit by companies, foundations, and so on. Again, applying in National Achievement is simple—just check the box indicating you're Black on the test answer sheet, and wait for further word.

Another large national program is that of the National Honor Society. Teachers and administrators in your school who compile the honor roll and run the school's society chapter should certainly know of this one. The National Honor Society Scholarship Program selects from among school nominees and makes one-time awards averaging $1,000 to about 200 students a year.

All schools are mailed annual announcements of another large program, the Betty Crocker Search for Leadership in Family Living. Young women interested in homemaking have a special advantage in it, and awards are not based on financial need, though they vary according to rank order in the selection of winners. It aids about 100 students a year in amounts ranging from some $500 to $5,000. You must apply for it by a deadline typically set at October 30 of your senior year. Request information about it in your school or from:

> The Betty Crocker Search for Leadership in Family Living
> General Mills, Inc.
> Box 113,
> Minneapolis, Minn. 55440.

High schools with especially dedicated science teachers are likely to know about the large problem called Science Talent Search of the Westinghouse Educational Foundation. It's through this program that schools or groups of schools often put on science fairs at which science research projects carried out by students are exhibited. Awards are based on project reports of up to 1,000 words by the students as well as recommendations of their science teachers and overall marks and test scores. In it, some forty students a year win amounts ranging from $250 to $10,000. Information on it is available from:

> Science Service, 1719 N St., N.W., Washington, D.C. 20036.

High school students in farming areas join widely in the National 4-H Awards Program, in which student agricultural projects are a key to winning awards. Students participate through their local 4-H clubs. Annual winners run to more than 200 students who receive awards of some $600 to $1,000. Applications usually close in October of your senior year, and details can be obtained from:

> National 4-H Service Committee, 150 N. Wacker Dr., Chicago, Ill. 60606.

A WORD ON OTHER POSSIBLE SCHOLARSHIP CONTESTS

Essay writing and other contests for scholarships—usually small prizes of $100 to $500—may come to your attention. If one or another such contest you learn of seems aboveboard and you're enthused, give it a try. But some of these contests in the past have been publicity gambits of the sponsors or even profit-making ventures for entry fees, with little or no benefits for students.

More than sixty contests endorsed as sound ones for you are described in a frequently revised booklet, "Advisory List of National Contests and Activities." You should be able to consult a copy of this booklet of the National Association of Secondary School Principals in your high school.

> Copies are available from the National Association of Secondary
> School Principals at:
> 1904 Association Dr.
> Reston, Va. 22091.

You might look in it to check out contests you hear about or to learn of ones you might enter if interested.

SCHOLARSHIP PROGRAMS ABOUT WHICH YOUR PARENTS CAN ASK

Your parents are in a good position to find out about possible private scholarship programs open to you in two senses: They'll help foot the bill on any college costs not covered by aid, and it's convenient for them to ask in organizations with which they're connected. These include such organizations as the following:

Companies or corporations where they work. Hundreds of employers across the country provide scholarship programs for children of employees. Your folks can find out if their employer has such an aid program by asking —their employer's personnel or employee-benefits manager, to be most certain, or some executive for whom they work.

Ford Motor Company Fund provides scholarships for the children of its hundreds of thousands of employees, for instance, as does Firestone Tire. IBM offers employee-children scholarships that are National Merit-sponsored awards. GE has provided an educational loan program for employee children.

Labor unions to which they belong. Your mom or dad can also ask local officers or national officers of any union to which they may belong. Union locals and unions sponsor scholarships for members' children in a great many cases. Among unions that have sponsored scholarships for members' children are the ILGWU (International Ladies Garment Workers Union), AFL-CIO (with sponsored National Merit awards), International Association of Machinists, United Steelworkers of America, and the National Maritime Union.

Fraternal organizations or lodges to which they belong. The Elks, Moose, Kiwanis, Lions, Rotary, and other fraternal orders or lodges sometimes sponsor scholarships either for members' children or for which members' children are given preference. Your parents can inquire at any such lodges to which they may belong.

Other community service organizations they have joined. Chambers of Commerce, PTAs (Parent-Teacher Associations), and other civic and service organizations not uncommonly raise funds for a few scholarships— ones in some cases awarded with preference for members' children and in other cases open generally to students in the community. The PTA in Parma, Ohio, for example, has offered a $250 scholarship to a Parma public school graduate going into teaching.

Any veterans organizations to which they belong. Local branches of veterans organizations like those of the American Legion or Veterans of Foreign Wars are occasionally the source of scholarships for the children of veterans. They also often have information about scholarships for veterans' children from other sources. Having your parents ask at their Legion Post or VFW headquarters shouldn't be much trouble for them and may uncover additional possibilities for you.

MORE SCHOLARSHIP PROGRAMS ABOUT WHICH YOU CAN ASK

Among other sources you might check out locally are these to which you can inquire directly.

Your church. Church organizations in some cases provide scholarships to members of the denomination, particularly those planning to attend colleges sponsored by the denomination. Such programs include those of the Aid Association for Lutherans (offering scholarships for study at any college; write the association at 222 W. College Ave., Appleton, Wisc. 54911), of the United Presbyterian Church (475 Riverside Dr., New York, N.Y. 10027), of the United Methodist Church (Box 871, Nashville, Tenn. 37202), and of the Knights of Columbus (for use at Roman Catholic colleges; write P.O. Drawer 1670, New Haven, Conn. 06507).

Any youth organizations to which you belong. You might also ask adult leaders of any youth organizations to which you belong if the organizations provide college financial aid programs for members or information about them. Nationwide scholarship programs of the 4-H farming youth clubs have already been mentioned as an example. Boys' clubs and girls' clubs in various cities have offered scholarships for their members. So have local chapters of Junior Achievement, in which young people learn the workings of business enterprises.

At companies where you may work. A few companies employing young people on a part-time or temporary basis offer scholarships. For instance, the *Philadelphia Bulletin* has provided *Bulletin* Contribution Scholarships for news carriers graduating from college. You might accordingly ask about possible similar aid where you yourself may work.

Two or more years' work as a golf caddie would make you eligible to compete for an award from the Evans Scholarship Foundation, which in past years has made grants to 250 students covering their college tuition and fees plus room costs. Information is available from the foundation at Golf, Ill. 60029.

STILL MORE WAYS FOR YOU TO HUNT PRIVATE-AGENCY AID PROGRAMS

Inquire about aid in your chosen college-study field. You would consider this possibility only if you have already reached a fairly final decision on a definite study field and related career area in which to concentrate in college. These would be fields like pharmacy, nursing, mechanical engineering, accounting, physical therapy, or one of many others. If you have settled on such a field, write to a national professional society in it for information on college financial aid offered for study in the field. While you're writing, you might want to ask as well for information on careers and lists of colleges offering approved programs in it, which these organizations also commonly provide on request.

You can find names and addresses for each of a great many of these societies in a book that should be in your school or community library, the latest edition of the *Occupational Outlook Handbook*, issued by the Bureau of Labor Statistics, U.S. Department of Labor. (Look in the book under the career for which you intend to study.) A librarian should be able to help you get the name and address for such an organization from this or other reference works.

As an additional step, you might ask the colleges to which you're applying to please be sure to consider you for any aid provided specifically for study in your chosen field that they may have to award.

Watching for word of aid programs locally. You and your parents may also find word of aid programs open to you just by generally keeping your eyes and ears open locally, especially through the spring and summer months when awards to scholarship winners are commonly announced and announcements are also made about the opening of application for the next year.

Watch for such word particularly in your local newspapers, your school newspaper, and house organs or newssheets of any company, union, church, club, lodge, civic, or social organization with which your parents are connected.

Watch also on bulletin boards—in your school, post offices, libraries, and where your parents work.

Small, new, local programs are being introduced constantly across the country. Keeping alert in this way might locate one of them for you.

Possibly search in a financial aid directory. You could also search in one of the few directories of financial aid for possible programs open to you. One of the disadvantages of this approach compared to inquiring locally is that the most numerous kind of private-agency programs—the small, local ones in which you're most likely to get aid—often come and go rather rapidly, so that published listings can quickly become outdated. Private aid programs may also be so obscure that many of them never get included in a book or other general information source, though they are quite well publicized among special groups eligible for them. The sheer numbers and varieties of such small aid programs also make poring through a directory that lists even some of them quite laborious.

There's no harm in trying, though, especially if you can find a recently issued directory in your school or community library. Among ones you might look for are the *Student Aid Annual* and *Student Aid Bulletins*, issued primarily for guidance offices by Chronicle Guidance Publications, Inc. (Moravia, N.Y. 13118), and *Financial Aids for Higher Education, 1976–77 National Catalog* by Oreon Keeslar and published by William Brown Co. (Dubuque, Iowa 52001).

Possibly use a computer search service for financial aid. As one more alternative, you could also use a computer search service to help find private-agency aid programs for which you are eligible. The computer data bank of such a service is in essence like the contents of a financial aid directory, and can have much the same drawbacks, namely, incomplete and out-of-date information about aid programs. It can spare you the tedium of directory searching, but replaces it with a fee charged for the service. In general, unless a computer service has an extraordinarily well-developed and constantly updated data bank, it probably can't locate any more financial aid programs open to you than would a very capable guidance counselor in your high school.

Should you be interested in trying such a computer service, however, one is the College Scholarship Information Bank, administered by the College Scholarship Service (of the College Entrance Examination Board). In its files are mainly private-agency aid programs. It contains some 10,000 aid sources in the New England states, with additional sources throughout Texas, New Jersey, and Illinois due to be added in late 1977. The service plans to extend its coverage to include all states eventually. The fee for a search by the bank (and printout of all aid sources on file that are open to you) is $12. Information about the bank may be obtained by writing:

> College Scholarship Information Bank
> College Entrance Examination Board
> 888 Seventh Ave., New York, N.Y. 10019.

Another computer service you might try is Scholarship Search. Its coverage is nationwide, and its fee for a search and printout is $40. Information about it is available from:

> Scholarship Search
> 1775 Broadway,
> New York, N.Y. 10019.

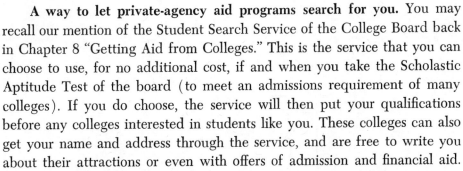

A way to let private-agency aid programs search for you. You may recall our mention of the Student Search Service of the College Board back in Chapter 8 "Getting Aid from Colleges." This is the service that you can choose to use, for no additional cost, if and when you take the Scholastic Aptitude Test of the board (to meet an admissions requirement of many colleges). If you do choose, the service will then put your qualifications before any colleges interested in students like you. These colleges can also get your name and address through the service, and are free to write you about their attractions or even with offers of admission and financial aid.

Use of the service like this is also open to sponsors of scholarship programs other than colleges, including reputable private agencies. Opting for the Student Search Service could thus put your qualifications before some private-agency scholarship sources that might then get in touch with you.

APPLYING AND QUALIFYING IN PRIVATE-AGENCY AID PROGRAMS

There's only one thing you might look out for generally in connection with private-agency aid programs—early aid appplication deadlines, ones often earlier than those of colleges. Many of these programs set deadlines for getting your first application form in as early as dates running from October 1 to December 1 of your high school senior year.

Again, as noted in the checklist at the start of this chapter, the things you'd be required to provide in most of these programs are much like those required in college and government aid programs. Requirements typically include an application form (often with one or more short essays characterizing yourself and your interests), high school transcript, college entrance test scores, and your school recommendation. Community programs especially are fond of required interviews for all applicants. Some private aid programs have special requirements, as you've seen in such cases as the 4-H clubs, Betty Crocker Search, and Science Talent Search programs. Essay or other scholarship contests have obvious special requirements.

Do be sure to apply early enough in any of these private-agency aid programs in which you're eligible. And unfailingly follow a schedule for meeting each requirement of the program.

Should you be fortunate enough to win, you'll probably hear the good news (in most cases) by or before mid-April of your last high school year. Here's hoping your news will be good.

11

BEYOND AID: STUDENT AND FAMILY SOURCES OF ADDITIONAL FUNDS DURING THE COLLEGE YEARS

BEYOND assets, grants, federally aided work-study programs, and guaranteed student loans, there are usually still money needs that must be met during the college years. This chapter and the next deal with meeting those needs.

For families with dependent students, the chief source of additional income can be the generation of additional funds through the return of the student's mother to the work force. This continues to be a major trend, fed by increasingly widespread job opportunities for women. It is somewhat undercut by a trend toward return to school on the part of women seeking career training and similarly by the increasing divorce rate, but it remains a major trend.

Sound long-range planning in this area can greatly enhance earnings when they are most needed and at the same time reconcile potential contradictions between career training or business building on the one hand and the need to earn college fund money for children's education on the other. Inadequate long-range planning can mean missed career opportunities, a far smaller contribution to college money than is reasonably possible, and sometimes enormous and unnecessary marriage strains.

Like all college financial planning, the key is an early start. Whether it's a business, a profession, or simply a relatively highly paid, marketable skill, the preparations should be undertaken before the college money is needed. This usually means a family decision to invest time and money in training or business building while potentially college-bound children are in their early high school or even their elementary school years.

As in any career choice, thought must be given not only to the career wanted for personal reasons but also to which careers will offer reasonably good job possibilities once training has been completed. Just as the college-bound student will at some point have to give thought to the practical value of a philosophy major (not that it should be abandoned because it may be impractical, but it's a factor to be considered), so too does a woman returning to the work force have to consider whether an undergraduate major in psychology or English is a practical choice.

FAST-GROWING JOB AREAS

Some very fast-growing areas that women returning to the work force have been choosing to enter are:

1. The health care fields. The Labor Department's Bureau of Labor Statistics projects continued very fast rates of growth in almost all health care areas. Growth rates projected between 1974 and 1985 for example, are:

- Dental hygienists—up from 23,000 to 58,000, a growth of 156.7 percent. Most dental hygienists take a two-year course in a school of dental hygiene and qualify for a state license by passing a state examination. Entry-level jobs pay $7,000–$9,000 per year; experienced dental hygienists are paid in the $10,000–$13,000 area.

- Respiratory therapy workers—up from 53,000 to 120,000, a growth of 121.7 percent. Respiratory therapists take American Medical Association-approved courses ranging from eighteen months to four years. Entry-level jobs pay $8,000–$10,000 per year; experienced respiratory therapists are paid in the $14,000–$17,000 area.

  There are a wide variety of potential careers open to women returning to work in the health care field, ranging from the hundreds of thousands of new practical nurses, medical records technicians, and medical laboratory technicians needed all the way to the relatively few who will go back to school, finish their interrupted professional educations, and become highly paid doctors and psychologists.

2. The computer industry, which continues to grow by leaps and bounds. For example, the number of computer programmers is expected to grow from 200,000 to 285,000 between 1974 and 1985, up 42.5 percent; the number of systems analysts, from 115,000 to 190,000, up 56.2 percent.

   Programmers usually do not have formal degrees, but rather some college or technical school training in programming, plus on-the-job training. Systems analysts are usually taken from the ranks of the programmers.

   Beginning programmers are paid in the $9,000–$13,000 range; experienced programmers, in the $14,000–$20,000 range. Systems analysts start in the $12,000–$14,000 range, then move up into the $17,000–$22,000 range.

3. Retail buying, which is expected to grow by close to 40 percent between 1974 and 1985. Buyers usually have bachelor's degrees, get on-the-job

training, can expect to start at $9,000–$10,000, then move into the $17,000–$23,000 range.

There are dozens of other fields returning women are entering, often fields that were closed or very nearly closed when they first entered the job market. They include such jobs as bank officer, accountant, and government health inspector, all fast-growing occupations requiring little beyond a two- or four-year college degree.

The fact is that women entering the job market anew can train for and often get jobs that pay rather well and are at the same time personally stimulating—if they and their families plan far enough ahead and are willing to invest sufficient time and money in that training. Of all the investments we've discussed, that training offers by far the highest return, whether return is measured in dollars alone or in both dollars and personal satisfaction, as it should be.

GOING INTO BUSINESS

Going into business should be viewed in much the same way as the investment in career training. For your business to succeed and not become just another hopefully started and soon failed small business, it must be done right.

Doing a small business right involves developing a number of skills and understandings that are quite special. The woman who thinks that she should open a restaurant because she is a fine cook and routinely entertains many guests at dinner may be in for an unneeded, costly set of surprises.

Sometimes a small business develops quite naturally out of career training. The newly trained cosmetologist gets a job, works for a while for someone else, learns the business side of the business, sets up for herself. It's done every day—a combination of formal skills training and business apprenticeship that can result in a successful small business.

One way or another, you must learn the business side of the business— the buying of materials, accounting, selling, advertising and promotion, people handling, financing, and all the other details that will make the difference between success and failure. And the best possible way to learn any business is to work in it long enough to see, understand, and learn how to handle all the problems and opportunities that come up in the course of the business year.

Yes, business year. There's absolutely no point in taking some of the family's savings and putting the money into an ill-prepared-for small business. You'll just use up money you should be saving for college, rather than preparing to make a substantial contribution to the family's total income during the years you'll need money most. By far the best way to enter any small business is to work in the same or a very similar kind of business first for at least six months to a year.

Small businesses that have proven quite substantial sources of additional family income without large financial risks are usually to be found in the service industries—catering and party giving, office temporary businesses, copying centers. Others can involve special skills and interests such as craft stores, art supply and framing stores, specialty food stores, some boutiques.

A successful small business can provide substantial income and equally large personal satisfactions. It should be planned carefully, financed adequately, and given a chance to get past the early dry period that must be expected of all beginning businesses. A caution here: If it is clearly failing, drop it and take your losses before they become an enormous drain on family resources and the potential graveyard of college money plans.

STUDENT JOBS

Students work in an extremely wide range of occupations, all the way from those paying considerably below federal minimum wages to the ownership of businesses yielding many thousands of dollars in profits every year.

Most on-campus college-connected jobs are paid for largely by government funds, handled as part of the "financial aid package" by the college, and given to those students proving greatest financial need. They usually average little more than the minimum wage. On some campuses, there are a few other jobs, and, of course, these are worth going after. But the fact is that most of the school year earnings opportunities that you can do anything about are not likely to involve direct employment by the college.

If you need to earn a significant amount of money during the school year, bear in mind that some colleges are better located than others for earnings purposes. The small liberal arts college located on a country campus five miles from the nearest small town and forty miles from the nearest medium-sized city may be a great place to go to school; however, it's not likely to offer many job opportunities during the school year. City and suburban campuses, especially those located in relatively prosperous areas, will offer a great many more ways of making money. And sometimes they won't require a car for getting to and from your work.

Planning to have moneymaking skills when you'll need them is as true for part-time and seasonal work as it is for long-term full-time careers. For example, the typing course you take in high school will be extremely useful for doing term papers in college. It can also be a source of considerable income during the college years. The computer course may result in relatively well-paid computer operator and programming work. And your interest in repairing automobiles may earn you a good deal of money during your college years.

For planning purposes, be aware that your earnings, especially if they are larger than the amounts indicated in your yearly "financial aid package," can result in cutting your financial aid. The amount cut, however, is not likely to be anything near the amounts made.

TREND TOWARD PART-TIME JOBS

Millions of Americans, including hundreds of thousands of college students, are employed as part-time workers. And the trend toward part-time work continues to grow. The Bureau of Labor Statistics points out that almost one-sixth of all American workers are part-timers, up from one-tenth fifteen years ago. One-fifth of all unemployed workers are seeking only part-time work, up from one-tenth twenty years ago.

The trend is especially strong in retailing and in a number of service industries. In 1977, S. S. Kresge estimated that 34,000 of 133,000 employees worked an average of twenty-four hours a week or less. Sixty-five percent of J. L. Hudson's employees in Detroit were part-timers. Gimbel's in the New York area had a work force composed of 40 percent full-timers, 25 percent part-time, and 35 percent extra on part-time.

And these are large employers with year round steady businesses. More seasonal employers, like Howard Johnson's, employ thousands of part-timers every summer, as do resorts, restaurants, camps, private clubs—some of the traditional sources of summer jobs for college students.

There are also the off-hours employers—the telephone company, which has used part-timers for many years; computer companies and departments of companies using computers, which rent computers and try to use them for more than one shift; the fast food restaurants.

Summer seasonal employers are not the only seasonal job possibilities. Students have always found employment with the post office and the retail stores to handle the Christmas rush. In recent years, they have also found considerable employment in the growing tax preparation industry as office workers and tax preparers. Accountants put on additional clerical help between Christmas and April 15. Tax preparation firms hire almost their whole work forces during that period, often training people as part of the entire process and rehiring as many as possible from previous years—excellent job opportunities for college students.

Ten years ago, during the prosperity of the sixties, college students had little trouble finding part-time jobs if they were willing to look hard and persistently for them. Then, in the early seventies, they became very hard to get indeed. Now, the tide has turned. Part-time jobs are a growing trend in American industry, and most college students are finding themselves once again able to get part-time work during the school year. It's still awfully hard if you're going to school way out on a country campus, but increasingly possible everywhere else.

SUMMER JOBS

Full-time summer jobs are quite another matter. They're hard to get, and don't seem to be getting much easier. As far as college students and full-time summer jobs are concerned, prosperity is still very much around the corner.

Still, there are a considerable number of summer income opportunities available. They tend to require some careful advance planning, but are often very much worth it.

Students often have an entirely understandable reluctance to work in the family business during the summer or at any other time. But if there is a family business, it's worth considering. Remember, every dollar legitimately paid rather than given to a dependent student may be worth almost two dollars, after taking into account the tax advantages to the entire family supporting that student. And the family business may need to hire extra help for vacations and summer business increases, as do other businesses.

Even if there's no family business, summer jobs often result from family ties. Corporations often give summer and part-time job preference to the children of employees. Uncles in the construction business may have to be approached well ahead of time, but can be sources of very good summer jobs.

For commuting students and those living away from home but staying all year in their college areas, it is often possible to work for only one employer, moving back and forth fairly easily between part-time school year and full-time summer employment. Employers who are normally wary of hiring students during the summer and training them only to see them quit to return to school look at year round part-timers quite differently and will often expand their employment during periods of full-time availability.

The traditional student summer jobs are still there—camp counseling, hotel, restaurant, private club work. They have been joined in recent years by office temporaries work, computer operating and programming, and such outdoor jobs as lawn care and house painting, which are often student-run small businesses.

STUDENT-RUN BUSINESSES

Student-run small businesses can be excellent sources of income. They can also be time- and money-consuming failures, like any other small businesses. As discussed earlier in this chapter, and allowing for less training time and investment in student businesses than in family businesses, they still must be done right—which involves learning the business side of the business as well as the kind of business.

A student who wants to run a lawn care and fix-it operation during the summer would be well advised to work for someone else first, to learn the ins and outs of the business, not the least of which is how to find the jobs. A student who thinks investing savings in a couple of vending machines around the college seems like a good business may not be able to apprentice in the vending machine business, but had best seek out others who have done so and try to learn something about the problems as well as the opportunities involved.

There are many businesses in which the student can act as representative and often salesperson for a larger business. They include such traditional businesses as magazine subscription agenting, appliance rentals, insurance selling, clothing and jewelry sales.

Large and active direct sales markets have grown up in and around most campuses today in such items as arts and crafts created directly by students for sale to other students and faculty members. Students also place their arts and crafts materials in retail stores, often in a very wide area around the schools. They also visit other campuses to sell their work. Some students also secure goods from other sources and act mainly as direct sales representatives on campus and in surrounding communities.

Students provide a large number of services for which they are paid directly, rather than as employees. They range from babysitting to bartending at parties and often develop into businesses. The babysitter who has too much work and secures other babysitters can soon be running an informal babysitting agency. The bartender at several parties can start a party catering business. The quick accurate typist who starts doing a few papers for friends often finds a substantial source of part-time income.

12

BEYOND GUARANTEED LOANS: OTHER SOURCES OF LOAN MONEY DURING THE COLLEGE YEARS

COLLEGE money is often a very iffy jigsaw puzzle—a no-strings grant perhaps, a mostly federally funded college job, a guaranteed student loan with the rate of interest sometimes sliding upward if your family income is too high, a summer job the student may or may not get. As in all financial planning, the only things you can be even reasonably sure of for planning purposes are your current assets and your current income.

Very often, you must make college decisions involving substantial long-term expenditures without having a very good idea of what financial aid, if any, will be forthcoming. As a practical matter, the financial side of that decision therefore rests on what you have, what you earn, and what you can borrow.

One of the most basic things to remember about credit is that the old saw about only being able to borrow money when you don't need it has a substantial kernel of truth in it. Beyond guaranteed student loans, in which the government pledges repayment of the loans, you are dealing with private lenders, all of whom will lend you money only if they think they have a good chance of repayment.

Students, then, usually with little in the way of assets, current income, or good credit history, have an extremely hard time borrowing any meaningful sums of money beyond the guaranteed student loan. And although those loans have often placed heavy post-graduation burdens upon students, they have often meant the difference between a college education and none.

The families of dependent students face a different problem. They often find it necessary to borrow to close the gap between all other sources of college money and the amount of money needed, and face significant timing and capability problems, often before knowing just how much money will be coming from all other sources.

Families can usually borrow most easily well before they need the money for college. That's when their financial positions are strongest, when savings and other assets are at their highest, when debts and expenses are lower than at any time during the college years. It is therefore usually good financing strategy to try to make the longest time kinds of financial arrangements and establish maximum reserves before college expenses begin to impact on family finances.

Good financing strategy also includes coming into potential major borrowing situations with other kinds of current debts and repayments as low as possible. It makes good sense for families to come into the year before college entrance without substantial installment purchases being repaid, with credit card balances low, with bank balances healthy. It doesn't make any sense at all, for example, to deplete current bank balances with an expensive vacation trip just when you may want to borrow a good deal of money, or to buy a new car and add substantial monthly payments as a burden on current income just when a banker may be evaluating your ability to repay large loans.

It also makes very good sense to try to borrow as much as you'll need (to bridge the gap between all other sources of college money and what the family will really need) just once from one lender. It is almost always far easier to borrow a substantial amount once, rather than to borrow inadequately and then have to come back for more, or even worse have to go elsewhere and wind up paying back two loans at once. Some family college loan arrangements encourage this kind of sound planning by making the total amounts loaned realistically large, paying the loaned amounts as needed rather than all at once, and providing for somewhat stretched out repayment.

CASH SURRENDER VALUE LOANS

If you have cash surrender value in a whole life insurance policy and you need college money, by all means borrow from the insurance company on the policy.

You will find the interest rate at which you'll be borrowing to be in the 4–6 percent simple interest range. That's far better than you'll do anywhere else.

You should be able to borrow 90–95 percent of the cash surrender value in the policy, with a minimum of red tape and no extra charges of any kind for "points" or "services" or legal and accounting fees.

The amount borrowed reduces the face amount of the policy by exactly what was borrowed. The net effect is therefore to leave something closer to pure insurance in the policy, taking out the savings.

One way to look at this kind of transaction is that the interest charges are so low on the borrowings from a whole life insurance policy that after taking the impact of inflation into account, your repayments will be in dollars that are likely to have lost enough value to make up for the interest. Putting it differently, you may not be paying any real interest for the use of the money.

Another factor to take into account is that the interest you do pay is tax deductible, which further decreases your borrowing cost.

WORK-CONNECTED LOANS

In recent years, an increasing number of companies have developed a very attractive fringe benefit—the low-interest, long-term-repayment college loan.

One major company offers employees up to $5,000 per year in family college loans, with a maximum loan at any time of $10,000. The loan is repayable over a ten-year period at 6 percent simple interest by means of a monthly payroll deduction.

This is an extremely valuable fringe benefit and highly prized by company employees. They know that after taking inflation and the deductibility of interest into account, they are paying at most a negligible amount for the use of substantial college money when they need it. And the payroll deduction feature makes repayment relatively painless, especially as the ten-year repayment period makes even the largest possible payments relatively easy to handle. The company reserves the right to limit amounts loaned when employee earnings might make repayment difficult and takes other precautions to limit company risk, but the net effect is the provision of a valuable benefit.

If you are employed by a company that has such a loan plan, explore it long before college money is needed to determine how much money may be available for your needs. It may not be possible to get an advance commitment from your company, anymore than a bank will be willing to give you a commitment until you actually apply for a loan, but it may be possible to get something very close to a commitment, which can help your college money planning considerably.

Should your company not have this kind of benefit, it's never too soon to start pushing for adoption of it. You're sure to find many co-workers facing college costs, just as you are, and willing to add their voices to your requests for institution of this kind of loan plan. It's an excellent employee relations device for the company, and its cost to the company compares very favorably with many other less highly prized fringe benefits.

Those owning or partially owning their own businesses may be able to create this kind of benefit for themselves by borrowing money at low rates from their own businesses. Consult your accountant before you do it, though, to be sure you comply with all applicable laws and regulations.

Another traditional source of fairly low-interest, easy-to-secure loan money has been the employee credit union. If you work in a company with a credit union, investigate it as a possible college money source.

COLLEGE MONEY LINES OF CREDIT

Some banks have instituted what amounts to a line of credit dedicated to college money needs. This sort of arrangement can function as a superb financial planning device for you, as the line of credit can be applied for as soon as acceptance has been received from any college or graduate school.

One such arrangement is that of the Irving Trust Company of New York. The line of credit offered goes up to $20,000, which is the current New York statutory limit for this kind of loan.

Repayment can take as long as seven years, with an interest rate of 1 percent per month on the outstanding loan balance and an effective annual interest rate of 12.17 percent.

The only other charges are life insurance charges of 60¢ per $1,000 per month on outstanding balances and credit available. That means, for example, a monthly insurance charge of $6.00 if you have balances owing and credits available adding up to $10,000.

Where credit lines extended total over $5,000 or carry repayment terms of over thirty-six months, family income must be over $15,000 per year or more. This is the New York State law, clearly designed to allow this kind of more expensive credit to take over for middle-income families where the guaranteed student loan leaves off. Of course, as is so often true in the illogical checkerboard of college financing arrangements, New York State has changed its rules to permit guaranteed loans to dependent students from families with anything less than $25,000 per year in adjusted income for student loan purposes, thus creating an "opportunity" for overlapping loans.

Those who may apply for this kind of credit line are parents of students or individual students attending school while holding full-time jobs.

Once the line of credit is granted, the bank supplies a book of checks—"school chex"—which are used by the borrower to pay for tuition, fees, room and board, books, and other educational costs. Checks can be issued up to the limit of the line of credit for any number of children at colleges, graduate schools, and private schools.

This is not an inexpensive means of getting college money, and all less-expensive ways of doing so should be preferred. But it does offer a borrowing base for financial planning to join relatively sure aspects of current assets and income. Like any other standby credit, it should be applied for while your financial position is strong—that is, before college costs really begin to impact strongly on your financial position.

EDUCATION LOANS

The bank-offered education loan works a little differently. Rather than functioning as a line of credit, it tends to offer a fixed sum loaned at the beginning of each year, with a total four-year bank commitment based on the credit granted on the basis of the original loan application.

Loan proceeds are usually sent directly to the borrower to be used to pay for college costs. As a practical matter, those funds will usually then be mingled with the other funds of the borrower and often used generally for family purposes during the college years. We would urge you not to handle borrowed college funds this way, but rather to hold them in a separate account with other college money to be sure that they are used for the purposes intended.

The amount of education loan money a bank will lend you may go as high as the line of credit previously discussed, and will depend on your financial strength and history at the time of application. These are not funds guaranteed by any government, but rather funds loaned in expectation of repayment by you.

Life insurance is usually attached to these kinds of loans, sometimes with and sometimes without additional charges.

Repayment can take up to seven years, with effective interest rates in the 12 percent range.

This kind of credit is relatively expensive, as is a college money line of credit. But, like the line of credit, it offers a reasonably sound planning base. It is not, however, standby credit, but actual borrowing, which means that considerably more care should be taken in estimating borrowing needs than in the line-of-credit instance. Once you borrow, you must pay back, including interest, and prepayment of money owed never offsets all the interest charges due.

SECURED PERSONAL LOANS

Bank loans that are secured by other personal assets are usually far easier to get than personal loans secured only by your signature, that is, by your simple promise to pay.

Assets that are usually acceptable for securing loans include savings accounts, some stocks, some bonds, some mutual funds. As we discussed in Chapter 4, stocks and bonds that are recognizably "blue chip" are very acceptable as security, up to as much as 70–80 percent of current market value.

College fund borrowings should be thought of as long-term. Therefore, passbook borrowings are not especially appropriate for this purpose. All you're doing is holding savings then, on which you're receiving a maximum of 7–8 percent in long-term interest, and probably more like 5 percent short-term, so that you can borrow funds on which you'll pay 9–12 percent in effective interest, depending on the bank, the time, and the arrangements you are able to make.

Stocks and bonds, on the other hand, often make excellent loan-securing assets. Sometimes, especially those stocks that are doing well, you don't want to sell and have to pay capital gains taxes on the appreciation in the value of the stocks. By borrowing on the stocks, you are able to hold them, continue to receive dividends and any gains in the value of the stock, and at the same time borrow money on that stock.

PERSONAL LINES OF CREDIT

The use of corporate and personal lines of credit, or "overdraft banking," has been widespread throughout the world for many years. Recently, the personal line of credit has been widely introduced into U.S. consumer banking and has become extremely popular.

A personal line of credit is an arrangement by which your bank extends you the privilege of overdrawing your account by a specified sum and then promises to honor your checks drawn on that account up to the limit established.

Personal lines of credit usually run in the $1,000–$5,000 range, with financing charges in the 12-percent annual area. Some banks are now offering those they consider their best credit risks lines of credit in the $10,000–$15,000 range or even higher, but that is rare so far.

These lines of credit revolve; that is, there is no periodic repayment or time limit on repayment, as long as credit limits are not exceeded. Interest and service charges are debited to your account and require no special payments.

Education lines of credit and direct education loans are better devices for paying college costs, but the personal line of credit also has an important function to perform.

The main advantage of the personal line of credit is that it can be applied for and secured long before college costs need be faced. A banking relationship can be built up that includes the line of credit. A history of use and repayment of the line of credit can be developed.

That can mean a somewhat expanded personal financial base for you during the college planning years—and a "back burner" source of personal funds for emergencies during the years in which you're straining every resource to provide funds for college.

Be sure, though, to be careful in using your personal credit line. It's a rather expensive, last resort source of quick funds, not a funding device for long-term obligations. It's reserve, not current grocery money.

And when it's time to go after an education credit line or a long-term education loan, be sure to have a healthy plus balance in your checking account, not a minus number showing your personal credit line in use. The presence of an unused personal credit line is unlikely to limit your ability to get other lines; it will rather show you to be a prudent money manager. Conversely, a heavily used personal credit line with a minus balance showing while you're trying to borrow substantial sums of college money can only work toward your disadvantage.

MORTGAGES

We have previously discussed the high cost of remortgaging. Do it if you must, but all the ways of borrowing we've discussed so far in this chapter are considerably less expensive in the long run.

On the other hand, some relatively high-income families, with many years of increasing earnings ahead, may get substantial tax advantages from the way interest charges are figured on remortgage, with much higher tax-deductible interest charges available in the early years of the new mortgage. In some cases, after-tax interest charges can be effectively cut by as much as 50 percent, representing taxes that won't be paid on the mortgage interest.

Second mortgages are a poor idea for college financing, as they result in double mortgage repayments just when you need the money for college costs. If you feel that you must use the store of value in your home to help meet college costs, it is almost preferable to remortgage.

COMMERCIALLY SPONSORED "PAYMENT PROGRAMS"

Parents of students about to enter college, who are in the process of figuring out how to pay for college, are often delighted to receive a very nice and helpful letter on the college's letterhead. The letter expresses a desire to help with the difficult problem of getting the money for college, and in very kindly fashion offers the services of this or that plan of payment.

The implied sponsorship of the college firmly established, the letter then proceeds to briefly but carefully disclaim any financial or operating connection or responsibility for the program. The letter then goes on to extol the dubious virtues of the payment plan being presented.

Thanks to the Truth In Lending Law, the "payment plans" are now forced to disclose that they are making loans and to give their rates of interest. For one of the largest of them, and one that has used hundreds of college letterheads to sell its services, those interest rates run from almost 14 percent to almost 18 percent, depending on the length of repayment time and the amount borrowed.

If you wonder how respectable, well-established colleges are willing to lend themselves to this sort of practice, consider that many colleges are having horrendous financial difficulties and that the problems they face aren't getting any easier to solve. After having allowed for that, you still have a right to wonder, though.

You may feel that you have to pay these high interest rates because you are otherwise a very poor credit risk and this is the only way to get the money to pay for college for your dependents. If so, fair enough. But take another look at all the other possibilities we've discussed before you do. And don't, like so many others over the years, pay these very high interest rates just because they seem college-approved and because you haven't taken the time and trouble to investigate other possibilities.

13

PUTTING IT ALL TOGETHER: SUCCESSFUL COLLEGE-COST PLANNING

SOME families correctly estimate the potentially crushing impact of coming college costs, generate enough income to make early planning truly meaningful, and are able to plan early and well.

Others, with just as large income possibilities, hardly plan at all, and wind up with children cheated of college opportunities, enormous debts, and sometimes both.

Some individuals and families have modest resources, make the most of them with sound planning and early study of financial aid possibilities. They often choose college options carefully and succeed in meeting college obligations without mortgaging student and family futures. Others manage to mortgage their futures and still not have enough money to complete college educations.

And many must depend almost wholly on financial aid possibilities, with the difference between going to college or not depending on how well they search out and make use of aid, loans, and whatever income they can generate.

THE PLANNERS

Sam and Marge Harris started a separate savings account for college costs the day they decided to have their first child. Both college graduates themselves, they were determined to provide as much college education as their children would want.

They had three children spaced two years apart and figured that at least one, and possibly all three, would want to go on to graduate school.

Sam was a young lawyer in the legal department of a large corporation in the early years of their marriage. He had good earnings prospects. Marge had been headed for some sort of career in teaching and intended to go back to it when the kids were off to college.

In those early years, Sam's salary was just about enough to meet current expenses. They bought a house and a couple of cars, and moved to one of the suburbs of the big eastern city in which Sam worked.

They investigated financial aid possibilities early and decided that the prospects of getting no-strings grants from federal or state sources were small, given the assets they were sure they'd build up over the years and the level of income Sam could reasonably expect by the time their first child was ready to apply for college.

That led to an early decision to build a tax-free college fund by systematically buying Series E bonds in their children's names (see Chapter 4). And, as they were therefore not concerned about building their children's assets to the detriment of possible available financial aid, they bought life insurance early, with their children as beneficiaries and later created modest trust funds in their children's names as tax avoidance devices, only after careful consultation with their accountant.

They continued to put money in the savings account and later began to put some of it into triple A–rated corporate bonds maturing during the college years. During the stock market's boom years in the mid-sixties, they bought some blue chip stocks, knowing that they could always borrow using these stocks as security if they needed to without selling the stocks at a tax- or current-value disadvantage. (Sam bought some speculative stocks in those years, too, and "lost his shirt" on them when the market collapsed in the late sixties and early seventies, but he always knew they were speculative and the college fund wasn't hurt.)

The college fund grew, but not as fast as the cost of putting children through college. In the early seventies, as their children began to enter high school, it began to be perfectly clear that they would need considerably more than Sam could make when the children were all in college.

In later years, they said that the most important financial decision they'd ever made was when Marge went back to school right after their first child entered high school. Marge, now fourteen years older than when she'd been headed for a career in teaching, took a second look and decided she wanted to be a school psychologist. It took a couple of years and some thousands of dollars, but by the time their first child had entered college, she was working in a nearby school district, making a professional's salary, and building an independent career.

Sam and Marge did several other things to prepare for the impact of college costs:

• They investigated scholarship opportunities—not the highly competitive national ones that their children would try for and make or not on a competitive basis, but the local and special purpose scholarships that have limited numbers of applicants. They found that most required some kind of financial need but that some did not.

• Sam discovered that his company was considering a college-loan plan for long-term employees and their families. He joined those who were pushing for it and was gratified to see the plan adopted while his children were still in high school.

• They investigated all available loans. On the basis of that investigation, they held off remortgage of their home, discarded the "college-sponsored" finance company loan plans, and developed a fairly large emergency line of credit with a local bank before any of the children were in college. In addition, realizing that federally guaranteed loans were available for their children, they discussed those loans with each child in turn, deciding to take some loans but not enough to cause any child to substantially mortgage his or her future.

• The college selection process was carefully and early discussed with each child in turn. Sam and Marge were both State University products, and while recognizing the value of "prestigious" colleges for some purposes, wanted the children to know that public colleges were in most cases at least as good and often better than private colleges for all normal educational purposes—and cost a great deal less.

• Their children were encouraged early to work and build college funds. Each developed some kind of special skill that paid a good deal more than the standard campus jobs, most of which they would not be eligible for because of their lack of "financial need." Sam, Junior, who took a computer programming course in high school, was a skilled and well-paid programmer throughout his college years and found that his computer knowledge was enormously useful in his chosen field of financial management. Ellen learned how to prepare tax returns from her lawyer father and worked for an accounting firm part-time all year and almost full time during "tax season." George worked for a local catering service during his high school years, then ran a lucrative part-time catering business during his college years.

Here's how it worked out:

Sam, Junior, decided he wanted to go into the business world and knew he wanted a high prestige M.B.A. He wasn't the best student in the world, though an adequate one, and the family decided that he would be best advised to go to a high cost, high prestige "feeder" school, one that would be likely to give him, with anticipated high but not outstanding undergraduate grades and exams, a shot at a graduate school like Harvard Business School or the Wharton School. It cost a little over $35,000 when they finished totaling it up, but all agreed it was worth it when Sam, Junior, was accepted at Harvard Business School. The money came out of savings, maturing bonds, student loans that Sam, Junior, would pay out of future earnings, and out of the current earnings of Sam, Marge, and Sam, Junior.

Ellen wasn't sure what she wanted to do or be, but there was a good chance she might want to be a doctor. Facing the possibility of having to pay for several years of medical school after four years of college, and at the same time wanting some career decision alternatives, she headed for the state university. A brilliant student, she qualified for several local and national scholarships, but chose the state university because given her lack of "financial need" and the enormous difference in costs between the private colleges and the state university, it made financial sense to pick the state university. Besides, it was a large school, with many course and career options. The family financed her undergraduate education as they had Sam, Junior's. She did ultimately go on to medical school, and that financing was greatly helped by a guaranteed student loan and a special interest scholarship that was granted on the basis of merit rather than financial need.

George, as it turned out, had the best business head in the family. His catering business came very close to financing him through four years at the state university. After that, he soon went into business for himself and now runs a string of fast food restaurants. He did use some of those family college funds, though—as borrowed capital to help finance his first restaurant.

THE HIGH FLYERS

Walter Bigelow really lost his shirt when the bottom fell out of the stock market in the late sixties. Of course, it wasn't a very expensive shirt, because Walter hadn't really saved enough to make any very substantial investments, which is probably why he went into speculative stocks that went way, way up—on paper—for a while and then came to earth with a thud.

It didn't have the slightest effect on the way Walter, Louise, and their two children lived, though.

Walter and Louise were always "borrowed up," which he had explained to her very early in their married life was a good idea, as the interest on borrowings was tax deductible. They had always lived in expensive houses, driven expensive cars, taken expensive vacations, and entertained a good deal.

As to college, well, their kids were both going to go to the best schools money could buy.

Jeannette, the older child, took a year off between high school and college. Her brother Richard entered college one year later. Both average students in high school, they wound up at "the best schools money could buy," small private colleges in the northeast, with limited curricula, smallish libraries, considerable social life, and very high total costs.

The year before Jeannette entered college, Louise went into her small business. Without ever having worked in one, she opened a boutique.

It lasted nine months and lost $6,000 in borrowed money before she decided to close. The decision to close was hastened by a look at tuition, board, and fees costs at the college that had accepted Jeannette.

Nonetheless, Walter insisted on taking a vacation in the Caribbean with Louise to "celebrate" the closing of the boutique and her liberation from the drudgery of small store ownership. The money for the vacation? From the generous overdraft privileges they enjoyed at the local bank, plus the "executive credit" extended them through a major credit card company.

And the money to pay for college? Well, Walter and Louise had heard of the high cost of college, but they just hadn't anticipated needing $8,000 in all for Jeannette's first year, then $16,000 a year for Jeannette and Richard together for three years, then $8,000 for Richard's final year—$64,000 in after-tax income in all. Actually, with inflation, it turned out to be a little more than that.

Oh, they raised the money, and their children went to the best colleges money could buy. They now enjoy a very expensive mortgage on their home and owe a finance company years of payments on a "college-approved" easy payment plan at close to 17 percent annually.

Jeannette and Richard have ten years of payments facing them on loans taken to pay for college costs from incomes that do not promise to be too substantial, considering the quality of the preparation they have received for life in the real world.

Neither Jeannette or Richard has mentioned graduate school—there doesn't seem to be much point in doing so.

Louise now works as a receptionist in a local doctor's office "to get out of the house." She and Walter aren't getting on too well lately.

Walter? Oh, Walter is doing what he did before—worrying himself sick about money and getting old too fast in a young man's business.

PEOPLE OF MODEST MEANS

Owen and Mary McKay don't have much money. Never have had. Aside from some small savings, all they have in the world is their restaurant. They've run it together for the past twenty-five years, with brief interruptions for the births of Nora and Sharon, their two daughters.

Neither Owen nor Mary went beyond high school, and they haven't been very anxious about their daughters' educations. Both have in the past confessed to close friends that they would have been happy to have seen their daughters through high school and into careers as wives and mothers without the bother and expense of college.

Nora did just that. She graduated from high school, worked for a year, and married her high school sweetheart.

Sharon was quite a different person. She'd always been a reader, always been bright, alert, headed for some kind of career. Since her first year in high school, she'd realized that her ticket out of the small town she'd grown up in was a college education, and probably graduate school beyond.

Her first job was to convince Owen and Mary to go along with her. That wasn't too hard. Then, with the help of an alert guidance counselor at the local high school, Sharon worked out a plan that took her through college and law school and into her chosen career.

To get into law school, Sharon had to have a degree from a good four-year college. Given her scholastic aptitudes and career drive, there was a good chance that her college record would be good enough to get her into a well-regarded law school.

But to be able to afford law school, even with maximum financial aid and borrowings, she had to go through four years of college as inexpensively as possible.

Sharon enrolled in a two-year community college near her home. During those two years, she worked in the family restaurant part-time all year and full time during holidays and summers. She wasn't paid a great deal, as that would have harmed some of her financial aid possibilities, but her work did free some of the family's income for her college needs. She got a local fraternal order scholarship, which was small, but was a four-year scholarship. In addition, she competed for and won a national scholarship. She applied for financial aid, just missed a Basic Grant because of her income and her parents' assets and income, but did get some state no-strings award money.

Her "financial aid package" included a guaranteed loan, which she did not apply for, and a federally financed campus job, which she did not take, as she was working in the restaurant.

At the end of those two years, she had borrowed nothing and her parents had borrowed nothing.

She then spent two years at the state university, located in a different area of the state. There, real costs were considerably higher than at the community college, as they included room and board, slightly higher tuition costs and student fees, and transportation costs.

In the state university situation, she qualified for a small Basic Grant, took a campus job as part of the financial aid package, used her restaurant skills to work as a cocktail waitress on weekends, and went home to work in the family restaurant summers as before. Once again, she was able to get by without borrowing.

She applied to and was accepted at several law schools, ultimately choosing a school located in a major city in which job prospects would be good. To get through law school, she worked part-time weekends, holidays, and summers as a cocktail waitress; borrowed as much as possible on a federally guaranteed loan basis; and got some no-strings financial aid from government and private sources. During her last year of law school, she asked her father to cosign a $2,000 bank loan at regular rates of interest, which he gladly did. Sharon came out of law school over $10,000 in debt, but with every probability of paying it off easily out of current earnings as a lawyer over a period of many years.

HOMER

Homer Jones is doing it the hard way. But he's doing it.

Homer was a street kid in Los Angeles in the sixties. He left home before he was sixteen, moved around the country, worked at all kinds of odd jobs, kept moving. Three years ago, he wandered back to Los Angeles, met a girl named Sue, married, and within a year had a son they named Homer, Junior. Now, at twenty-seven for the first time he feels the need to have some skills, to be more than a dishwasher and bean picker, to get a house and a car and send a boy named Homer to college some day.

He's taken and passed a high school equivalency test and has enrolled in a two-year community college course with the aim of becoming an occupational therapy assistant.

Like too many other independent students, his financial obligations go far beyond college costs. In his instance, they include a contribution toward the support of his wife and child during the two years he'll be in college. Sue is working, but is unskilled and unable to make enough money to support them both.

Here's how Homer and Sue are doing it:

Sue is continuing to work. She works nights as a waitress, on a heavy part-time schedule. Homer stays home while Sue works, studying and taking care of Homer, Junior.

Homer, with the help of the college financial aid office, has put together an aid package that consists of:

Basic Educational Opportunity Grant of $1,400 yearly
Federal Supplementary Educational Opportunity Grant of $500 yearly
State outright grant of $800 yearly
State scholarship of $400 yearly
Private scholarship of $500 yearly
College Work-Study Program, which pays him $500 yearly for doing a campus job

The yearly direct aid package totals $4,100, which with Sue's earnings takes them within striking distance of the money Homer and Sue need to meet college and living costs during the two years Homer attends college.

But it's not quite enough, and Homer has borrowed to finance the balance he and Sue need. He's taken $2,500 a year in federally guaranteed loans, half at 3 percent simple interest and half at 7 percent simple interest, which he must start to repay nine months after graduation. He and Sue think they will be able to handle the payments all right.

Homer is very sure that he wouldn't have been able to go to college without the financial aid he's getting—and Sue is thinking hard about going to college herself once Homer is finished with school. She's always had a good head for figures and is beginning to explore the possibility of becoming a financial aid administrator.

APPENDIX A

Calendar-Countdown

Time Before Your Child Enters College	Action	Situation	Chapters
10 years	Start college fund by investing in low-risk securities (e.g., U.S. Savings Bonds Series E)	You have family income over $15,000 or liquid family assets over $25,000	1, 13
4 years	Plan & start further training of student's mother for high income work	You want to avoid the mother starting work at a minimum wage later	1
3 years	Start deciding on the range of college cost options acceptable to you	You might want to avoid paying $30,000 for college	2
2½ years	Analyze your assets as money-for-college sources	You don't want to be forced into high-cost expedients at the last minute	3
2¼ years	Estimate whether you can prove financial need at one or more of your college cost options	You have family income under $30,000	4
2 years	Start developing a strategy for college and financial aid applications; begin choosing specific colleges	You want the greatest chances for minimum college costs & maximum college aid	5
2 years	Establish line of credit with a bank	You won't be able to prove financial need and want low-interest credit to help pay tuition	3, 12
1½ years	Begin using search strategy to check all possible sources of financial aid	You may or may not have financial need	6
1¼ years	Revise college choices to maximize chances of college-provided aid; request current catalogs & applications (Spring of the student's junior year in high school)		8

Time Before Your Child Enters College	Action	Situation	Chapters
1¼ years	Identify all Federal and State aid programs for which the student is eligible; request current details & applications	You may or may not have financial need	9
1¼ years	Hunt down any private-agency scholarship programs in which the student is eligible; request current details & applications	You have financial need	10
12-10 months	Send for admission and financial aid applications to each college chosen (Fall of the student's senior year)	You may or may not have financial need	8
12-10 months	Send applications for Federal aid programs (but not Basic Grants program), State aid programs, and private-agency aid programs	You may or may not have financial need	9, 10
9 months	Begin working on current year's income tax returns (Dec. of student's senior year)	You will have financial need	4
8 months	Send completed Financial Aid Form (FAF) or Family Financial Statement (FFS) right after Jan. 1 (*not* before), as the colleges and programs you're applying to require (fill out using data from income tax returns); use FAF or FFS to apply for Basic Grants Program (Federal)	You will have financial need	4, 9
7-5 months	Receive early college aid-and-admission offers; resist or resolve	You may or may not have financial need	8

Time Before Your Child Enters College	Action	Situation	Chapters
	pressures to commit to an early offer before you may have received better ones		
5 months	Receive aid offers (or regrets) by about Apr. 15 from most-sought-after colleges & most private-agency & government aid programs	You may or may not have financial need	8-10
5-4 months	Accept your most attractive aid offers (decline others) by about May 15; report final choice of college to aid sources	You may or may not have financial need	8-10
4-2 months	Arrange to fill in college-financing gaps with funds beyond aid (e.g., mother's earnings, extra-high student earnings)	You have college-financing gaps by this time	11
4-2 months	Arrange to fill in college-financing gaps beyond guaranteed loans with special low-cost loans	Gaps remain beyond guaranteed loans	12
1 month	Receive letter copies confirming payment of scholarship & grant awards to the college (awards that may total up to $7,500/year)	You have applied and qualified for such aid	13

APPENDIX B
WORKSHEET

Line 1. Choose your target college/program.

    1a. Prestige college (see page 12).
    1b. Less-expensive private college (see page 14).
    1c. U.S. Service Academies (see page 15).
    1d. Credits by examination (see page 16).
    1e. Extension degree programs (see page 20).
    1f. Night/weekend colleges (see page 22).
    1g. Commuting to a community college (see page 24).
    1h. State university (see page 25).
    1j. Cooperative work-study programs (see page 26).
    1k. Special low-cost colleges (see page 26).
    (See also the financial cost/option summary table, page 30).

Line 2. Calculate your personal resources available to pay college costs (see page 33).
    (For *advance* financial and tax-planning information, see page 35).

☞ Calculate separately below Line 2 for each Option or College from Line 1.

☞ Name of Option/College _____

Line 3. Enter the *Student Expense* budget figure (see page 57).

Line 4. Enter the *Total Expected* figure
    (see page 57 using figure & worksheet from Line 2).

Line 5. Subtract Line 4 from Line 3.

This is your FINANCIAL NEED for this Option/College.

☞ For planned *contributions* to your Financial Need for this Option/College, compute the following line items 6 through 18:

Line 6. College scholarships (see page 82).   _____

Line 7. College loans (see page 84).   _____

Line 8. College work programs (see page 115).   _____

Line 9. Federal no-need grants (see page 104).   _____

Line 10. Federal need-basis scholarships (see page 111).   _____

Line 11. Federal loan programs (see page 109).   _____

Line 12. State need-basis scholarships (see page 116).   _____

Line 13. State loan programs (see page 116).   _____

Line 14. State job aid (see page 116).   _____

Line 15. Special aid for students handicapped by
    poverty or discrimination (see page 73).   _____

Line 16. Private agencies (see page 131).   _____

Line 17. Students jobs through the Option/College
    (see page 142).   _____

Line 18. Personal or special loans and mortgages
(does not include college, federal or
state loans on Lines 7, 11 and 13)
(see page 149).

Line 19. TOTAL Contribution to Financial Need
(add Lines 6 throught 18).

Line 20. Enter *Financial Need* figure from Line 5 above.

Line 21. Subtract Line 20 from Line 19.

☞ If the figure on Line 21 is a *plus* figure, your chosen Option/College is attainable.

☞ If the figure on Line 21 is a *minus* figure, your chosen Option/College is not yet reasonably attainable.

Try other Option/Colleges from Line 1
                    or
Re-evaluate your personal resources on Line 2
                    or
Review possible overlooked contributions to Financial Need on
Lines 6 through 18.

INFORMATION SOURCES

Advisory List of National Contests and Activities, National Association of Secondary School Principals, 1904 Association Drive, Reston, Va. 22091.

Air Force ROTC, Maxwell Air Force Base, Ala. 36112 (for ROTC scholarship applicant information).

Army ROTC Scholarships, P.O. Box 12703, Philadelphia, Pa. 19134 (for applicant information).

Basic Educational Opportunity Grant, P.O. Box 84, Washington, D.C. 20044 (for requesting "Student Guide" booklet, "Basic Grant Eligibility" booklet, and application form).

Cash for College by Robert Freede, Prentice-Hall, Inc., Englewood Cliffs, N.J. 07632.

College Admissions Center, National Association of College Admissions Counselors, 801 Davis St., Evanston, Ill. 60201 (service at which you can apply and have interested colleges offer you admission and financial aid).

Collegian's Guide to Part-Time Employment by Russell H. Granger, Arco Publishing Co., Inc., 219 Park Ave. South, New York, N.Y. 10003.

The College Handbook (issued every other fall in odd-numbered years), College Entrance Examination Board, Publication Orders, Box 2815, Princeton, N.J. 08540.

College Scholarship Information Bank (computer search service), 888 Seventh Ave., New York, N.Y. 10019.

Education Fund, American Institute of Certified Public Accountants, 1211 Avenue of the Americas, New York, N.Y. 10036.

Financial Aids for Higher Education, National Catalog, by Oreon Keeslar, William Brown Co., Dubuque, Iowa 52001.

Five Federal Financial Aid Programs, U.S. Office of Education, Room 1069, 400 Maryland Ave., S.W., Washington, D.C. 20202.

Getting It All Together, A No-Sweat Guide to a Better Deal for Ex-GI's, Veterans Education and Training Service, National League of Cities, 1620 I St., Washington, D.C. 20006.

Going Right On, College Entrance Examination Board, Publication Orders, Box 2815, Princeton, N.J. 08540.

Guaranteed Student Loan Program, Office of Education, U.S. Dept. of HEW, Washington, D.C. 20202 (for requesting a list of regional branches providing loan program information).

Guide to Colleges, by Gene R. Hawes, New American Library, 1301 Avenue of the Americas, New York, N.Y. 10019.

Guide to Financial Aid for Students and Parents, by Elizabeth W. Suchar, Simon & Schuster, Inc., 1 W. 39th St., New York, N.Y. 10018.

Guide to Financial Aids for Students in Arts and Sciences, by Aysel Searles, Jr., and Anne Scott, Arco Publishing Co., Inc., 219 Park Ave. South, New York, N.Y. 10003.

How to Beat the High Cost of College, by Claire Cox, The Dial Press, 1 Dag Hammarskjold Plaza, New York, N.Y. 10017.

How to Pay for Your Health Career Education; A Guide For Minority Students, Bureau of Health Resources Development, Health Resources Administration, U.S. Dept. of HEW, 9000 Rockville Pike, Bethesda, Md. 20014.

Making It: A Guide to Student Finances, Harvard Student Agencies, 4 Holyoke St., Cambridge, Mass. 02138.

Meeting College Costs: A Guide for Parents and Students, College Board Publications Orders, Box 2815, Princeton, N.J. 08540.

The Money Book, by Robert Rosefsky, Follett Publishing Company, 1010 W. Washington Blvd., Chicago, Ill. 60607.

National Scholarship Service and Fund for Negro Students, 1776 Broadway, New York, N.Y. 10019. Southeastern regional office: 931½ Hunter St., Atlanta, Ga. 31314.

Navy ROTC Scholarships, Commander, Navy Recruiting Command, (Code 314), 4015 Wilson Blvd., Arlington, Va. 22203 (for applicant information).

Need A Lift? American Legion, Dept. S, Box 1055, Indianapolis, Ind. 46206 (for information about college financial aids for veterans and their children).

The New York Times Book of Money, by Richard E. Blodgett, Quadrangle/The New York Times Book Company, 3 Park Ave., New York, N.Y. 10016.

The New York Times Guide to Personal Finance, by Sal Nuccio, Harper & Row, 10 E. 53rd St., New York, N.Y. 10022.

Occupational Outlook Handbook (latest edition), Bureau of Labor Statistics, U.S. Dept. of Labor, Superintendent of Documents, U.S. Government Printing Office, Washington, D.C. 20402.

Scholarship Search, (computer search service), 1775 Broadway, New York, N.Y. 10019.

Sources of Information on Student Aid, National Education Association, 1201 16th St., N.W., Washington, D.C. 20036.

Student Aid Annual, Student Aid Bulletins, Chronicle Guidance Publications, Inc., Moravia, N.Y. 13118.

Student Expenses at Postsecondary Institutions (annual edition), by Elizabeth Suchar et al., College Scholarship Service, College Entrance Examination Board, 888 Seventh Ave., New York, N.Y. 10019.

Sylvia Porter's Money Book, Avon Books, 959 Eighth Ave., New York, N.Y. 10019.

Undergraduate Programs of Cooperative Education in the United States And Canada, National Commission for Cooperative Education, 360 Huntington Ave., Boston, Mass. 02115.

U.S. Bureau of Indian Affairs, Room 201, 5301 Central Ave., N.E., Albuquerque, N. Mex. 87108 (for requesting addresses of area offices responsible for Bureau of Indian Affairs grants).

U.S. Dept. of the Interior, Bureau of Indian Affairs, Division of Student Service, 123 4th St., S.W., P.O. Box 1788, Albuquerque, N. Mex. 87103.

VEA (Veterans Education Assistance Act) Benefits Program, REACT Center, P.O. Box 1000, Mt. Vernon, N.Y. 10550.

Veterans Administration, Washington, D.C. 20420 (for information about veterans' educational benefits programs).

INDEX